> "Nolo's home page is worth bookmarking."
> —WALL STREET JOURNAL

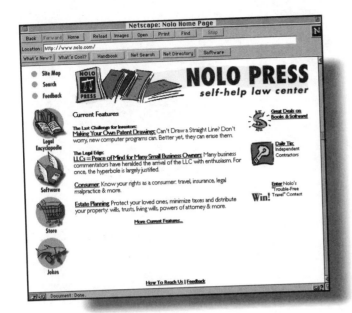

LEGAL INFORMATION ONLINE

www.nolo.com

24 HOURS A DAY

AT THE NOLO PRESS SELF-HELP LAW CENTER ON THE WEB, YOU'LL FIND:

○ Nolo's comprehensive **Legal Encyclopedia**, with links to other online resources

○ Downloadable demos of Nolo software and sample chapters of many Nolo books

○ An online law store with a secure online ordering system

○ Our ever-popular lawyer jokes

○ Discounts and other good deals,
our hilarious SHARK TALK game

THE NOLO NEWS

Stay on top of important legal changes with Nolo's quarterly magazine, *The Nolo News*. Start your free one-year subscription by filling out and mailing the response card in the back of this book. With each issue, you'll get legal news about topics that affect you every day, reviews of legal books by other publishers, the latest Nolo catalog, scintillating advice from Auntie Nolo and a fresh batch of our famous lawyer jokes.

1st Edition

The Financial Power of Attorney Workbook

BY ATTORNEY SHAE IRVING

EDITED BY MARY RANDOLPH

Nolo Press Berkeley

Your Responsibility When Using a Self-Help Law Book

We've done our best to give you useful and accurate information in this book. But laws and procedures change frequently and are subject to differing interpretations. If you want legal advice backed by a guarantee, see a lawyer. If you use this book, it's your responsibility to make sure that the facts and general advice contained in it are applicable to your situation.

Keeping Up to Date

To keep its books up to date, Nolo Press issues new printings and new editions periodically. New printings reflect minor legal changes and technical corrections. New editions contain major legal changes, major text additions or major reorganizations. To find out if a later printing or edition of any Nolo book is available, call Nolo Press at 510-549-1976 or check the catalog in the *Nolo News*, our quarterly publication. You can also contact us on the Internet at www.nolo.com.

To stay current, follow the "Update" service in the *Nolo News*. You can get a free one-year subscription by sending us the registration card in the back of the book. In another effort to help you use Nolo's latest materials, we offer a 25% discount off the purchase of the new edition of your Nolo book if you turn in the cover of an earlier edition. (See the "Special Upgrade Offer" in the back of this book.) This book was last revised in **December 1997**.

First Edition	DECEMBER 1997
Editor	MARY RANDOLPH
Illustrations	MARI STEIN
Cover Design	TONI IHARA
Layout Design	TERRI HEARSH
Index	SAYRE VAN YOUNG
Proofreading	ROBERT WELLS
Printing	CUSTOM PRINTING COMPANY

Irving, Shae.
    The financial power of attorney workbook : who will handle your finances if you can't? / by Shae Irving. -- 1st ed.
        p.   cm.
    Includes index.
    ISBN 0-87337-409-6
    1. Power of attorney--United States--Popular works. I. Title
KF1347.Z9I78   1997
346.7302'9--dc21
                                                    97-24099
                                                      CIP

For information on bulk purchases or corporate premium sales, please contact the Special Sales Department. For academic sales or textbook adoptions, ask for Academic Sales. Call 800-955-4775 or write to Nolo Press, Inc., 950 Parker Street, Berkeley, CA 94710.

Acknowledgments

My deepest gratitude goes to Mary Randolph, a meticulous editor who offers an abundance of good humor and good heart.

Also, thanks to Mary and to Denis Clifford for writing Nolo's *Who Will Handle Your Finances If You Can't?* and to Denis Clifford for Nolo's *Power of Attorney Handbook*. These two books are no longer in print, but my work is based on them. Without this strong foundation, I wouldn't have known where to begin.

Finally, thanks to Terri Hearsh for her skillful formatting and design.

About the Author

Shae Irving graduated from Boalt Hall School of Law at the University of California at Berkeley in 1993 and joined the editorial staff at Nolo Press in 1994. She is the author or co-author of several Nolo publications, including *Take Control of Your Student Loans* and the forthcoming version of Nolo's *WillMaker* software. Shae is also the editor of many Nolo books, among them *Nolo's Everyday Law Book*, *Nolo's Pocket Guide to California Law*, *A Legal Guide for Lesbian and Gay Couples* and *Money Troubles*.

Table of Contents

1 What This Book Does

A. Choosing the Right Power of Attorney Form 1/2

B. Will You Need a Lawyer? 1/5

C. Icons Used in This Book 1/5

2 Do You Need a Durable Power of Attorney?

A. Avoiding Conservatorship Proceedings 2/2

B. If You Think You Don't Need a Durable Power of Attorney 2/3

C. When You Shouldn't Rely on a Durable Power of Attorney 2/5

D. How a Durable Power of Attorney Fits Into an Estate Plan 2/5

3 How Durable Powers of Attorney Work

A. The Mental Competency Requirement 3/2

B. The Expense of a Durable Power of Attorney 3/3

C. What the Attorney-in-Fact Does 3/3

D. When the Attorney-in-Fact Takes Over 3/5

E. Will Your Power of Attorney Be Accepted? 3/8

F. If You Move to Another State 3/10

G. When the Power of Attorney Ends 3/10

4 Your Attorney-in-Fact

A. Choosing Your Attorney-in-Fact 4/2

B. Your Attorney-in-Fact's Responsibilities 4/6

C. Paying Your Attorney-in-Fact 4/10

5 Granting Powers to the Attorney-in-Fact

A. Granting Specific Financial Powers 5/2

B. Special Instructions for the Attorney-in-Fact 5/7

C. The Attorney-in-Fact's Power to Delegate 5/12

6 Preparing Your Durable Power of Attorney

A. What Forms to Use 6/2

B. Step-by-Step Instructions 6/2

C. What's Next? 6/10

7 Making Your Durable Power of Attorney Legal

A. Before You Sign 7/2

B. Sign and Notarize the Durable Power of Attorney 7/2

C. Putting Your Durable Power of Attorney on Public Record 7/4

D. What to Do With the Signed Document 7/5

E. Making and Distributing Copies 7/5

F. Keeping Your Document Up to Date 7/5

8 Conventional Powers of Attorney

A. When to Use a Conventional Power of Attorney 8/2

B. How Conventional Powers of Attorney Work 8/3

C. Choosing Your Attorney-in-Fact 8/5

D. The Attorney-in-Fact's Responsibilities 8/6

E. Granting Powers to the Attorney-in-Fact 8/6

F. Preparing Your Document 8/6

G. Making It Legal 8/20

H. When to Make a New Power of Attorney 8/24

9 Powers of Attorney for Real Estate

A. When to Use a Power of Attorney for Real Estate 9/2

B. How Powers of Attorney for Real Estate Work 9/3

C. Choosing Your Attorney-in-Fact 9/4

D. The Attorney-in-Fact's Authority 9/5

E. Preparing Your Document 9/5

F. Making It Legal 9/10

10 Powers of Attorney for Child Care

A. When to Use a Power of Attorney for Child Care 10/2

B. How Powers of Attorney for Child Care Work 10/3

C. The Attorney-in-Fact's Authority 10/5

D. Preparing Your Document 10/5

E. Making It Legal 10/8

11 Revoking a Power of Attorney

A. Special Considerations for Durable Powers of Attorney 11/2

B. When to Revoke a Power of Attorney 11/3

C. How to Revoke a Power of Attorney 11/5

12 Help Beyond the Book

A. Legal Typing Services 12/2

B. Finding a Lawyer 12/2

C. Working With a Lawyer 12/4

D. Lawyers' Fees 12/4

E. Doing Your Own Legal Research 12/5

A How to Use the Forms Disk

1. Copying the Disk Files Onto Your Computer .... Appendix A/2

2. Creating Your Documents With the Forms Disk Files .... Appendix A/3

B Power of Attorney Forms

1. Financial Power of Attorney

2. Financial Power of Attorney: Alaska

3. Financial Power of Attorney: Arizona

4. Financial Power of Attorney: District of Columbia

5. Financial Power of Attorney: New Mexico

6. Financial Power of Attorney: North Carolina

7. Financial Power of Attorney: Oklahoma

8. Limited Power of Attorney

9. Power of Attorney for Real Estate

10. Power of Attorney for Child Care: Single Parent

11. Power of Attorney for Child Care: Two Parents

12. Information for an Attorney-in-Fact

13. Physician's Determination of Incapacity (All States Except New Mexico)

14. Healthcare Professional's Determination of Incapacity (New Mexico)

15. Delegation of Authority

16. Resignation of Attorney-in-Fact

17. Notice of Revocation: Unrecorded

18. Notice of Revocation: Recorded

What This Book Does

A. Choosing the Right Power of Attorney Form 1/2

   1. Durable Power of Attorney for Finances 1/3

   2. Conventional Power of Attorney for Finances 1/4

   3. Power of Attorney for Real Estate 1/4

   4. Power of Attorney for Child Care 1/5

B. Will You Need a Lawyer? 1/5

C. Icons Used in This Book 1/5

This book can help you in a number of situations:

- You are concerned about what will happen if you become seriously ill or otherwise incapacitated, and you want to be sure your financial affairs will be handled by someone you trust.
- You will be temporarily unavailable—due to a trip out of town, for example—and you need someone to take care of financial matters in your absence.
- You want someone to handle a real estate transaction for you.
- You must leave your children in someone else's care for a period of time, and you want to be certain the caretaker has the authority to pay bills and make medical and school-related decisions on their behalf.

You can take care of any of these concerns with a simple legal document called a power of attorney. This book provides all the information, fill-in-the-blanks forms and instructions you need to create your own financial power of attorney. It includes several different powers of attorney, each geared to a particular situation. You can choose the one that best meets your needs.

Begin by reviewing the different power of attorney forms. They're described just below in Section A. Once you've found the power of attorney that's right for your circumstances, you need read only the chapters that apply to your document. The process of making a power of attorney is fairly straightforward and will probably be easier and less time-consuming than you think.

And after your power of attorney is complete, you can rest easier, knowing your important affairs are secure in the hands of a trusted person you've chosen.

A. Choosing the Right Power of Attorney Form

A power of attorney is a powerful legal document. With it, you give another person legal authority to act on your behalf. The person to whom you give this authority is called your attorney-in-fact. The word "attorney" here means anyone authorized to act on another's behalf; it's most definitely not restricted to lawyers. Your attorney-in-fact can perform a wide variety of duties for you, from paying your bills to watching over your real estate. Exactly what your attorney-in-fact can do depends on the authority you grant in the power of attorney document.

Because a power of attorney can transfer so much power, it's important to choose the right document for your situation. This section provides a brief overview of different types of powers of attorney and helps you pick the one that's right for you.

Important Terms

Making a financial power of attorney doesn't require a lot of complicated legal language. But there are a few basic terms you'll want to know.

Principal: The person who creates and signs the power of attorney document, authorizing someone else to act for him or her. If you make a financial power of attorney, *you* are the principal.

Attorney-in-Fact: The person who is authorized to act for the principal. In many states, the attorney-in-fact is also referred to as an "agent" of the principal.

Alternate Attorney-in-Fact: The person who takes over as attorney-in-fact if the principal's first choice cannot or will not serve. Alternate attorneys-in-fact are frequently called "successor" attorneys-in-fact.

Conventional Power of Attorney: A power of attorney that automatically ends if the principal becomes incapacitated.

Durable Power of Attorney: A power of attorney that will remain valid and in effect even if the principal becomes incapacitated, or will take effect only if the principal becomes incapacitated.

Incapacitated: Unable to handle one's own financial matters or healthcare decisions. Also called "disabled" or "incompetent" in some states. Generally, incapacity isn't precisely defined by state law. Usually, a physician makes the determination.

Generally, drafting a financial power of attorney is not complicated. Once you figure out what type of document you need, it shouldn't take you long to prepare it. This book contains fill-in-the blanks forms that let you create:

- a durable power of attorney for finances,
- a conventional power of attorney for finances,
- a power of attorney for real estate, or
- a power of attorney for child care.

Let's look at each one.

1. Durable Power of Attorney for Finances

The primary focus of this book is the durable power of attorney for finances. This document allows you to name someone to take care of your financial matters if you become incapacitated and can't handle them yourself. You can make the document effective immediately, or you can make what's known as a "springing" durable power of attorney—a document that doesn't take effect unless and until you become incapacitated.

The trusted person you name—your attorney-in-fact—will take responsibility for paying bills (with your assets), making bank deposits and handling many other important financial matters for you. The document does *not* allow you to name someone to make healthcare decisions for you. To do this, you will need to make a different document, called a durable power of attorney for healthcare. (See "Making Medical Decisions," below.)

Most people with property or an income can benefit from establishing a durable power of attorney for finances. The document will be a great help if you unexpectedly become unable to manage your financial affairs, temporarily or permanently. If you haven't made a durable power of attorney for finances and you become incapacitated, a court will choose someone to manage your finances for you.

Making a durable power of attorney is particularly important for those who have reason to believe that they may become incapacitated soon: the elderly, for example, and anyone who has a life-threatening health condition or is facing a serious operation.

Members of unmarried couples—straight or gay—may also feel a strong need for the document. If you want to be sure that your partner takes responsibility for your finances in the event of your incapacity, a durable power of attorney is a good idea. Without it, a court could choose another family member to make financial decisions on your behalf.

If you're interested in making a durable power, Chapter 2 contains more information to help you decide whether the document is right for your situation. Chapters 3 through 7 explain the document in detail and show you how to prepare it.

Making Medical Decisions

If you're thinking ahead and planning for incapacity, you'll want to make a durable power of attorney for finances—but you shouldn't stop there. You'll also want to create documents in which you set out your wishes for medical care and name someone to make medical decisions for you if you become unable to make them yourself. These documents are typically known as a "durable power of attorney for healthcare" and a "living will." This book does not contain healthcare documents, but you can get more information about them—including where to get forms—in Chapter 2, Section D.1.

2. Conventional Power of Attorney for Finances

Unlike a durable power of attorney, a conventional power automatically ends if you become incapacitated. So it's the document to make if you want to give someone authority to manage your financial affairs on a temporary basis. For example, if you're planning a long trip away from home, you might want your spouse or partner to have clear authority over your bank accounts and other assets.

You can use a conventional power of attorney to give your attorney-in-fact as much or as little authority as you choose. You may want your attorney-in-fact to handle all of your financial matters for you while you are out of town. Or, you may want simply to authorize someone to handle a single transaction for you, such as selling your car. To help you create a document that will work well in your situation, this book contains two different conventional power of attorney forms:

- a broad form that you can use to grant a wide range of powers, and
- a limited form that you can tailor to a very specific need.

Chapter 8 helps you decide which conventional power of attorney form is best for you, and shows you how to complete your document.

Check With Your Financial Institutions

Many financial institutions—banks and brokerage houses, for example—have their own power of attorney forms. If yours does, we recommend that you use it. If you want to give your attorney-in-fact broad powers over your finances, you'll probably want to use the financial institution's form in addition to one of the broader power of attorney forms in this book.

By using your financial institution's form, you'll head off problems for your attorney-in-fact, because the financial institution will have no need to examine and quibble with the power of attorney; it will know exactly what powers its own form grants.

3. Power of Attorney for Real Estate

A power of attorney for real estate is the document to use if you want your attorney-in-fact to handle real estate transactions—and nothing else. If your needs are limited in this way, it makes good sense to use the real estate document rather than a broader power of attorney that encompasses real estate transactions. Mortgage lenders and title companies are less likely to fuss about a power of attorney that's designed exclusively for real estate business.

A power of attorney for real estate allows your attorney-in-fact to buy or sell real estate on your behalf, or to conduct any other business concerning real estate that you own. The document is a type of conventional power of attorney, meaning that it automatically expires if you become incapacitated and unable to manage your own financial affairs.

Powers of attorney for real estate are discussed in Chapter 9.

4. Power of Attorney for Child Care

If you have young children, you're likely to face situations when you must leave them in somebody else's care for a period of time. If this time amounts to weeks or months, you'll probably want to make a power of attorney for child care. The document helps to ensure that the caretaker you've chosen has full authority to make medical and school-related decisions for your child, and to pay his or her expenses. While a power of attorney for child care doesn't have the force of a court ordered guardianship, the document should be enough to authorize your attorney-in-fact to take care of your child's needs for a limited period of time.

To learn how to make a power of attorney for child care, read Chapter 10.

B. Will You Need a Lawyer?

Most people can prepare a financial power of attorney without a lawyer. If, however, you have specific questions or unusual circumstances—for example, a very large amount of property or unusu-

ally contentious family members—you may need legal advice. As you read this book, you'll be alerted to circumstances where you may run into trouble or benefit from a lawyer's help. If you do need to see a lawyer, Chapter 12 contains information on how to find a good one.

C. Icons Used in This Book

Throughout this book, the following icons will help you along.

 You may be able to skip some material that doesn't apply to your situation.

 Slow down and consider potential problems.

 Alerts you to important tips.

 Refers you to additional sources of information about the particular issue or topic discussed in the text.

 Refers you to related information in another chapter of this book.

 Circumstances when you may want to consult with an attorney. ■

Do You Need a Durable Power of Attorney?

A. Avoiding Conservatorship Proceedings 2/2

B. If You Think You Don't Need a Durable Power of Attorney 2/3

    1. If You Are Married 2/3

    2. If You Have a Living Trust 2/3

    3. If You Own Joint Tenancy Property 2/4

C. When You Shouldn't Rely on a Durable Power of Attorney 2/5

    1. You Want Court Supervision of Your Finances 2/5

    2. You Fear Family Fights 2/5

D. How a Durable Power of Attorney Fits Into an Estate Plan 2/5

    1. Making Medical Decisions 2/5

    2. Arranging Care for Young Children 2/7

    3. Protecting Assets 2/7

    4. Leaving Property to Family, Friends or Charities 2/7

    5. Winding Up Your Affairs After Death 2/7

Almost everyone with property or an income can benefit from a durable power of attorney for finances. It's particularly important, however, to have a durable power of attorney if you fear that health problems may make it impossible for you to handle your financial matters.

Making a durable power of attorney will ensure that someone you trust will be on hand to manage the many practical, financial tasks that will arise if you become incapacitated. For example, bills must be paid, bank deposits must be made and insurance and benefits paperwork must be handled. Many other matters may need attention as well, from property repairs to managing investments or a small business. In most cases, a durable power of attorney for finances is the best way to handle tasks like these.

The main reason to make a durable power of attorney for finances is to avoid court proceedings if you become incapacitated. If you don't have a durable power of attorney, your relatives or other loved ones will have to ask a judge to name someone to manage your financial affairs. These proceedings are commonly known as "conservatorship" proceedings. Depending on where you live, the person appointed to manage your finances is called a conservator, guardian of the estate, committee or curator.

A. Avoiding Conservatorship Proceedings

Conservatorship proceedings can be complicated, expensive and even embarrassing. Your loved ones must ask the court to rule that you cannot take care of your own affairs—a public airing of a very private matter. Court proceedings are matters of public record; in some places, a notice may even be published in a local newspaper. If relatives fight over who is to be the conservator, the proceedings will surely become even more disagreeable, sometimes downright nasty. And all of this causes costs to mount up, especially if lawyers must be hired.

If a judge decides that a conservator is necessary, there is no guarantee that the person she appoints will be the person you would have chosen for the job. A judge may ask you to express a preference for conservator—and will strongly consider what you say—but even this will not ensure that your choice will serve. State law generally provides a priority list for who should be appointed. For example, a number of states make the person's spouse the first choice as conservator, followed by an adult child, parent and brother or sister.

In many states, the law allows the court to appoint whomever it determines will act in your "best interests." Because of this, it's possible that some crony of the judge could end up managing your finances. Because a conservator is entitled to payment for his or her services (from your assets), there's a chance that such a conservator will pay himself handsomely for less than dedicated service.

The appointment of a conservator is usually just the beginning of court proceedings. Often the conservator must:

- post a bond—a kind of insurance policy that pays if the conservator steals or misuses property
- prepare (or hire a lawyer or accountant to prepare) detailed financial reports and periodically file them with the court
- get court approval for certain transactions, such as selling real estate or making slightly risky investments.

All of this, of course, costs money—your money.

A conservatorship isn't necessarily permanent, but it may be ended only by the court.

The good news is that you can avoid the troubles of a conservatorship if you take the time to create a durable power of attorney for finances now. When you make a durable power of attorney, you give your attorney-in-fact full legal authority to handle your financial affairs. A conservatorship proceeding would be necessary only if no one were willing to serve as attorney-in-fact, the attorney-in-fact wanted guidance from a court, or a close relative thought the attorney-in-fact wasn't acting in your best interests.

Faking It. If someone becomes incapacitated, panicky family members may consider just faking the signatures necessary to carry on routine financial matters. After all, what's wrong with signing Aunt Amanda's name to a check to pay her phone bill? It's not stealing.

No, it's forgery, which is just as illegal. It can get well-meaning relatives into a lot of trouble. The law is strict in this area to guard against dishonest family members who might loot a relative's assets.

Forging a signature on checks, bills of sale, tax returns or other financial documents may work for a while, but it will probably be discovered eventually. The court proceeding everyone was trying to avoid will still be necessary—and the court will not be eager to put a proven liar in charge of a relative's finances.

B. If You Think You Don't Need a Durable Power of Attorney

You may not think that you need a durable power of attorney for finances if you're married, or if you've put most of your property into a living trust or hold it in joint tenancy. But the truth is that in all of these situations, a durable power of attorney can make life much easier for your family if you become incapacitated. All these issues are discussed below.

1. If You Are Married

If you are married, don't assume that your spouse will automatically be able to manage your finances if you can't.

Your spouse does have some authority over property you own together—for example, your spouse may pay bills from a joint bank account or sell stock in a joint brokerage account. There are significant limits, however, on your spouse's right to sell property owned by both of you. For example,

in most states, both spouses must agree to the sale of co-owned real estate or cars. Because an incapacitated spouse can't consent to such a sale, the other spouse's hands are tied.

And when it comes to property that belongs only to you, your spouse has no legal authority. You must use a durable power of attorney to give your spouse authority over your property.

EXAMPLE 1: New York residents Michael and Carrie have been married for 47 years. Their major assets are a home and stock. The home is owned in both their names as joint tenants. The stock was bought only in Michael's name, and the couple has never transferred it into shared ownership.

Michael becomes incapacitated and requires expensive medical treatment. Legally, Carrie cannot sell the stock to pay for medical costs.

She could take a loan against her interest in the house, but doesn't want to. And as a practical matter, a bank would probably be very reluctant to grant a mortgage that wasn't signed by both spouses.

EXAMPLE 2: Janice's husband, Hal, is incapacitated and living in a nearby nursing home. Janice wants to raise money by selling Hal's old car, which he can no longer drive, but she can't because the title is in Hal's name.

2. If You Have a Living Trust

The primary purpose of a revocable living trust is to avoid probate. But the trust can also be useful if you become incapable of taking care of your financial affairs. That's because the person who will distribute trust property after your death (called the successor trustee) can also, in most cases, take over management of the trust property if you become incapacitated. Usually, the trust document gives the successor trustee authority to manage all property in the trust and to use it for your needs.

EXAMPLE: Jasmine creates a probate-avoidance living trust, appointing herself as trustee (the person in charge of the property that technically is owned by the living trust). The trust document states that if she becomes incapacitated, and a physician signs a statement saying she no longer can manage her own affairs, her daughter Joy will replace her as trustee.

The successor trustee has no authority over property that the trust doesn't own. Most people transfer into a living trust assets that are expensive to probate, such as real estate and valuable securities, but few people transfer all their property to a living trust. So although it's helpful, a living trust isn't a complete substitute for a durable power of attorney for finances.

The two documents work well together, however, especially if you name the same trusted person to be your attorney-in-fact and the successor trustee of your living trust. That person will have authority to manage property both in and out of your living trust. You can also give your attorney-in-fact the power to transfer items of your property into your living trust. (See Chapter 5, Section A.8.)

EXAMPLE: Consuela, a widow, owns all the stock of a prosperous clothing manufacturing corporation. To avoid probate, she transfers the stock into a living trust, naming her brother, Rodolfo, as successor trustee. If Consuela becomes incapacitated, Rodolfo will become acting trustee, and manage the trust property (the stock) for Consuela's benefit.

Consuela also prepares a durable power of attorney for finances and names Rodolfo as her attorney-in-fact. That gives him authority over whatever assets she does not transfer to the trust—for example, her bank accounts and car. In her durable power of attorney, she also gives Rodolfo the power to transfer property into her living trust, if he feels that's in her best interest.

3. If You Own Joint Tenancy Property

Joint tenancy is a way that more than one person can own property together. The most notable feature of joint tenancy is that when one owner dies, the other owners automatically inherit the deceased person's share of the property. But if you become incapacitated, the other owners have very limited authority over your share of the joint tenancy property.

For example, if you and someone else own a bank account in joint tenancy and one of you becomes incapacitated, the other owner is legally entitled to use the funds. The healthy joint tenant can take care of the financial needs of the incapacitated person simply by paying bills from the joint account. But the other account owner has no legal right to endorse checks made out to the incapacitated person. In practice, it might be possible—if not technically legal—to get an incapacitated person's checks into a joint account by stamping them "For Deposit Only," but that's not the easiest way to handle things.

Matters get even more complicated with other kinds of joint tenancy property. Real estate is a good example. If one owner becomes incapacitated, the other has no legal authority to sell or refinance the incapacitated owner's share.

By contrast, with a durable power of attorney, you can give your attorney-in-fact authority over your share of joint tenancy property, including real estate and bank accounts.

C. When You Shouldn't Rely on a Durable Power of Attorney

The expense and intrusion of a conservatorship are rarely desirable. In a few situations, however, special concerns justify the process.

1. You Want Court Supervision of Your Finances

If you can't think of someone you trust enough to appoint as your attorney-in-fact, with broad authority over your property and finances, don't create a durable power of attorney. A conservatorship, with the built-in safeguard of court supervision, is worth the extra cost and trouble.

2. You Fear Family Fights

A durable power of attorney is a readily accepted and powerful legal document. Once you've finalized yours, anyone who wants to challenge your plans for financial management will face an uphill battle in court. But if you expect that family members will challenge your document or make continual trouble for your attorney-in-fact, a conservatorship may be preferable. Your relatives may still fight, but at least the court will be there to keep an eye on your welfare and your property.

Is a durable attorney right for you? If you expect family fights and feel uncomfortable making a durable power of attorney for finances, you may want to talk with a knowledgeable lawyer. He or she can help you weigh your concerns and options, and decide whether a durable power of attorney is the best option for you.

D. How a Durable Power of Attorney Fits Into an Estate Plan

A durable power of attorney for finances serves a very important purpose by arranging for the management of your finances and avoiding the need for a conservatorship. But it is only part of an estate plan—that is, a plan for taking care of your property and your family at your death or incapacity. You need other documents to accomplish other goals. This section summarizes some basic estate planning tasks you should consider when you create your durable power of attorney. It does not cover every aspect of estate planning—reducing estate tax, for example, is not covered—but it's a place to start thinking about the documents you may need to thoroughly take care of your affairs.

1. Making Medical Decisions

If you become incapacitated, you'll need someone to make medical as well as financial decisions for you. Your durable power of attorney for finances does *not* give your attorney-in-fact legal authority to make medical decisions for you.

To make sure that medical decisions—including decisions about life-prolonging medical care such as respirators and surgery—are in keeping with your wishes, you should prepare healthcare directives. These are generally known as a living will and a durable power of attorney for healthcare, although in many states the two are combined in a single document called a Directive to Physicians or Declaration. These directives allow you to set out written wishes for your medical care—and to name a person to make sure those wishes are carried out.

Even if you want the same person to make both financial and medical decisions for you, you should sign two separate powers of attorney: one for finances and one for healthcare. In some states, separate documents are required by law. While you may be tempted to put all your wishes in one comprehensive document, it's not a good idea, for several reasons:

- State laws that regulate healthcare directives change rapidly as legislatures strive to keep up with new medical technology and new court decisions. More importantly, you may want to change your healthcare documents to keep current with your changing needs, adjustments in your personal life, or to more accurately reflect new treatment choices that become available.
- Combined (medical and financial) durable power of attorney forms do not permit you to be very specific about your wishes regarding medical treatment.
- Healthcare documents often have different validation requirements—for example, they may have to be signed in front of witnesses, while a financial durable power of attorney doesn't have to be witnessed in most states.
- Each durable power of attorney will be used for a very different purpose and presented to different people and organizations, often at different times.
- By using two documents, you don't have to show your medical wishes to people who are concerned only with your finances, and vice versa.

a. Living Wills

A living will, which may be called a Healthcare Directive, Advance Directive or Directive to Physicians in the state where you live, is a statement of your wishes about certain kinds of medical treatments and life-sustaining procedures. It becomes effective if you can't communicate your own healthcare decisions. A living will is directed to your doctors; if it is properly prepared, they are legally bound to follow your wishes for medical treatment or to transfer you to a doctor who will. Most states now provide fill-in-the-blanks living will forms; if your state does, you can use the official form.

Many states allow you to name a "proxy" or "patient advocate" in a living will either to oversee the wishes you set out or to use discretion in pick-

ing and choosing your medical care. This means you will need only one healthcare document. If your state does not use this simplified approach, however, you'll get the best protection by writing both a living will and a durable power of attorney for healthcare, which does let you appoint someone to make sure your wishes are respected.

b. Durable Powers of Attorney for Healthcare

A durable power of attorney for healthcare lets you choose someone to make medical decisions for you when you can't. People frequently use this document to name the person who will make sure that doctors respect their decisions about whether or not life-sustaining procedures should be administered if they cannot express their wishes on their own.

Where to Get Healthcare Forms. Local senior centers may be good resources. Many of them have trained healthcare staff on hand who will be willing to discuss your options for medical care. The patient representative at a local hospital may also be a good person to contact for help. Hospitals and senior centers often provide free help for people making healthcare documents. And if you have a regular physician, you can discuss your concerns with him or her.

Local special interest groups and clinics may also provide help in obtaining and filling out healthcare directives—particularly organizations set up to meet the needs of the severely ill, such as AIDS or cancer organizations. Check your telephone book for a local listing, or call one of the group's hotlines for more information or a possible referral.

Beware of any organization that offers a seminar for a hefty fee. The decisions needed to complete your healthcare documents are intensely personal and yours alone to make.

You can also make your healthcare documents using Nolo's *WillMaker* (software for Windows and Macintosh). The program walks you step-by-step through the process of creating healthcare documents that are valid in your state.

2. Arranging Care for Young Children

You cannot use a durable power of attorney to give anyone authority to care for your minor children if you become incapacitated. Your attorney-in-fact will have authority over your property, not your family. You can, however, authorize your attorney-in-fact to use your property to pay for your children's needs while you are incapacitated. (See Chapter 5, Section A.10.) And you can use a limited power of attorney to authorize someone to care for your children on a temporary basis when you're not incapacitated but temporarily unavailable—for example, if you go out of town. (See Chapter 10.)

If you become incapacitated, the children's other parent will be responsible for caring for them. If he or she cannot care for them, a court will appoint someone—a close family member, if possible—to do it.

3. Protecting Assets

Within legal limits, your attorney-in-fact can try to prevent all of your money from being used up for medical or housing costs, to preserve assets for your family. For example, Medicaid rules exempt some property when determining eligibility for benefits, but there are detailed rules that must be followed to qualify for the exemption. The attorney-in-fact should get advice from an expert before jumping into any complex asset-saving strategies.

4. Leaving Property to Family, Friends or Charities

Your attorney-in-fact cannot make a will (the document that designates how your property should be distributed after your death) for you, or change your existing will. You can, however, give the attorney-in-fact authority to make gifts of your property while you are still alive, including gifts designed to save on estate taxes. (See Chapter 5, Section B.1.)

5. Winding Up Your Affairs After Death

All durable powers of attorney end when the principal dies. That means that you can't give your attorney-in-fact authority to handle tasks after your death, such as paying your debts, making funeral or burial arrangements or transferring your property to the people who inherit it.

If you want your attorney-in-fact to have authority to wind up your affairs after your death, use your will to name that person as your executor. If you also want to avoid probate—extensive court involvement after your death—you may want to prepare a living trust and name that person as your successor trustee.

More Information About Estate Planning.
Nolo Press offers numerous books and software programs designed to help you with basic estate planning tasks:

WillMaker (software for Windows or Macintosh) lets you create a valid will, healthcare directive and final arrangements document using your computer.

Nolo's Will Book, by Denis Clifford, contains a detailed discussion of wills and all the forms you need to create one. You can choose from several standard forms or create your own customized document.

The Quick and Legal Will Book, by Denis Clifford, contains forms and instructions for creating a basic will.

Nolo's Law Form Kit: Wills, contains a simple fill-in-the-blanks will.

Plan Your Estate, by Denis Clifford and Cora Jordan, is a detailed guide to estate planning, including a discussion of probate and probate avoidance methods, trusts, estate taxes, charitable gifts and other topics.

Living Trust Maker (software for Windows or Macintosh) lets you make a simple revocable probate-avoidance trust using your computer.

Make Your Own Living Trust, by Denis Clifford, contains forms and instructions for preparing two kinds of living trusts: a basic probate-avoidance trust and an estate tax-saving AB trust. ■

How Durable Powers of Attorney Work

A. The Mental Competency Requirement 3/2

B. The Expense of a Durable Power of Attorney 3/3

    1. Up-Front Costs 3/3

    2. Ongoing Costs 3/3

C. What the Attorney-in-Fact Does 3/3

D. When the Attorney-in-Fact Takes Over 3/5

    1. You Want Someone to Take Over Now 3/5

    2. You Want Your Attorney-in-Fact to Take Over
       If You Become Incapacitated 3/5

E. Will Your Power of Attorney Be Accepted? 3/8

F. If You Move to Another State 3/10

G. When the Power of Attorney Ends 3/10

    1. You Revoke the Power of Attorney 3/10

    2. A Court Invalidates Your Power of Attorney 3/11

    3. After a Divorce 3/11

    4. No Attorney-in-Fact Is Available 3/11

    5. After Your Death 3/11

This chapter explains in more detail how durable powers of attorney work in the real world.

A. The Mental Competency Requirement

You can create a valid power of attorney if you are an adult (at least 18 years old) and of sound mind.

When you sign the document, no one makes a determination about your mental state. The issue will come up later only if someone goes to court and challenges the durable power of attorney, claiming that you weren't of sound mind when you signed it. That kind of lawsuit is very rare.

Even in the highly unlikely event of a court hearing, the requirement is not difficult to satisfy. If you understood what you were doing when you signed your durable power of attorney, that's enough. To make this determination, a judge would probably question the witnesses (if any) who watched you sign the document and others who knew you well at the time. There would be no general inquiry into your life. It wouldn't matter, for example, that you were occasionally forgetful or absentminded around the time when you signed your power of attorney document.

Heading Off Problems

If you think someone is likely to go to court and challenge your durable power of attorney or claim that you were coerced into signing it, you can take several steps to head off problems.

See a Lawyer. You may want the lawyer to review the estate planning documents you've created yourself, or to draw up some documents for you. An experienced estate planning lawyer can answer questions about your durable power of attorney and about your other estate planning documents as well. For example, you may also be expecting challenges to your will, a trust or healthcare wishes. You can talk with a lawyer about all of these issues. The point is to have the lawyer put your fears to rest by answering your questions and confirming that your estate plan will hold up under the challenges of your stubborn relatives. Your attorney can also testify about your mental competency, should the need arise.

Sign Your Document in Front of Witnesses. You can sign your document in front of witnesses, even if your state does not require it. (See Chapter 7.) After watching you sign, the witnesses themselves sign a statement that you appeared to know what you were signing and that you did so voluntarily. If someone later challenges your competency, these statements will be strong evidence that you were of sound mind at the time you signed your document.

Get a Doctor's Statement. You may also want to get a doctor's statement around the time you sign your durable power of attorney. The doctor should write, date and sign a short statement saying that he or she has seen you recently and believes you to be of sound mind. You can attach this statement to your power of attorney document. Then, if necessary, your attorney-in-fact can produce the statement as proof that you were of sound mind when you signed your power of attorney.

Make a Videotape. You can also videotape a statement of your intent to make and sign the durable power of attorney. Such a step should not be necessary, but going to this length may further minimize the chances of a successful challenge to your competency. Be warned, however, that using a videotape may work against you. The person challenging your power of attorney document will want to use any visible quirks of behavior or language as evidence that you were not in fact competent when you made your document. If you do make a videotape, keep this tape with your power of attorney document.

Helping Someone Prepare a Durable Power of Attorney

If you are concerned that someone close to you—perhaps a parent, relative or friend—will become incapacitated soon, it is a kindness to recommend that he or she prepare and sign a durable power of attorney now. This is particularly true if you'll be the one to deal with a legal tangle if no durable power of attorney is prepared. You can explain how the durable power works and how it can give the person a say in his or her affairs—now, before it's too late. If it helps, you can also offer reassurance that the document does not need to take effect until a doctor or someone else the person absolutely trusts decides it's needed.

But if a loved one resists your honest attempts to help, there is nothing you can do. You should never coerce a person into giving up the right to handle his or her own affairs. Problems are especially likely to develop if you urge an ill person to sign a durable power of attorney and will also serve as the attorney-in-fact. An angry relative or close friend could file a lawsuit claiming you exerted "undue influence" over the person who signed the durable power of attorney, and a legal battle could ensue.

B. The Expense of a Durable Power of Attorney

In most instances, the only expense of creating a durable power of attorney is the price of this book and a few dollars for a notary to verify your signature on the document. In some situations, however, there may be other costs.

1. Up-Front Costs

If you file (record) the power of attorney in the local public land records office, you'll have to pay a small fee. You'll need to record your durable power of attorney if your state requires it (most don't), or if you give your attorney-in-fact power over your real estate. Recording your document is explained in Chapter 7, Section C.

Although it's not usually necessary, you may decide that you want a lawyer to review or modify your durable power of attorney. The fee for this service shouldn't be large, at least by lawyers' standards.

2. Ongoing Costs

If you become incapacitated and someone must handle your financial affairs for you, additional expenses will crop up. But if you have a durable power of attorney, the cost will be less than if a court-appointed conservator had to take over.

Attorney-in-Fact's Payment. If you decide your attorney-in-fact is to be paid for his or her services, those fees will be paid from your assets. (See Chapter 4, Section C.)

Fees for Accountants and Other Experts. If the attorney-in-fact must hire professionals, such as accountants or financial advisers, to help with managing your property and finances, their fees will be paid from your assets.

C. What the Attorney-in-Fact Does

Commonly, people give an attorney-in-fact broad power over their finances. But you can give your attorney-in-fact as much or as little power as you wish. With the durable power of attorney forms in this book, you can give your attorney-in-fact authority to do some or all of the following:

- use your assets to pay your everyday expenses and those of your family
- handle transactions with banks and other financial institutions
- buy, sell, maintain, pay taxes on and mortgage real estate and other property
- file and pay your taxes
- manage your retirement accounts

- collect benefits from Social Security, Medicare or other government programs or civil or military service
- invest your money in stocks, bonds and mutual funds
- buy and sell insurance policies and annuities for you
- operate your small business
- claim or disclaim property you inherit
- make gifts of your assets to organizations and individuals that you choose
- transfer property to a living trust you've already set up, and
- hire someone to represent you in court.

These powers are discussed in detail in Chapter 5, *Granting Powers to the Attorney-in-Fact.*

You can also place conditions or restrictions upon the attorney-in-fact. For example, you can give your attorney-in-fact authority over your real estate, with the express restriction that your house may not be sold.

Under the law, the attorney-in-fact must act in your best interests, keep accurate records, keep your property separate from his or hers, and avoid conflicts of interest. These legal requirements are discussed in more detail in Chapter 4.

What Your Attorney-in-Fact Can't Do

There are a few powers you can't give to your attorney-in-fact under your durable power of attorney for finances.

Healthcare Decisions. A durable power of attorney for finances does not give your attorney-in-fact legal authority to make healthcare decisions for you. To make sure that your wishes for healthcare are known and followed, you should create healthcare directives. (See Chapter 2, Section D.1.)

Marriage, Adoption, Voting, Wills. You cannot authorize your attorney-in-fact to marry, adopt, vote in public elections or make a will on your behalf. These acts are considered too personal to delegate to someone else.

Powers You've Already Delegated. If you've already given someone legal authority to manage some or all of your property, you cannot delegate that authority to your attorney-in-fact. Here are two common examples:

- You created a living trust that gives the successor trustee power over trust property if you become incapacitated. (See Chapter 2, Section B.2.)
- You signed a partnership agreement that gives your partners authority to manage your interest in the business if you can't. (See Chapter 5, Section A.5.)

Create, Modify or Revoke a Trust. Nolo's power of attorney forms don't allow you to give your attorney-in-fact permission to create, modify or revoke a trust on your behalf—with one notable exception. If you've already set up a revocable living trust, you may give your attorney-in-fact the power to transfer property to that trust. (See Chapter 5, Section A.8.)

D. When the Attorney-in-Fact Takes Over

There are two kinds of durable powers of attorney for finances: those that take effect immediately, and those that never take effect unless a doctor (or two, if you wish) declares that you can no longer manage your financial affairs. Which to choose depends, in part, on when you want your attorney-in-fact to begin handling tasks for you.

If you want someone to take over some or all of your affairs now, you should make your document effective as soon as you sign it. Then, your attorney-in-fact can begin helping you with your financial tasks right away—and can continue to do so if you later become incapacitated.

On the other hand, you may feel strongly that your attorney-in-fact should not take over unless you are incapacitated. In this case, you have two options. If you trust your attorney-in-fact to use his or her authority only when it's absolutely necessary, you can go ahead and make your durable power of attorney effective immediately. Legally, your attorney-in-fact will then have the authority to act on your behalf—but won't do so unless he or she ever decides that you cannot handle your affairs yourself.

If you're uncomfortable making a document that's effective immediately, you can make what's known as a "springing" power of attorney. It doesn't take effect until a physician examines you and declares, in writing, that you can't manage your finances.

There are some real inconveniences involved in creating a springing power of attorney, and it's wise to consider them before you decide to make one. If you truly trust your attorney-in-fact, you may find that it makes more sense to create a document that takes effect immediately and then make clear to your attorney-in-fact when he or she should take action under the document.

1. You Want Someone to Take Over Now

You don't have to be incapacitated to benefit from a durable power of attorney. If you make your document effective immediately, your attorney-in-fact can step in right away to help you manage your financial affairs. This may make sense in a number of different situations, including when:

- you are suffering from a short- or long-term illness and you don't have the energy to deal with day-to-day financial tasks
- you have an injury that makes it difficult to get to the bank or government agency offices to take care of important money matters, or
- you've been occasionally forgetful and feel that it would be safer to have someone else keeping an eye on your finances.

Even if you give your attorney-in-fact permission to start handling your finances before you become incapacitated, you don't have to turn over complete control. Explain to your attorney-in-fact exactly how much help you need, and with which specific tasks. He or she should follow your wishes carefully. And if you want your attorney-in-fact to consult you before taking action under the power of attorney, he or she is legally obligated to do so. If you become dissatisfied with the arrangement, you can revoke the durable power and end the attorney-in-fact's authority to act for you.

2. You Want Your Attorney-in-Fact to Take Over If You Become Incapacitated

There's no precise legal definition of incapacity. It means that you have lost some physical or mental abilities, but it is not a recognized medical condition. The general understanding is summed up by New Mexico's law, which says you're incapacitated if you can no longer "effectively manage personal care, property or financial affairs." For example, you may still be in command of your mental faculties, but unable, because of injury, illness, old age or blindness, to care for your property. You might be unable to handle financial matters, but still be able to make personal medical decisions. Or you might be able to handle personal day-to-day finances, but not manage investments.

Common physical causes of incapacity are problems associated with advancing age, such as heart attacks, strokes and Alzheimer's disease. Incapacity can also be caused by serious accidents, drug or alcohol addiction, degenerative diseases such as AIDS or mental illness. People sometimes move in and out of periods of incapacity. (For information about what happens if you regain capacity and want to revoke your power of attorney, see Chapter 11.)

Many people don't want their attorney-in-fact to take any action under their power of attorney unless they become incapacitated. But even if that's what you want, you may still want to make your document effective as soon as you sign it.

a. Making Your Document Effective Immediately

If you know, or reasonably believe, that you are likely to become incapacitated soon, it's probably a good idea to make your durable power of attorney effective right away. For example, if you or someone you love has a serious degenerative disease and is rapidly losing the ability to manage business affairs, a durable power of attorney that is effective immediately would be appropriate. Or, if you are facing major surgery, you will probably want to sign an immediately effective document.

Even if you're 100% healthy now, if you're comfortable giving another person the authority to manage your affairs and your attorney-in-fact is as trustworthy as he or she should be, you're probably better off making your document effective immediately. Signing an immediately effective document avoids the hassles creating a springing power of attorney, discussed below. You can agree with your attorney-in-fact that no action will be taken under the document until in the attorney-in-fact's opinion, you are unable to take care of yourself and your property—or you otherwise direct. If you don't trust

that your attorney-in-fact will refrain from using the document for as long as you are able to handle your own affairs, you may want to think about naming someone else to represent you.

If you choose to make your document effective immediately, you and your attorney-in-fact should discuss what "incapacity" means to you. You'll want a clear understanding of when your attorney-in-fact should take matters into his or her own hands. For example, you may want to have your attorney-in-fact take over when he or she sees that you're too ill to pay your bills on time or have lost the mental acuity to make responsible decisions about your investments. Explore various scenarios with your attorney-in-fact until you reach an understanding of when and how your attorney-in-fact should exercise authority under the document.

b. Making a Springing Power of Attorney

You may not want your attorney-in-fact to take over your financial affairs until a doctor states that you are no longer able to manage them on your own. If this is so, you can make a "springing" power of attorney. It has absolutely no effect unless and until at least one physician signs a sworn statement that you are incapacitated.

Some people prefer this kind of durable power of attorney because they're not in immediate danger of incapacity. The document simply acts as a kind of risk-free legal insurance—something to protect you if you ever need it.

And some people may like the idea of a springing document because requiring at least one doctor's statement removes any danger that your attorney-in-fact will make his or her own judgment that you are incapacitated—even if you disagree. Ideally, however, you will trust your attorney-in-fact so well that this will not be a serious concern.

There are some drawbacks to springing powers of attorney that you should consider.

First, for your document to spring into effect, your attorney-in-fact will have to obtain statements from one or two doctors certifying that you can no longer handle your financial affairs. The process of getting the doctors' statements may be time-consuming and complicated for your attorney-in-fact.

In addition, some people may be reluctant to accept a springing power of attorney, even though your attorney-in-fact has obtained the required doctors' statements and your document is perfectly legal. A bank, for example, might question whether you have, in fact, become incapacitated. These hassles could delay your attorney-in-fact and disrupt the handling of your finances.

i. Who Decides That You're Incapacitated

To make a springing durable power of attorney, you must decide who will be responsible for judging whether or not you are incapacitated. Otherwise, there's no way for your document to go into effect. When you make a durable power of attorney using this book, you have a couple of options:

- You may name (in your power of attorney document) one or two doctors to make the determination, or
- You may allow your attorney-in-fact to choose one or two doctors if the need arises.

Alaska Residents. In Alaska, two licensed physicians must certify that you are incapacitated before your springing durable power of

attorney takes effect. You may be stumped as to whom these doctors should be. If you know just one doctor that you trust, ask him or her to recommend the second. Or let your attorney-in-fact choose two doctors if the time comes.

If you live in a remote area, and your attorney-in-fact cannot find two doctors to make the determination that you're incapacitated, one doctor's statement is acceptable as long as that doctor's statement says that it was not possible to find a second opinion.

New Mexico Residents. In New Mexico, two healthcare professionals must sign statements that you are incapacitated before your document can spring into effect. One of the healthcare professionals must be a licensed physician. Beyond that, state law does not specify who qualifies as a healthcare professional—except to say that the person you choose must be licensed. Presumably, other professionals involved in your care—such as licensed nurses or therapists—would qualify. Use your good judgment and name someone only if they have a license to practice in the area of physical or mental health care.

If you're not sure who to name, ask people you trust for recommendations. Or, let your attorney-in-fact choose the healthcare professionals if the need ever arises.

Why Must a Doctor Make the Decision?

Because incapacity isn't really a medical condition, it may seem unnecessary to have a physician make the determination that you can no longer handle your finances. But it's almost always done that way, even though only Alaska and New Mexico require, by law, statements from physicians or healthcare professionals.

A doctor's statement is familiar and reassuring to the people your attorney-in-fact will have to deal with. Banks and other institutions would probably be unwilling to rely on a statement by a family member or close friend that you are unable to handle your affairs.

If you don't want to involve doctors, you can let your attorney-in-fact decide when to start using the authority granted by the durable power of attorney. See Section 2.a, above.

One Doctor or Two?

If you're comfortable with the idea of naming one doctor to make this determination, there's no need to require a second physician's statement. Require it only if it worries you to leave the decision in the hands of just one person.

And if that's the case, take a moment to consider whether you're comfortable making this power of attorney document. Do you truly trust the person who will be your attorney-in-fact? Do you fear that family members will make trouble for your attorney-in-fact and try to interfere with your plans? If you are experiencing a lot of anxiety about making the document, talk with family members and the person who will be your attorney-in-fact to get a clearer idea of whether they support what you are doing. If you're still uncomfortable after you've tried to talk things out, you may want to consult a lawyer about your fears.

A form for the doctor to sign is included in this book. A sample is below; you can find a blank tear-out form in Appendix B or on the enclosed computer disk. Once the physician has signed a statement documenting your incapacity, the attorney-in-fact can attach it to the original power of attorney. Then, if anyone questions the attorney-in-fact's authority to act for you, the attorney-in-fact can produce the statement and confirm his or her authority.

If you name the doctor yourself, be sure to ask whether he or she is willing to make the incapacity determination for you. And be certain you and the doctor are in basic agreement about what "incapacitated" means to you. If you decide to let your attorney-in-fact choose the doctor, you should have a conversation about incapacity with your attorney-in-fact. Be sure your attorney-in-fact understands what "incapacity" means to you. He or she will need to discuss the issue with the doctor if the time comes.

ii. If the Doctor Is Unavailable

If you name a specific doctor to certify your incapacity and that doctor is not available when a physician's statement is needed, your attorney-in-fact can choose another doctor to make the determination.

If no one objects to the doctor's statement that you are incapacitated, your document should take effect without any trouble. But if third parties raise a fuss, a court may have to make the final decision about your ability to take care of yourself and your property.

E. Will Your Power of Attorney Be Accepted?

Durable powers of attorney are common; financial institutions, insurance companies and government agencies are used to them. Your attorney-in-fact, armed with a signed and notarized power of

Physician's Determination of Incapacity

I, _____,

of the City of _____, County of _____,

State of _____, declare under penalty of perjury that:

1. I am a physician licensed to practice in the state of _____.

2. I examined _____

   on _____, _____. It is my professional opinion that

   _____

   is currently incapacitated and unable to mange his/her finances and property.

Dated: _____

_____
(Signature of Physician)

_____, Physician

CERTIFICATE OF ACKNOWLEDGMENT OF NOTARY PUBLIC

State of _____

County of _____ } ss

On _____, _____, before me, _____

_____, a notary public in and for said state, personally appeared

_____, personally

known to me (or proved on the basis of satisfactory evidence) to be the person whose name is

subscribed to the within instrument, and acknowledged to me that he or she executed the same in

his or her authorized capacity and that by his or her signature on the instrument the person, or the

entity upon behalf of which the person acted, executed the instrument.

WITNESS my hand and official seal.

_____

Notary Public for the State of _____

[NOTARIAL SEAL]   My commission expires: _____

attorney document (and, if the durable power of attorney is springing, a signed statement from your physician that you are incapacitated), should have no problem getting people to accept his or her authority.

But certain questions may come up when an attorney-in-fact tries to exercise his or her authority.

Is the document still valid? It's reasonable for someone to want to make sure that your durable power of attorney is still valid and hasn't been changed or revoked. To reassure a third party, your attorney-in-fact can show that person the power of attorney document. To lay these fears to rest, it clearly states that any person who receives a copy of the document may accept it without the risk of legal liability—unless he or she knows that the document has been revoked.

Laws in many states also protect people who rely on apparently valid powers of attorney. For example, an Indiana statute states that a written, signed power of attorney is presumed valid, and a third party may rely on it. Other states have similar laws.

As a last resort, the attorney-in-fact can sign a sworn statement (an affidavit) in front of a notary public, stating that as far as he or she knows, the durable power of attorney has not been revoked and that you are still alive. Most states have laws that make such a statement conclusive proof that the durable power of attorney is in fact still valid.

Does the attorney-in-fact have the authority he or she claims? Any third party who relies on a durable power of attorney must be sure that the attorney-in-fact has the power he or she claims to have. That means the third party must examine the document, to see what power it grants.

Nolo's power of attorney document is very specific about the attorney-in-fact's powers. For example, if you give your attorney-in-fact authority over your banking transactions, the document expressly states that the attorney-in-fact is empowered to write checks on your behalf. Your attorney-in-fact can point to the paragraph that grants that authority, so a doubting bank official can read it in black and white.

An attorney-in-fact who runs into resistance should seek, politely but insistently, someone higher up in the bureaucracy.

Were you of sound mind? If you weren't of sound mind when you signed your durable power, the document has no legal effect. (See Section A, above.) If you think that someone might raise this issue later, and demand proof that you were competent when you signed your durable power, you may want to follow the suggestions in Section A; they are designed to help your attorney-in-fact prove that you were competent when you signed your document.

F. If You Move to Another State

If you move to another state, it's best to revoke your old durable power of attorney and create a new one, complying with all regulations of your new state. (Revocation is explained in Chapter 11.) This is true even though your old power of attorney may be acceptable under your new state's laws.

When carrying out his or her duties, your attorney-in-fact may run into problems that are more practical than legal. For example, the document may need to be recorded (put on file) with the local land records office in the new state. If the document does not meet certain requirements, the recorder's office in the new state may not accept it. Making a new document will ensure that things will go smoothly for your attorney-in-fact.

G. When the Power of Attorney Ends

A durable power of attorney for finances is valid until you revoke it, you die or there is no one to serve as your attorney-in-fact. Very infrequently, a court invalidates a power of attorney.

1. You Revoke the Power of Attorney

As long as you are mentally competent, you can revoke a power of attorney for finances at any time, whether or not it has taken effect. All you need to do is fill out a simple form, sign it in front of a notary public, and give copies to the attorney-in-fact and to people or institutions the attorney-in-fact has been dealing with. This book contains revocation forms for you to use. (Sample forms are shown in Chapter 11; you can find blank tear-out forms in Appendix B and on the enclosed computer disk.) Keep these forms on hand in case you need them later.

> **EXAMPLE:** Susan prepares a springing durable power of attorney naming her closest friend, Tina, as her attorney-in-fact. Three years later, they have a bitter fight. Susan prepares a one-page document that revokes the durable power of attorney, and gives Tina a copy. She destroys the old document and then prepares a new one, naming her sister Joan as her attorney-in-fact.

2. A Court Invalidates Your Power of Attorney

Even if you sign a durable power of attorney for finances, if you become incapacitated there is a remote possibility that a disgruntled relative could ask a court to appoint a conservator to manage your financial affairs. (See Chapter 2, Section A.)

It's rare, but a power of attorney could be ruled invalid if a judge concludes that you were not mentally competent when you signed the durable power of attorney, or that you were the victim of fraud or undue influence. The power of attorney could also be invalidated for a technical error, such as the failure to sign your document in front of witnesses if your state requires it. If that happens, the judge could appoint a conservator to take over management of your property.

In most states, if a court appoints a conservator, the attorney-in-fact becomes accountable to the conservator—not just to you—and the conservator has the power to revoke your durable power of attorney if he or she doesn't approve of the way

your attorney-in-fact is handling your affairs. In a few states, however, your durable power of attorney is automatically revoked, and the conservator assumes responsibility for your finances and property. (For a list of the rules in each state, see Chapter 11.)

3. After a Divorce

In California, Illinois, Indiana and Missouri, if your spouse is your attorney-in-fact and you divorce, your ex-spouse's authority is immediately terminated. If you named an alternate (successor) attorney-in-fact in your power of attorney, that person takes over as attorney-in-fact.

In any state, however, third parties may question the validity of a document created before a divorce that names the ex-spouse as attorney-in-fact. For this reason, if you get divorced you should revoke your durable power of attorney and make a new one.

4. No Attorney-in-Fact Is Available

A durable power of attorney must end if there's no one to serve as the attorney-in-fact. To avoid this, you can name up to two alternate (successor) attorneys-in-fact, who will serve if your first choice can't. (See Chapter 4, Section A.)

For a bit of extra insurance, you can also allow the alternate attorney-in-fact to delegate his or her duties to someone else. (See Chapter 5, Section C.)

5. After Your Death

A durable power of attorney ends when the principal dies. In most states, however, if the attorney-in-fact doesn't know of your death and continues to act on your behalf, his or her actions are still valid.

If you want your attorney-in-fact to have any authority over winding up your affairs after your death, you must grant that authority in your will or living trust. (See Chapter 2, Section D.5.) ∎

Your Attorney-in-Fact

A. Choosing Your Attorney-in-Fact 4/2

    1. General Considerations 4/2

    2. If You're Married 4/3

    3. If You Have a Living Trust 4/3

    4. Appointing More Than One Person 4/4

    5. Poor Choices for Attorney-in-Fact 4/5

    6. If You Can't Think of Anyone to Name 4/5

    7. Naming Alternate Attorneys-in-Fact 4/5

B. Your Attorney-in-Fact's Responsibilities 4/6

    1. Basic Responsibilities: Honesty and Prudence 4/6

    2. Supervision of the Attorney-in-Fact 4/8

    3. Resignation 4/8

    4. The Alternate Attorney-in-Fact's Duties 4/10

    5. Information for Your Attorney-in-Fact 4/10

C. Paying Your Attorney-in-Fact 4/10

This chapter helps you choose an attorney-in-fact and explains the basic legal rules your attorney-in-fact must follow while acting on your behalf. It is written primarily for those who are using this book to make a durable power of attorney for finances—a document that remains effective even if you become incapacitated. If you are making a durable power, it's best to carefully read the entire chapter.

If you are using this book to make a conventional power of attorney—a document that automatically ends if you become incapacitated—this chapter will help by introducing the basic issues to consider when appointing an attorney-in-fact. If you're making a general conventional power of attorney that grants long-term powers, you can skip the discussions involving incapacity. Those making a limited conventional power of attorney can skip the information about incapacity or extensive, long-term financial management; it doesn't apply to your situation.

A. Choosing Your Attorney-in-Fact

The most important decision you must make when you create any kind of financial power of attorney is who will serve as your attorney-in-fact.

Depending on the powers you grant, the attorney-in-fact may have tremendous power over your property. You need to choose someone you trust completely. Fortunately, most of us know at least one such person—usually a spouse, partner, relative or close friend. Or, perhaps one member of your family is particularly good at managing business affairs and routinely helps you and other family members with them. If there's no one you trust completely with this great authority, a financial power of attorney isn't for you.

If you are making a durable power of attorney, remember that no one will be keeping an eye on the attorney-in-fact once he or she takes over your finances. If your attorney-in-fact handles your affairs carelessly or dishonestly while you are incapacitated, the only recourse of your family or friends

would be a lawsuit—obviously, not a satisfactory approach. Lawsuits are burdensome and expensive, and would entangle your loved ones in all the legal red tape a power of attorney is designed to avoid. And there's no guarantee that money lost by a bungling attorney-in-fact would ever be recovered. All this is not said to frighten you needlessly, but simply to underscore the need to make a careful choice about who will represent you.

No matter what type of document you make, if you are of sound mind, you can always "fire" a troublesome or dishonest attorney-in-fact by revoking the power of attorney document. But choosing wisely from the start will help you avoid both hard feelings and monetary losses.

1. General Considerations

Any competent adult can serve as your attorney-in-fact; the person most definitely doesn't have to be a lawyer.

But don't name someone to serve as your attorney-in-fact without first discussing it with that person and making sure he or she accepts this serious responsibility. This book contains a sheet of information you can copy and give to your attorney-in-fact explaining what the job is about. (See Section B.5; a tear-out copy is in Appendix B, or you can print it from the enclosed computer disk.)

In most situations, the attorney-in-fact does not need extensive experience in financial management; common sense, dependability and complete honesty are enough. If necessary, your attorney-in-fact can get professional help—from an accountant, lawyer or tax preparer, perhaps—and pay for it out of your assets. If, however, you want the attorney-in-fact to help run your small business or manage extensive investments, be sure you choose someone with enough experience to handle the job.

Sometimes it's tough to know whom to choose. Perhaps your mate is ill, or just wouldn't be a good choice for other reasons. Or you may not know anyone that you feel entirely comfortable asking to take over your financial affairs. Or, if you have an active, complex investment portfolio or own a business, you might decide that your attorney-in-fact needs business skills, knowledge or management abilities beyond those of the people closest to you.

If you're not sure whom to choose, read the rest of this chapter and discuss the issue with those close to you. Keep in mind that it's better not to make a power of attorney than to entrust your affairs to someone in whom you don't have complete confidence.

Avoiding Family Conflicts. If there are long-standing feuds among family members, they may object to your choice of attorney-in-fact or the extent of the authority you delegate. If you foresee any such personal conflicts, it's wise to try to defuse them in advance. A discussion with the people who are leery of the power of attorney might help. If you still feel uncomfortable after talking things over, you may want to discuss the troubles with a knowledgeable lawyer. A lawyer can review your estate planning documents and might help you feel reassured that your plans will be carried out as you wish.

2. If You're Married

If you're married, you'll probably want to make your spouse your attorney-in-fact unless there is a compelling reason not to. There are powerful legal and practical reasons, in addition to the emotional ones, for appointing your spouse. The main one is that naming anyone else creates the risk of conflicts between the attorney-in-fact and your spouse over how to manage property that belongs to both spouses. (Your spouse's authority over your property, if you become incapacitated, is discussed in Chapter 2, Section B.1.)

EXAMPLE: Henry and Amelia, a married couple, each create a durable power of attorney for finances. Henry names Amelia as his attorney-in-fact, but Amelia names her sister Anna. Later,

Amelia becomes unable to manage her affairs, and Anna takes over as her attorney-in-fact. Soon Anna and Henry are arguing bitterly over what should be done with the house and investments that Henry and Amelia own together. If they can't resolve their differences, Henry or Anna may have to go to court and ask a judge to determine what is in Amelia's best interests.

If your spouse is ill, quite elderly or simply not equipped to manage your financial affairs, you may have to name someone else as attorney-in-fact. The wisest course is for you and your spouse to agree on who the attorney-in-fact should be, perhaps one of your grown children.

Divorce does not end your spouse's authority in most states. If your spouse is your attorney-in-fact, that designation does not automatically end if you get divorced, except in California, Illinois, Indiana and Missouri. In any state, after a divorce you should revoke the power of attorney and create a new one, naming someone else as your new attorney-in-fact. (See Chapter 11.)

3. If You Have a Living Trust

If you have created a revocable living trust to avoid probate or minimize estate taxes, the "successor trustee" you named in the trust document will have power over the trust property if you become incapacitated. Or, if you and your spouse made a living trust together, the trust document almost certainly gives your spouse authority over trust property if you become incapacitated. (Living trusts are discussed in Chapter 2, Section B.2.)

Creating a financial power of attorney doesn't change any of this. Your attorney-in-fact will not have authority over property in your living trust. To avoid conflicts, it's advisable to have the same person managing both trust property and non-trust property if you become incapacitated. So normally, you'll name the same person as successor trustee and as your attorney-in-fact.

EXAMPLE: Carlos, a widower, prepares a revocable living trust to avoid probate and a durable power of attorney for finances in case he becomes incapacitated. He names his son, Jeffrey, as both successor trustee of the living trust and attorney-in-fact under the durable power of attorney.

Several years later, Carlos has a stroke and is temporarily unable to handle his everyday finances. Jeffrey steps in to deposit his father's pension checks and pay his monthly bills, using his authority as attorney-in-fact. As successor trustee, he also has legal authority over the property Carlos transferred to his living trust, including Carlos's house.

4. Appointing More Than One Person

In general, it's a bad idea to name more than one attorney-in-fact, because conflicts between them could disrupt the handling of your finances. Also, some banks and other financial institutions prefer to deal with a single attorney-in-fact.

If you're tempted to name more than one person simply so that no one feels hurt or left out, think again. It may be better to pick one person for the job and explain your choice to your loved ones now. If you name more than one person and they don't get along, they may wind up resolving their disputes in court. This might result in more bad feelings than if you had just picked one person to be attorney-in-fact, and explained your choice, in the first place.

a. How Multiple Attorneys-in-Fact Make Decisions

If you name more than one attorney-in-fact, you'll have to grapple with the question of how they should make their decisions. You can require co-agents to carry out their duties in one of two ways:

- they must all reach agreement before they take any action on your behalf, or

- they may make decisions independent of one another.

Both methods have strengths and pitfalls. Requiring your attorneys-in-fact to act jointly ensures that decisions are made carefully and with the knowledge of everyone involved, but coordinating multiple decision-makers can be burdensome and time-consuming. On the other hand, allowing your attorneys-in-fact to act separately makes it easy to get things done, but allowing more than one person to make independent decisions about your finances can lead to poor recordkeeping and general confusion. For example, one attorney-in-fact could independently take money out of your bank accounts or sell stock without full knowledge of what the other is doing to manage your investments.

There's no hard and fast rule on which strategy is better. Choose the method that feels most comfortable to you.

b. If Your Attorneys-in-Fact Disagree

If your attorneys-in-fact get into a dispute that interferes with their ability to represent you properly, they may need help working things out. Getting help could mean submitting the dispute to mediation or arbitration—or going to court to have a judge decide what's best. Your attorneys-in-fact can decide how to handle the matter, keeping in mind that their foremost responsibility is to act in your best interest. The downside of all this is not just that there could be confusion and delays in handling your finances, but also that you'll probably be the one to pay the costs of settling the dispute.

c. If One or More of Your Attorneys-in-Fact Can't Serve

If you name more than one attorney-in-fact, and one of them can't serve, the others will continue to serve alone. If none of them can serve, an alternate can take over. (See Section 7, below, for more information about naming alternates.)

5. Poor Choices for Attorney-in-Fact

Here are some suggestions on whom to avoid when you're choosing an attorney-in-fact.

a. Someone Who Lives Far Away

To carry out duties and responsibilities properly and promptly, it's best that the attorney-in-fact live nearby. Although overnight mail, faxes, email and other technological wonders have made it easier to conduct business long-distance, it's still best to be close at hand. After all, this is the person who will be responsible for day-to-day details of your finances: opening your mail, paying bills, looking after property and so on.

Of course, many families are spread across the country these days. If there's only one person you

trust enough to name as attorney-in-fact, and he or she lives far away, you may have to settle for the less than ideal situation.

b. An Institution

Don't name an institution, such as a bank, as attorney-in-fact. It isn't legal in some states, and is definitely not desirable. Serving as attorney-in-fact is a personal responsibility, and there should be personal connection and trust between you and your attorney-in-fact. If the person you trust most happens to be your banker, appoint that person, not the bank.

6. If You Can't Think of Anyone to Name

If you can't come up with a family member or close friend to name, you may want to consider asking your lawyer, business partner or banker to serve as attorney-in-fact. If you really know and trust the person, it may be a good option for you. Otherwise, it's better not to make a power of attorney.

7. Naming Alternate Attorneys-in-Fact

If you're making a durable power of attorney or granting long-term powers with a general conventional power of attorney, it's a good idea to name someone who will take over as your attorney-in-fact in case your first choice can't serve or needs to resign after serving for a period of time. (Naming an alternate is not an option if you are making a limited conventional power of attorney using one of the short forms in this book.) You can name a second alternate as well. Your first alternate would take over if your initial choice can't serve. The second alternate would take the job only if both your first and second choices can't keep it.

When naming alternates, use the same criteria that you used to make your first choice for attorney-in-fact. Your alternates should be every bit as trustworthy and competent. If you don't know anyone you trust well enough, skip the matter altogether.

If You Name More Than One Attorney-in-Fact

If you name more than one attorney-in-fact, the person you name as a first alternate will take over only if all of your attorneys-in-fact must give up the job. If any of your first choices can continue to serve, they may do so alone, without the addition of your alternate.

If you name a second alternate, that person will take over only in the extremely unlikely event that all of your named attorneys-in-fact and your first alternate cannot serve.

As a further precaution, you can authorize your attorney-in-fact to appoint someone to serve if all those you named cannot. You do this by giving your attorney-in-fact permission to delegate tasks to others. (See Chapter 5, Section C.) Allowing your attorney-in-fact to delegate authority to someone else eliminates the minimal risk that the position might become vacant because of the original attorney-in-fact's death, disability or resignation. If this occurs, and you haven't named an alternate or none of your alternates are available, your power of attorney would be useless. If you are incapacitated, there would have to be a court action, such as a full-scale conservatorship proceeding, to find someone to manage your affairs.

B. Your Attorney-in-Fact's Responsibilities

How much authority you want to give your attorney-in-fact is up to you. But whatever the attorney-in-fact's duties, he or she must always act in your best interests.

1. Basic Responsibilities: Honesty and Prudence

The attorney-in-fact you appoint in your power of attorney is a "fiduciary"—someone who holds a position of trust and must act in your best interests. The law requires your attorney-in-fact to:

- handle your property honestly and prudently
- avoid conflicts of interest
- keep your property completely separate from his or her own, and
- keep adequate records.

These standards do not present problems in most simple situations. For example, if you just want your attorney-in-fact to sign for your pension check, deposit it in your bank account and pay for your basic needs, there is slight possibility of uncertainty or dispute.

Sometimes, however, these rules impose unnecessary hardships on an attorney-in-fact. For example, your property may already be mixed with that of your attorney-in-fact and it may make good sense for that to continue. You can use your power of attorney document to give your attorney-in-fact permission to deviate from some of the rules.

These rules and exceptions are discussed below.

a. Managing Your Property Prudently

The attorney-in-fact must be careful with your money and other property. State laws generally require an attorney-in-fact to act as a "prudent person" would under the circumstances. That means the attorney-in-fact has no obligation to make canny investment moves with your cash. The primary goal is not to lose your money.

The attorney-in-fact may, however, take careful actions on your behalf. For example, if your money is in a low-interest bank account, the attorney-in-fact might invest it in government bonds, which pay higher interest but are still very safe.

Because most people choose a spouse, close relative or friend to be attorney-in-fact, your power of attorney makes the attorney-in-fact liable only for losses resulting from willful misconduct or gross negligence—not for a well-meaning decision that turned out badly. Essentially, that means that the attorney-in-fact is liable only for intentional wrong-doing or extreme carelessness with your assets.

b. Avoiding Conflicts of Interest

Normally, an attorney-in-fact has no right to engage in activities where he or she personally stands to benefit. Such activities, which create conflicts of interest between the principal and attorney-in-fact, are called "self-dealing." The attorney-in-fact's motive is irrelevant. If the transaction is challenged in court, it is presumed fraudulent until the attorney-in-fact proves otherwise.

> **EXAMPLE:** David is the attorney-in-fact for his elderly mother, Irene. After Irene's failing eye-sight makes it impossible for her to drive, David decides to buy her car from her. He looks up the car's fair market value to make sure he is paying a fair amount, writes a check and deposits it in her bank account.
>
> This transaction is forbidden, even though David isn't cheating Irene, unless Irene's power of attorney specifically allows David to benefit from his management of her property and finances.

The ban on self-dealing is intended to protect you—after all, the attorney-in-fact is supposed to be acting on your behalf. It's quite sensible, however, to give the attorney-in-fact permission for self-dealing if your attorney-in-fact is your spouse, a close family member, a business partner or other person whose affairs are already intertwined with yours. For example, if your attorney-in-fact is also your wife, or your child who will someday inherit most or all of your property, you don't want her to have to worry because selling an item of property you own jointly will benefit her as well as you. You can grant this permission in your power of attorney document.

> **EXAMPLE:** Maurice wants Alice, his best friend, to serve as his attorney-in-fact. They have been involved in many real estate transactions to-gether, and they have several current projects in the works. Maurice doesn't want to risk disrupt-ing these projects or curtailing Alice's ability to do business, so he specifically states in his power of attorney that Alice may benefit from transactions she undertakes on Maurice's behalf as his attorney-in-fact.

c. Keeping Funds Separate

An attorney-in-fact is never allowed to mix (com-mingle) your funds with his or her own unless the power of attorney specifically authorizes it. You will probably want to grant that authority if you appoint your spouse, mate or immediate family member as attorney-in-fact, and your finances are already thoroughly mixed together in joint bank or security accounts.

> **EXAMPLE:** Jim and Eduardo have been living together for 25 years. They have a joint check-ing account and share all basic living expenses. Each names the other as his attorney-in-fact in springing durable power of attorney documents. To avoid any possible problems, Jim and Eduardo both include, in their powers of attorney, specific provisions that allow commin-gling of funds.

d. Keeping Good Records

Your attorney-in-fact is legally required to keep accurate and separate records for all transactions made on your behalf. This is true whether or not the attorney-in-fact is paid to serve as attorney-in-fact. (Paying your attorney-in-fact is discussed in Section C, below.) Good records are particularly important if the attorney-in-fact ever wants to resign and turn the responsibility over to a successor.

Recordkeeping isn't an onerous requirement. All the attorney-in-fact must be able to do is show where and how your money has been spent. In most instances, it's enough to have a balanced checkbook and receipts for bills paid and claims made. And because the attorney-in-fact will probably file tax returns on your behalf, income and expense records may be necessary.

> EXAMPLE: Keiji appoints Kathryn, his niece, to serve as his attorney-in-fact. Keiji receives income from his savings, two IRAs, Social Security and stock dividends. Kathryn will have to keep records of the income for bank and tax purposes.

You and your prospective attorney-in-fact should discuss and agree on what recordkeeping is appropriate. The attorney-in-fact may also want to review your current records now to find out where they're kept and make sure they're in order. If you don't have clear records, the attorney-in-fact may have to spend a lot of time sorting things out later.

As part of managing your finances, the attorney-in-fact may hire a bookkeeper, accountant or other financial advisor and pay for the services from your property.

Nolo's *Personal RecordKeeper.* If, like many people, your records are in haphazardly labeled shoeboxes and file folders, this may be a good time to get organized. One way to start is with Nolo's *Personal RecordKeeper,* a computer program (Windows or Macintosh) that helps you organize family, medical, financial and insurance records and inventory your property.

2. Supervision of the Attorney-in-Fact

An attorney-in-fact is not directly supervised by a court; that's the whole point of appointing one. The attorney-in-fact is not required to file reports with any courts or government agencies.

If you make a durable power of attorney and become incapacitated, a court may become involved only if someone close to you fears that the attorney-in-fact is acting dishonestly or not in your best interests. It's rare, but close relatives or friends may ask a court to order the attorney-in-fact to take certain actions. Or they may ask the court to terminate the power of attorney and appoint a conservator to look after your affairs. If a conservator is appointed for you, the attorney-in-fact will have to account to the conservator—or the conservator may revoke your durable power of attorney altogether. (See Chapter 11.) Disgruntled family members or friends may also challenge the durable power of attorney itself, on the ground that you weren't mentally competent when you signed it or were the victim of some kind of fraud.

Some states have statutes that set out specific procedures for such court actions. For example, a California statute authorizes certain people—the principal, the attorney-in-fact, a spouse or child of the principal, and any person who would inherit property from the principal if he or she died without a will (close family members, in most cases)—to ask a court to resolve questions relating to the durable power of attorney. In Tennessee, the next of kin can ask a court to require an attorney-in-fact to post a bond (basically, an insurance policy, generally issued by a surety company).

3. Resignation

No one can be forced to serve as an attorney-in-fact—it's a voluntary job, and in theory, the attorney-in-fact can resign at any time.

If you're making a durable power of attorney or a general conventional power of attorney, resignation is simplest when the document names a successor to take over as attorney-in-fact, and the successor is willing and able to serve. A resignation form, which your attorney-in-fact can sign and send to the successor, is contained in Appendix B and on the enclosed disk. A sample form is shown below.

Resignation of Attorney-in-Fact

I, _____,

of the City of _____, County of _____,

State of _____, resign as attorney-in-fact under the

Financial Power of Attorney created by _____

_____

and dated _____. My resignation is effective _____

_____.

Dated: _____

_____
Signature of Attorney-in-Fact

_____, Attorney-in-Fact

CERTIFICATE OF ACKNOWLEDGMENT OF NOTARY PUBLIC

State of _____ }

County of _____ } ss

On _____, _____, before me, _____

_____, a notary public in and for said state, personally appeared

_____, personally

known to me (or proved on the basis of satisfactory evidence) to be the person whose name is

subscribed to the within instrument, and acknowledged to me that he or she executed the same in

his or her authorized capacity and that by his or her signature on the instrument the person, or the

entity upon behalf of which the person acted, executed the instrument.

WITNESS my hand and official seal.

_____

Notary Public for the State of _____

[NOTARIAL SEAL]   My commission expires: _____

For durable powers of attorney, if your attorney-in-fact resigns after you are incapacitated and your document doesn't name a successor, or the successor cannot serve, a conservatorship proceeding may be necessary. (See Chapter 2, Section A.) Leaving a disabled principal in the lurch without a good reason could be considered a breach of duty, and a court might order an attorney-in-fact to continue serving until a conservator can be appointed and take over.

4. The Alternate Attorney-in-Fact's Duties

Someone who is asked to serve as an alternate attorney-in-fact (see Section A.7, above) may be worried about possible liability for the acts of the original attorney-in-fact. To protect against this, Nolo's Financial Power of Attorney form states that a successor attorney-in-fact is not liable for any acts of a prior attorney-in-fact.

5. Information for Your Attorney-in-Fact

The person you ask to be your attorney-in-fact may not have a clue about what the job entails. That's why you should give him or her some important background information like that in the information

sheet below. This information is appropriate for attorneys-in-fact appointed under durable or conventional powers of attorney. (A tear-out version is in Appendix B; you can also print it from the enclosed computer disk.) It explains, in general terms, what your attorney-in-fact's responsibilities will be.

But don't just hand it over and walk away. Take some time to sit and talk with your attorney-in-fact about the issues involved in managing your finances. Use the information sheet to help you remember the main issues, and be sure to touch on each of them in your conversation.

C. Paying Your Attorney-in-Fact

In family situations, an attorney-in-fact is normally not paid if the duties won't be complicated or burdensome. If your property and finances are extensive, however, and the attorney-in-fact is likely to devote significant time and effort managing them, compensation seems fair—and you can probably afford it. You should discuss and resolve this issue with the proposed attorney-in-fact before you finalize your document.

If you're making a durable power of attorney or a general conventional power of attorney, and you want to pay your attorney in fact, you can and should specify the payment arrangement in your power of attorney form. You can set your own rate—for example, $10,000 per year, $10 per hour or some other figure that you and your attorney-in-fact agree on. Or, if you don't want to decide on an amount right now, you can allow your attorney-in-fact to determine a reasonable wage when he or she takes over. No single strategy works best for everyone. Choose the approach—and the amount—that feels right to you.

> EXAMPLE 1: Frederick is quite wealthy. He owns and operates a successful chain of convenience stores in a large city. He also owns a house, several pieces of investment property and a wide array of stocks. When he is diagnosed

Information for an Attorney-in-Fact

An attorney-in-fact is someone who agrees to manage financial matters for someone else. Some attorneys-in-fact assist a relative or friend who just wants some help with paying bills or managing investments. Others take over complete control of the financial matters of someone who can no longer handle them. It all depends on the circumstances and on the document, called a "power of attorney for finances," which sets out your duties.

Serving as an attorney-in-fact is a serious responsibility, but in most situations, it involves little legal risk. In most cases, you don't need special financial or legal knowledge. Common sense, dependability and complete honesty are more important.

Your Duties as an Attorney-in-Fact

The power of attorney document is prepared and signed by the person who is granting you authority over his or her finances. (This person is called the principal.) It spells out exactly what authority has been granted. Read the document carefully. If there is anything you don't understand, talk to the principal or ask a lawyer to explain it to you.

Depending on the circumstances, your duties may include, among others:

- Handling banking transactions for the principal—writing checks, paying bills, depositing checks.
- Claiming Social Security and other benefits for the principal.
- Managing the principal's investments.
- Paying everyday expenses of the principal and his or her family.
- Managing real estate.
- Preparing and filing tax returns for the principal.
- Running the principal's small business.

Keep in mind that you can hire experts, if necessary, to help you with any of these tasks. Their fees are paid out of the principal's assets.

Your Legal Responsibilities

An attorney-in-fact holds a position of great trust. As you perform your duties, the law requires you to be scrupulously honest and act only in the best interests of the principal. Specifically, you must:

- Manage the principal's assets prudently, steering well clear of risky investments. You don't, however, need to worry about getting sued for honest mistakes you make while handling someone else's money. Under the Nolo Press power of attorney form, you will be liable for losses only if you are extremely careless or intentionally do wrong.
- Avoid conflicts of interest. If you benefit personally from an action taken on the principal's behalf, the transaction is presumed to be fraudulent—no matter how pure your motives. You must avoid all such transactions unless the durable power of attorney document specifically allows them.
- Keep your property and the principal's separate, unless the power of attorney document expressly allows you to mix them.
- Keep in contact with the principal, to the extent possible. If you are acting on behalf of a principal who is incapacitated, and he or she gives you instructions that you believe are not in his or her best interest, you should seek court approval before you disobey his or her wishes.
- Keep good records. You must keep accurate and separate records of all transactions made on the principal's behalf. This shouldn't be an onerous requirement. In most situations, it's enough to have a balanced checkbook and receipts for bills paid and claims made. You may, however, be required to furnish periodic reports of income and expenses to persons the principal named in the durable power of attorney.

Should You Take the Job?

You do not have to accept the responsibility of serving as an attorney-in-fact. Before you decide, discuss these issues with the principal:

- How the principal wants you to make financial decisions.
- The potential for conflicts and tension if others close to the principal disapprove of your actions.
- If you would become attorney-in-fact only if the principal becomes incapacitated, how the determination of incapacity will be made, and by whom.
- What expertise you need to manage the principal's property and keep necessary records.
- How much time your duties will require. If you are to be paid for your time, the power of attorney document should spell out the terms of the agreement.

Resigning

You can resign at any time. If you do, the alternate (successor) named in the power of attorney document will take over. If no alternate is named or none is available, you can, if the power of attorney allows it, delegate the job to a person you choose. Otherwise, the principal or a court (if the principal is incapacitated) will have to turn the job over to someone else.

If you need to step down temporarily, the power of attorney document may allow you to delegate your duties to someone else for a certain period of time. If the document doesn't permit this, you will have to resign and the principal or a court (if the principal is incapacitated) will assign the job to another person.

---

with a life-threatening illness, he creates a durable power of attorney appointing his close friend Barbara as his attorney-in-fact. Because he expects Barbara to watch over his business as well as tend to his other financial affairs, he feels it's appropriate to pay her for her services. Frederick and Barbara settle on a rate of $15,000 per year for her services.

EXAMPLE 2: Martin creates a springing durable power of attorney naming his brother, Andrew, as attorney-in-fact. Martin owns a complex investment portfolio, and the brothers agree that Andrew should be paid if he has to manage Martin's finances. They consider an hourly wage, but decide not to be that specific now. In his durable power of attorney, Martin states that Andrew may pay himself "reasonable" fees for his services.

If You Named More Than One Attorney-in-Fact

If you named more than one attorney-in-fact and you want to pay them, the amount you choose—for example, $5,000 per year or $12 per hour—applies to each one. If you want to allow your attorneys-in-fact to determine a reasonable amount for their services, each is allowed to set his or her own salary.

If you're making a limited conventional power of attorney and you want to pay your attorney-in-fact, you and your attorney-in-fact should decide on an appropriate amount and write up a separate agreement that spells out what you've decided. ■

5

Granting Powers to the Attorney-in-Fact

A. Granting Specific Financial Powers 5/2

   1. Real Estate Transactions 5/2

   2. Tangible Personal Property Transactions 5/3

   3. Stock, Bond, Commodity and Option Transactions 5/3

   4. Banking and Other Financial Institution Transactions 5/3

   5. Business Operating Transactions 5/4

   6. Insurance and Annuity Transactions 5/4

   7. Estate, Trust and Other Beneficiary Transactions 5/5

   8. Living Trust Transactions 5/5

   9. Claims and Litigation 5/5

  10. Personal and Family Maintenance 5/6

  11. Government Benefits 5/6

  12. Retirement Plan Transactions 5/6

  13. Tax Matters 5/7

B. Special Instructions for the Attorney-in-Fact 5/7

   1. Gift Transactions 5/7

   2. Restricting the Sale of Your Home 5/10

   3. Restrictions on Running a Small Business 5/11

   4. Making Periodic Reports 5/11

   5. Nominating a Conservator or Guardian 5/12

C. The Attorney-in-Fact's Power to Delegate 5/12

This chapter discusses the specific powers you can give your attorney-in-fact using Nolo's broad financial power of attorney form. If you're making a durable power of attorney or a general conventional power of attorney, you should carefully read the material that follows. But if you're using one of the shorter forms in this book—the limited conventional power of attorney, the power of attorney for real estate, or the power of attorney for child care—you can skip this chapter altogether.

A. Granting Specific Financial Powers

Nolo's financial power of attorney form lists 13 specific financial powers. You can give your attorney-in-fact some or all of them. Many people choose to give all the powers, so their attorney-in-fact will have authority to handle any transaction concerning their property or finances. But because the powers put an enormous amount of control over your finances into the hands of your attorney-in-fact, it's important to review each power and be sure you understand what it allows your attorney-in-fact to do.

If you grant all the powers, your attorney-in-fact will be able to handle your investments, real estate, banking and so on. The attorney-in-fact can use your assets to pay for any of your debts and expenses, including home maintenance, taxes, insurance premiums, wage claims, medical care, child support, alimony and your personal allowance. The attorney-in-fact can sign deeds, make gifts, pay school expenses, and endorse and deposit checks.

Here is a general explanation of each of the financial powers. They are numbered as they appear in the financial power of attorney document; you'll find a detailed definition of each power in the document itself. To grant some or all of these powers, you must simply initial the appropriate blank lines on your power of attorney form. Instructions are in Chapters 6 (for durable powers) and 8 (for conventional powers).

1. Real Estate Transactions

This power puts the attorney-in-fact in charge of managing any real estate you own. Your attorney-in-fact must, for example, pay your mortgage and taxes (with your assets) and arrange for necessary repairs and maintenance. Most important, the attorney-in-fact may sell, mortgage, partition or lease your real property.

The attorney-in-fact may also take any other action connected to real estate. For example, your attorney-in-fact may:

- buy or lease real estate for you
- refinance your mortgage to get a better interest rate
- pay off liens (legal claims) on your property
- buy insurance for your property
- build, remodel or remove structures on your property
- grant easements over your property
- bring or defend lawsuits over real estate.

Remember, however, that the attorney-in-fact has a legal obligation to take only those actions that are in your best interests.

2. Tangible Personal Property Transactions

Tangible personal property means physical items—for example, cars, furniture, jewelry, computers and stereo equipment. It does not include real estate or intangible kinds of property such as stocks or bank notes. If you grant this power, your attorney-in-fact can buy, sell, rent or exchange personal property on your behalf. Your attorney-in-fact can also insure, use, move, store, repair or pawn your personal things. Again, all actions must be taken in your best interest.

> **EXAMPLE:** Paul names his wife, Gloria, as his attorney-in-fact for financial matters. When he later goes into a nursing home, his old car, which he can no longer use, becomes an expense Gloria cannot afford. As Paul's attorney-in-fact, she has legal authority to sell the car.

3. Stock, Bond, Commodity and Option Transactions

This power gives your attorney-in-fact the power to manage your securities, including stocks, bonds, mutual funds, certificates of deposit, commodities and call and put options. Your attorney-in-fact can buy or sell securities on your behalf, accept or transfer certificates or other evidence of ownership and exercise voting rights.

Brokers may have their own power of attorney forms. Many brokerage houses have their own power of attorney forms. If yours does, it's a good idea to use it, in addition to your Nolo power of attorney. Using your broker's form will make things easier for your attorney-in-fact, because your broker will have no need to investigate your power of attorney and quibble over its terms. The broker will already have its form on file and will understand exactly what your attorney-in-fact is authorized to do.

4. Banking and Other Financial Institution Transactions

One of the most common reasons for making a power of attorney is to arrange for someone to handle banking transactions. If you give your attorney-in-fact authority to handle your bank accounts, your bills can be paid, and pension or other checks can be deposited in your accounts even if you are not able to take care of these matters yourself.

> **EXAMPLE:** Virginia, who is in her 70s, is admitted to the hospital for emergency surgery. She's too weak to even think about paying her bills or depositing her social security check—and anyway, she can't get to the bank. Fortunately, she earlier created a durable power of attorney for finances, naming her niece Marianne as her attorney-in-fact. Marianne can deposit Virginia's check and sign checks to pay the bills that come while Virginia is in the hospital.

> **EXAMPLE:** Theo, a successful songwriter, is heading off to Europe for six months of vacation. While he's away, his friend Angela will housesit for him and watch after his financial affairs. Among other things, Theo wants Angela to deposit his royalty checks and pay his rent and other bills from his checking account. Theo creates a general conventional power of attorney and grants the banking power so Angela will have no trouble making deposits and signing checks to pay the bills.

Your attorney-in-fact may open and close accounts with banks, savings and loans, credit unions or other financial institutions on your behalf. The attorney-in-fact may write checks on these accounts, endorse checks you receive, and receive account statements. The attorney-in-fact also has access to your safe deposit box, to withdraw or add to its contents.

In most states, the attorney-in-fact may also borrow money on your behalf, and pledge your assets as security for the loan.

⚠️ **Ask your financial institutions about their power of attorney forms.** Many banks and other financial institutions have their own power of attorney forms. Even though granting the banking power will give your attorney-in-fact authority to act on your behalf at any financial institution, it's a good idea to use the financial institution's form in addition to Nolo's form. Using the form that your financial institution is most familiar with will make it easier for your attorney-in-fact to get things done.

5. Business Operating Transactions

This power gives your attorney-in-fact authority to act for you in operating a business that you own yourself or that you run as a partnership, limited liability company or corporation. Subject to the terms of a partnership agreement, operating agreement or corporate rules (bylaws and shareholders' agreements), your attorney-in-fact may:

- sell or liquidate the business
- merge with another company
- prepare, sign and file reports, information and returns with government agencies
- pay business taxes
- enforce the terms of a partnership agreement, if any, in court
- exercise any power or option you have under a partnership agreement.

If your business is a sole proprietorship, the attorney-in-fact may also:

- hire and fire employees
- move the business
- change the nature of the business or its methods of operation, including selling, marketing, accounting and advertising
- change the name of the business
- change the form of the business's organization—that is, enter into a partnership agreement or incorporate the business
- continue or renegotiate the business's contracts
- contract with lawyers, accountants or others
- collect and spend money on behalf of the business.

If you're a sole proprietor, a power of attorney is a very useful way to let someone else run the business if you're unable to do so, either for a short time or due to incapacity. Be sure to work out a business plan with the person you plan to appoint as your attorney-in-fact; explain what you want for your business and how you expect it to be managed.

⚠️ **Check your partnership agreement, operating agreement or corporate bylaws and shareholders' agreements.** If you operate your business with other people as a partnership, limited liability company or closely held corporation, your business agreement should cover what happens if a partner or shareholder becomes unavailable. Typically, the other business owners can operate the business during the person's absence or even buy out his or her share. These rules can't be overridden by a power of attorney.

> **EXAMPLE:** Mike wants his wife, Nancy, to be his attorney-in-fact to manage his finances if he becomes incapacitated. Mike, a house painter, runs the M-J Painting Co. with his equal partner, Jack. Mike and Jack's partnership agreement provides that if one partner becomes incapacitated, the other has exclusive authority to operate the business.
>
> If Jack and Nancy have conflicts over money, however, there could be some problems. Mike, Jack and Nancy should think through the arrangement carefully, and may want to consult a lawyer. Whatever they decide on should be spelled out in detail in the partnership agreement. They may also want to create a customized durable power of attorney, with the lawyer's help, that sets out the details of the business arrangements.

6. Insurance and Annuity Transactions

This power allows your attorney-in-fact to buy, borrow against, cash in or cancel insurance policies or annuity contracts for you and your spouse, children and other dependent family members. The attorney-in-fact's authority extends to all your policies and contracts, whether they name you or someone else as the beneficiary. Beneficiaries are the people who will receive any proceeds of the policy when you die.

The one exception to this rule covers any insurance policies you own with your spouse. Under these policies, your spouse must consent to any transaction that affects the policy. So if your attorney-in-fact is not your spouse, he or she will have to obtain your spouse's permission before taking action. In community property states, policies that are in one spouse's name may in fact be owned by both spouses. If you have questions about who owns your insurance policies, consult a lawyer.

If you already have an insurance policy or annuity contract, your attorney-in-fact can keep paying the premiums or cancel it, whichever he or she decides is in your best interests.

Your attorney-in-fact is also permitted to change and name the beneficiaries of your insurance policies or annuity contracts. This is a broad power, and it's a good idea to discuss your wishes about it with your attorney-in-fact. If you don't want your attorney-in-fact to change your beneficiary designations, you should make that clear. If you have strong feelings about whom the beneficiary of any new policies should be, you can discuss that as well.

There is one important limitation on your attorney-in-fact's ability to designate beneficiaries. Your attorney-in-fact cannot name himself or herself as beneficiary on a renewal of, extension of or substitute for an existing policy unless he or she was already the beneficiary before you signed the power of attorney.

7. Estate, Trust and Other Beneficiary Transactions

This power authorizes your attorney-in-fact to act on your behalf to claim or disclaim property you inherit or are entitled to from any other source. For example, if you were entitled to money from a trust

fund, your attorney-in-fact could go to the trustee (the person in charge of the trust) and press your claim on your behalf. Or, if you don't really need the money and it would cause your eventual estate tax bill to rise, your attorney-in-fact could turn down the cash.

Disclaiming property—saying that you don't want it—can be a good idea if you're worried about increasing the size of your estate and generating a big estate tax bill at your death. Of course, your attorney-in-fact can't turn away property you inherit unless he or she feels that it's in your best interest to do so.

8. Living Trust Transactions

If you've already set up a revocable living trust to avoid probate or minimize estate taxes, this power gives your attorney-in-fact the authority to transfer items of your property to that trust.

> EXAMPLE: Maureen, an Illinois resident, sets up a revocable living trust to avoid probate at her death, and transfers her house and some valuable antiques to the trust. She also makes a durable power of attorney for finances. Years later, when Maureen becomes incapacitated from a stroke, her son Paul takes over as her attorney-in-fact. While she is incapacitated, Maureen inherits a house from her elder sister. Paul, as attorney-in-fact, is able to transfer the house to Maureen's living trust—avoiding a substantial probate bill for Maureen's heirs when she dies.

9. Claims and Litigation

This provision allows your attorney-in-fact to act for you in all matters that involve courts or government agencies. For example, your attorney-in-fact can bring or settle a lawsuit on your behalf. He or she can also accept court papers intended for you, and hire an attorney to represent you in court, if necessary. (Unless your attorney-in-fact is a lawyer, he or she may not actually represent you in court, but must hire someone to do so.) If you lose a lawsuit, the attorney-in-fact can use your assets to pay the winner whatever you are obligated to pay.

10. Personal and Family Maintenance

This is an important power. It gives the attorney-in-fact the authority to use your assets to pay your everyday expenses and those of your family. The attorney-in-fact can spend your money for your family's food, living quarters, education, cars, medical and dental care, membership dues (for churches, clubs or other organizations) vacations and travel. The attorney-in-fact is allowed to spend as much as it takes to maintain your customary standard of living and that of your spouse, children and anyone else you usually support.

You may normally support people other than your legal dependents. If you regularly take care of others—for example, you are the primary caretaker for a disabled sibling or an aging parent—your attorney-in-fact can use your assets to continue to help those people. You should talk with your attorney-in-fact and explain exactly what your support obligations are.

11. Government Benefits

This power allows your attorney-in-fact to apply for and collect any government benefits you may be entitled to from Social Security, Medicare, Medicaid or other governmental programs, or civil or military service. Your attorney-in-fact must send the government office a copy of the financial power of attorney to prove his or her authority.

Social Security Checks

If you want your Social Security checks paid directly to a person or business, not your attorney-in-fact, you may appoint that person or business to be your "representative payee." This practice is common when the recipient of the check is in a nursing home and would just pay it over to the home anyway. Another simple approach is to have your Social Security checks deposited directly into your bank account each month. For more information, call the Social Security Administration at 800-772-1213.

12. Retirement Plan Transactions

This power gives your attorney-in-fact authority over retirement plans such as IRAs and Keogh plans. The attorney-in-fact may select payment options, designate beneficiaries (the people who will inherit any money left in the fund at your death) and change current beneficiary designations, make voluntary contributions to your plan, change the way the funds are invested and roll over plan benefits into other retirement plans. If authorized by the plan, the attorney-in-fact may make withdrawals, borrow from, sell assets to and buy assets from the plan.

Be aware of how broad some of these powers are. For example, the power to change the beneficiaries of your retirement funds is a drastic one. You should talk with your attorney-in-fact to make your wishes clear with respect to this power.

13. Tax Matters

This provision gives your attorney-in-fact authority to act for you in all state, local and federal tax matters. The attorney-in-fact can prepare and file tax returns and other documents, pay tax due, contest tax bills and collect refunds. (To file a tax return on your behalf, the attorney-in-fact must include a copy of the power of attorney with the return.) The attorney-in-fact is also authorized to receive confidential information from the IRS.

The IRS Power of Attorney Form

The IRS has its own power of attorney form, but you don't need to use it. It is primarily designed to allow attorneys, accountants and other professionals to receive confidential tax information on behalf of clients. It is not a comprehensive, durable power of attorney for tax matters. The Nolo form gives your attorney-in-fact the power to receive confidential information from the IRS, plus the authority to handle any tax matters that arise.

B. Special Instructions for the Attorney-in-Fact

You can add your own restrictions or additions to the powers you grant from the list discussed just above. For example, if a power seems too broad, you can check the box that grants the power but add restrictions in the "special instructions" section of your form. Or, you can skip a power altogether and then describe just the parts you want in the special instructions section. Finally, you may want to add a whole new power in the special instructions section. For example, giving your attorney-in-fact the power to make gifts of your property is an extremely personal decision and may be best handled in this way. The gift-giving power is explained below, along with a few other common special instructions.

That said, you'll want to be judicious in your use of special instructions. We've given great thought to constructing and defining powers that will work well in most circumstances, and the form includes enough space to make just a few additions or modifications of your own. (If you run out of room and want to add still more instructions, you'll need to retype the form.) If you add many special instructions, you run the risk of making your document confusing.

1. Gift Transactions

You may want your attorney-in-fact to be able to give away your property under some circumstances. On the other hand, allowing your attorney-in-fact to make gifts might feel like giving up too much control. This section discusses the pros and cons of allowing your attorney-in-fact to make gifts, and shows you how to add the appropriate legal clause to your power of attorney form.

a. Allowing Your Attorney-in-Fact to Make Gifts

There are many reasons why you might want to permit your attorney-in-fact to make gifts of your property. Here are a few of the most common.

Estate tax savings. Many people with substantial assets make an estate plan with a careful eye toward reducing their eventual estate tax liability. One popular way to reduce estate taxes is to give away some of your property while you are still alive. If you have set up this sort of gift-giving plan, you'll probably want to authorize your attorney-in-fact to continue it.

If you have a plan to reduce estate taxes by giving gifts, make sure your attorney-in-fact understands your intentions and goals. Your attorney-in-fact should know who should receive your property, how often and in what amounts. You may want to explicitly limit the people and organizations to whom your attorney-in-fact may give gifts by listing them in your power of attorney document. (This is explained below.)

Other gift-giving plans. Of course, there are lots of reasons to give gifts that have nothing to do with estate planning and avoiding taxes. You may, for example, want to donate regularly to your church or a favorite charity. Or perhaps you've made a commitment to help a family member with college or starting up a business. Allowing your attorney-in-fact to make gifts means that he or she will be able to carry out your plans for you.

But again, you'll want to talk with your attorney-in-fact about your intentions. Give as much guidance as you can. And remember that you can use your form to name the specific people and organizations to whom your attorney-in-fact may give your money or property.

Family emergencies. All of us are occasionally caught off guard by unexpected financial troubles. You may want your attorney-in-fact to be able to help out if a loved one faces such an emergency. This is fine. But be sure your attorney-in-fact knows whom you'd want to help, what you consider an emergency and what your limits are. Again, you may want to use your power of attorney form to limit the people to whom your attorney-in-fact can make gifts.

b.   Beware of Gift Taxes

If your attorney-in-fact gives away more than a certain amount (currently $10,000) to any one person (except your spouse) or organization in one calendar year, a federal gift tax return will have to be filed. Gift tax may eventually have to be paid, but unless you make hundreds of thousands of dollars worth of taxable gifts during your life, no tax will actually be due until after your death. Because your attorney-in-fact is required to act in your best interest, making large gifts could put him or her in a bind. On one hand, your attorney-in-fact may feel that you would want to make a sizable gift—even if it's

a taxable one—to a particular person or organization. On the other hand, if you have a large estate that is likely to owe estate tax at your death, he or she won't want to increase your eventual tax liability.

For this reason, if you do permit your attorney-in-fact to make gifts, it's particularly important that you explain, ahead of time, what you intend, and what your limits are, if any.

Plan Your Estate, by Denis Clifford and Cora Jordan (Nolo Press), is a detailed guide to estate planning, including all major methods of reducing or avoiding estate and gift taxes. If it doesn't answer your specific questions, talk with a knowledgeable attorney.

c.   Gifts to the Attorney-in-Fact

If you allow your attorney-in-fact to make gifts of your property, you must specifically decide whether or not your attorney-in-fact will be allowed to make gifts to himself or herself. This question raises some unique issues.

If you want to allow gifts to your attorney-in-fact, you must place an annual limit on those gifts. This is because of a tricky legal rule that involves something called a "general power of appointment." If your attorney-in-fact has an unlimited power to give your property to himself or herself, *all* your property could be considered to belong to the attorney-in-fact if he or she dies before you do. This means that the estate of your attorney-in-fact would be subject to taxes based not only on the attorney-in-fact's own assets, but on yours as well.

To avert this problem, you must limit the amount of money your attorney-in-fact may accept in any given year. The sample clauses, below, show you how to include the limit in your form. To avoid trouble with gift taxes you may want to let the current gift tax threshold be your guide and set the limit at $10,000 or less. Whatever amount you choose, be sure it's far less than what you're worth. If you set the limit too high, you may inadvertently create a general power of appointment—and increase the chances that your attorney-in-fact will use too much of your property for his or her own purposes.

d. Gifts to Others

If you're comfortable giving your attorney-in-fact broad authority, you can allow gifts to anyone whom your attorney-in-fact chooses. Or, you may want to provide a list of approved recipients.

If you give your attorney-in-fact broad authority to make gifts, be sure to discuss your intentions with him or her. Your attorney-in-fact should have a sound understanding of your gift-giving goals, including the recipients you have in mind, under what circumstances gifts should be made and in what amounts.

Remember that any gifts your attorney-in-fact makes must be in your best interest or according to your explicit instructions. For example, your attorney-in-fact may make annual gifts to each of your three children to reduce your estate tax liability. Or, he or she may make periodic gifts to your niece because you promised to help her with college costs. Your attorney-in-fact should follow the guidelines you give in the power of attorney document and in conversations between you.

Loan Forgiveness

When you give your attorney-in-fact the power to make gifts, you also give the power to forgive (cancel) debts owed to you. If anyone owes you money and you've authorized your attorney-in-fact to make gifts to them, be sure you let your attorney-in-fact know how you feel about those debts. Must they be paid, or may your attorney-in-fact forgive them under some circumstances?

If you authorize gifts to your attorney-in-fact and he or she owes you money, your attorney-in-fact can forgive those debts, too. But for these debts to you, your attorney-in-fact can't cancel an amount worth more than his or her maximum gift amount in any calendar year. For example, say your son, whom you've named as attorney-in-fact, owes you $20,000. You've placed the annual gift limit at $7,000. He can forgive his debt to you at the rate of $7,000 per year.

---

e. Sample Clauses

Following are a several sample clauses. You can include one of them in your form if you want to authorize your attorney-in-fact to make gifts of your property. Which clause you should choose depends on whom you want to authorize to receive gifts, and on whether you want to name those people in your form. Remember, any gifts your attorney-in-fact makes must be in your best interest.

- **Your attorney-in-fact may make gifts to people other than himself or herself.**
  My attorney-in-fact may make gifts of my property, including forgiveness of debts owed to me and completion of charitable pledges that I have made. However, my attorney-in-fact shall not (i) appoint, assign or designate any of my assets, interests or rights directly or indirectly to himself or herself, or his or her estate or creditors, or the creditors of his or her estate, (ii) disclaim assets to

which I would otherwise be entitled if the effect of the disclaimer is to cause the assets to pass directly or indirectly to my attorney-in-fact or his or her estate, or (iii) use my assets to discharge any of his or her legal obligations, including any obligation of support owed to others, excluding me and those I am legally obligated to support.

- **Your attorney-in-fact may make gifts to recipients that you list, but not to himself or herself.**
  My attorney-in-fact may make gifts of my property, including forgiveness of debts owed to me and completion of charitable pledges that I have made. However, the recipients of such gifts shall be limited to *[type the names of people to whom your attorney-in-fact may make gifts, joined with "or"]*.

  My attorney-in-fact shall not (i) appoint, assign or designate any of my assets, interests or rights directly or indirectly to himself or herself, or his or her estate or creditors, or the creditors of his or her estate, (ii) disclaim assets to which I would otherwise be entitled if the effect of the disclaimer is to cause such assets to pass directly or indirectly to my attorney-in-fact or his or her estate, or (iii) use my assets to discharge any of his or her legal obligations, including any obligation of support owed to others, excluding me and those I am legally obligated to support.

- **Your attorney-in-fact may make gifts only to himself or herself.**
  Except as specified below, my attorney-in-fact may not give away or transfer my property without consideration or with less than full consideration, and may not forgive debts owed to me. However, my attorney-in-fact may make gifts of my property to himself or herself as long as those gifts are not worth more than a total of $_____ in any calendar year.

- **Your attorney-in-fact may make gifts to anyone, including himself or herself.**
  My attorney-in-fact may make gifts of my property, including forgiveness of debts owed to me and

completion of charitable pledges that I have made. However, my attorney-in-fact shall not make gifts of my property to himself or herself, or anyone he or she is legally obligated to support, worth more than a total of $_____ in any calendar year.

- **Your attorney-in-fact may make gifts to himself or herself, and to other people that you name.**
  My attorney-in-fact may make gifts of my property, including forgiveness of debts owed to me and completion of charitable pledges that I have made. However, the recipients of any such gifts shall be limited to *[type the names of people to whom your attorney-in-fact may make gifts, joined with "or"]*. My attorney-in-fact may also make gifts of my property to himself or herself, provided that any gifts to my attorney-in-fact, or anyone he or she is legally obligated to support, are not worth more than a total of $_____ in any calendar year.

2. Restricting the Sale of Your Home

Selling your home, especially if you've lived there many years, can be a disturbing prospect. Some people feel quite strongly that the attorney-in-fact should not sell their home—no matter what happens. If you want to grant the real estate power, but forbid your attorney-in-fact from selling or mortgaging your home, you can include a provision like the one below.

My attorney-in-fact shall have no authority to sell, convey, exchange, transfer or partition the real property, or any rights or security interest therein, of my principal place of residence, located at *[type the full address of your home]*.

But think carefully before you tie the hands of your attorney-in-fact in this way. Of course you don't want to lose your home—but if a financial emergency makes it necessary, you may not want to leave your attorney-in-fact without options.

Especially if your spouse or other co-owner of your home will be your attorney-in-fact, you probably want to trust that person to make a decision that's in your best interests.

3. Restrictions on Running a Small Business

If you have given your attorney-in-fact power over your small business interests but want to restrict the attorney-in-fact's freedom to sell or encumber the business, you can include a clause like this one:

> My attorney-in-fact shall have no authority to sell, transfer, or otherwise encumber my business, *[type the name and address of your business]*.

If you don't want to include an outright ban on selling the business, you may still want someone—your spouse or financial advisor, perhaps—notified if the attorney-in-fact wants to sell it. If that's the case, include a clause like this:

> If my attorney-in-fact deems it necessary to sell *[whatever you specify]* he or she shall give written notice of the intent to sell, before the sale and as soon as reasonably possible, to: *[type the names and addresses of the people your attorney-in-fact must notify]*.

4. Making Periodic Reports

Unless you require it, your attorney-in-fact doesn't have to report to anyone about your finances. Usually, that's fine. In some circumstances, though, you may want to require reports. For example, if the attorney-in-fact is in charge of your business, investors may need to receive periodic financial statements, audited or reviewed by an accountant. Or perhaps you want to defuse a potentially explosive personal conflict by reassuring mistrustful family members that they'll receive regular reports

about your finances. You can use your power of attorney form to authorize periodic reports to people that you name.

> **EXAMPLE:** Theodore, who is ill, appoints his son, Jason, as his attorney-in-fact for finances. Theodore's two other children, Nancy and Ed, live out of state and aren't on the best of terms with Jason.
>
> To prevent suspicion or conflict between his children over Jason's handling of Theodore's finances, Theodore decides to require Jason to give Nancy and Ed semi-annual reports of all financial transactions he engages in as attorney-in-fact.

a. Are Reports Necessary?

The idea of making your attorney-in-fact accountable to people may be appealing to you. But before you type up a long list of names of people to whom your attorney-in-fact must make reports, ask yourself whether these reports are truly necessary.

One of the most important reasons for making a power of attorney is to give control of your finances to someone you trust completely, bypassing the court system. One big advantage of this tactic is that you spare your attorney-in-fact the hassle and expense of preparing reports and accountings for a court.

If you want your attorney-in-fact to prepare reports so that someone can keep tabs on what he or she is doing, think again about the person you've named. Do you really trust him or her?

b. What Goes in the Report

If you want your attorney-in-fact to make reports, have a talk about your expectations. The language we suggest you add to your power of attorney document requires that reports include income received by you and expenses incurred. If you want other details included, you can add them.

c. How Often Should Your Attorney-in-Fact Make Reports?

Unless the timing of reports is governed by a business agreement or other legally binding document, you are free to decide how often you want your attorney-in-fact to prepare reports. You'll probably want to weigh the need for the reports against the inconvenience to your attorney-in-fact, and the expense of preparing the reports. If you have a very anxious relative, for example, you may want to authorize quarterly reports. Making these reports could be less hassle for your attorney-in-fact than dealing with constant interference from your mistrustful family member. If the situation is not so tense, semi-annual or annual reports will probably do just fine.

d. Sample Clause

Here is an example of a clause authorizing periodic reports.

> My attorney-in-fact shall prepare written *[quarterly, semi-annual, annual]* reports regarding my finances, including the income received and expenses incurred by my attorney-in-fact for me during the previous *[three months, six months, twelve months]*. These reports shall be mailed within 30 days of each *[quarter, six-month period, year]* to *[type the names and addresses of people to whom your attorney-in-fact must make reports]*.

5. Nominating a Conservator or Guardian

This part applies only to durable powers of attorney. If you're making a general conventional power, skip ahead to Section C.

One last clause that you may want to include isn't really a special instruction to the attorney-in-fact, but it does concern the attorney-in-fact. It deals with what you want to happen in the highly unlikely event that a court proceeding is ever brought to set aside or override your durable power of attorney. (See Chapter 2, Section A.) If your durable power of attorney is declared invalid, the court will appoint a conservator to handle your financial affairs.

To guard against the possibility that your plans for financial management might be thwarted if a court appoints a conservator, you can provide, in your durable power of attorney, that you want the person you choose as attorney-in-fact to be named as the conservator. Even if it's not required by law, most courts will honor your request absent a powerful reason not to.

Here's a clause you can include in the special instructions section of your form to nominate your attorney-in-fact as conservator or guardian:

> If, in a court proceeding, it is ever resolved that I need a conservator, guardian or other person to administer and supervise my estate, I nominate my attorney-in-fact to serve in that capacity. If my attorney-in-fact cannot serve, I nominate the successor attorney-in-fact nominated in Part 1 to serve.

C. The Attorney-in-Fact's Power to Delegate

If your attorney-in-fact resigns from the job, the alternate you named will take over. But if there is no alternate available, or if your attorney-in-fact is only temporarily unavailable, the attorney-in-fact will need to find a stand-in.

If you allow it, your attorney-in-fact can turn over all or part of his or her duties to someone else in this situation. This reassignment of duties is called "delegation." Delegation may be necessary at times when your attorney-in-fact is unable to act for you—for example, if he or she goes out of town or becomes temporarily ill.

An attorney-in-fact who is allowed to delegate tasks is free to turn over any or all of the job to a competent third person. This person may step in on a temporary basis or permanently, depending on the situation.

EXAMPLE 1: Caroline names her son, Eugene, as her attorney-in-fact for finances, effective immediately. She names a close friend, Nicole, as alternate attorney-in-fact. A year later, Eugene goes to Europe for three weeks' vacation, so he delegates his authority over Caroline's bank accounts to Nicole until he returns.

EXAMPLE 2: Anthony names his wife, Rosa, as his attorney-in-fact; his son Michael is the alternate attorney-in-fact. When Rosa declines to serve because of her own ill health, Michael takes over, but soon finds that other responsibilities make it impossible to continue. He delegates all his authority to his sister, Theresa.

This book contains a form that your attorney-in-fact can use to delegate authority to someone else. (A sample form is shown below; a blank tear-out form is in Appendix B, or you can print out the form using the disk that's included with the book.) The new representative will use the signed form, along with your power of attorney document, to act on your behalf.

If You Named More Than One Attorney-in-Fact

Delegation becomes more complicated if you name more than one attorney-in-fact. Here are some issues to think about.

Attorneys-in-Fact Who Must Act Jointly

If you require your attorneys-in-fact to act together in all that they do, it's a good idea to give them the power to delegate responsibilities. This is to avoid trouble in the event that one or more of your attorneys-in-fact becomes temporarily unable to act on your behalf. If this happens, the unavailable attorney-in-fact can use the Nolo delegation form to give his or her authority to the remaining attorneys-in-fact. Your remaining attorneys-in-fact can use the delegation form to prove that they are permitted to act alone. If you don't grant the delegation power, an attorney-in-fact who will be unavailable will have to write and sign an affidavit—a sworn, notarized statement—saying that he or she cannot act for you. (If one of your attorneys-in-fact permanently resigns, he or she can sign a resignation form; the remaining attorneys-in-fact can use that form to prove their authority.)

In the unlikely event that all of your attorneys-in-fact will be temporarily unavailable, they can choose a person to take over. Because your attorneys-in-fact must act together, they must agree on any person who will take over some or all of their job.

Attorneys-in-Fact Who May Act Separately

If you've authorized your attorneys-in-fact to act independently, allowing them to delegate tasks is probably not necessary or wise. The main reason for allowing delegation is to ensure that someone will always be on hand to take care of your finances. In your situation, if just one of your attorneys-in-fact is temporarily unable to act on your behalf, the others may simply act alone, without any special documents or fuss. And you can name up to two alternate attorneys-in-fact to take over if all of your attorneys-in-fact must step down. (See Chapter 4, Section A.)

Allowing delegation in your situation could, in fact, create much unnecessary confusion. Because your attorneys-in-fact may act independently, they could each delegate tasks to individuals that they choose—without consulting each other. When it comes to your finances, it's better not to open the door to that sort of chaos.

Delegation of Authority

I, _____,

of the City of _____, County of _____,

State of _____, am currently serving as attorney-in-fact for

_____

under the Financial Power of Attorney dated _____.

    Under the power granted to me in that document, I delegate the following authority to

_____

for the period beginning _____ and ending

_____:

_____

_____

_____

_____

_____

_____

_____

_____

_____

_____

_____

_____

_____

_____

Dated: _____

_____
Signature of Attorney-in-Fact

_____, Attorney-in-Fact

Preparing Your Durable Power of Attorney

A. What Forms to Use 6/2

   1. The General Power of Attorney 6/2

   2. Limited Powers of Attorney 6/2

B. Step-by-Step Instructions 6/2

   Part 1.   Principal and Attorney-in-Fact 6/3

   Part 2.   Authorization of Attorneys-in-Fact 6/4

   Part 3.   Delegation of Authority 6/4

   Part 4.   Effective Date 6/4

   Part 5.   Determination of Incapacity 6/6

   Part 6.   Powers of the Attorney-in-Fact 6/6

   Part 7.   Special Instructions to the Attorney-in-Fact 6/8

   Part 8.   Compensation and Reimbursement of the Attorney-in-Fact 6/8

   Part 9.   Personal Benefit by Attorney-in-Fact 6/8

   Part 10. Commingling by the Attorney-in-Fact 6/10

   Part 11. Liability of the Attorney-in-Fact 6/10

   Part 12. Reliance on This Power of Attorney 6/10

   Part 13. Severability 6/10

   Part 14. Definition of Powers of the Attorney-in-Fact 6/10

C. What's Next? 6/10

Once you've chosen your attorney-in-fact and thought about what powers to give him or her, preparing the durable power itself is easy.

All you have to do is tear out the appropriate form from the back of the book or print it from the enclosed disk. Then follow the instructions in this chapter. It probably won't take you more than an hour.

Remember that this chapter covers only durable powers of attorney. If you want to make a conventional power of attorney, see Chapter 8, 9 or 10.

A. What Forms to Use

There are two kinds of durable power of attorney forms: general and limited. You may want to use both.

1. The General Power of Attorney

The durable power of attorney forms in this book are called general powers of attorney, because they can be used to give your attorney-in-fact a broad range of powers. The form called *Financial Power of Attorney* is valid in most states. If you live in one of the states listed below, however, use the special *Financial Power of Attorney* form for your state. All of these forms are in the Appendix at the back of this book and on the enclosed computer disk.

Special State Forms

Alaska
Arizona
District of Columbia (use only if you grant power over real estate)
New Mexico
North Carolina
Oklahoma

2. Limited Powers of Attorney

In addition to your general power of attorney, you may want to use a limited power of attorney form provided by your bank, brokerage house or other financial institution. Limited powers, as the name suggests, grant a much narrower authority to your attorney-in-fact. Many financial institutions have their own limited durable power of attorney forms. If yours does, we recommend that you use it, as well as the broader power of attorney form in this book. If, for example, your bank has its own form, using it will head off any problems for your attorney-in-fact, because the bank will have no need to examine and quibble with the power of attorney. The bank will know exactly what authority its form grants.

B. Step-by-Step Instructions

It's not hard to prepare a durable power of attorney correctly, but it is important to follow the instructions carefully. If you don't, your attorney-in-fact might not be able to get a bank, title company, insurance company or government agency to accept his or her authority. Remember, if your durable power of attorney is in effect, it means you may have become incapacitated, and you won't be able to fix any mistakes in the document.

Here are some tips to help you get the job done right.

1. **Make copies of the blank form.** Tear out the form you want to use and make a few photocopies. You can use one for a draft and save a clean one for the final document—the one you will sign and have notarized. Or, use the disk at the back of the book to generate a form with your computer.

Check the last page of your form. Each of Nolo's tear-out and computer generated forms (except the Power of Attorney for Child Care) has multiple last pages that may, at first glance, appear to be duplicates. Each of these pages is slightly different, however. Choose only the last page that has room for the number of witnesses your state requires—none, one or two. (You can find the number of witnesses required by your state in Chapter 7, Section B.2.) Then, check the page numbers of your documents to make sure everything's in proper order and you aren't missing pages or including any extras.

2. **Use a typewriter or word processing program to fill in the blanks.** It's not a legal requirement that a durable power of attorney be typed, but your attorney-in-fact is much less likely to run into trouble if it is. People expect legal documents to be typed and may be suspicious of handwritten ones.

3. **Don't erase anything.** Your final form should not contain any words that have been erased or whited-out. If the instructions tell you to cross out something, type a string of x's through the words.

⚠️ **Get help if you need it.** A durable power of attorney can transfer tremendous power either now or, in the case of a springing durable power of attorney, sometime in the future. Even though you can revoke it at any time (as long as you are mentally competent), never create a durable power of attorney unless you thoroughly understand what you're doing. If you have questions, see an expert.

Here are instructions for filling in each part of the Nolo financial power of attorney form. You may want to refer to the discussions in earlier chapters as you make the choices necessary to fill out the form. At the end of the instructions for each item, you'll find the name of the chapter that discusses the topic in more detail.

Part 1. Principal and Attorney-in-Fact

In the first blank on the form, fill in your name. Enter your name as it appears on official documents such as your driver's license, bank accounts or real estate deeds. This may or may not be the name on your birth certificate. Enter it first, middle (if you choose), then last.

EXAMPLE: Your birth certificate lists your name as Rose Mary Green. But you've always gone by Mary, and always sign documents as Mary McNee, your married name. You would use Mary McNee on your durable power of attorney.

Be sure to enter all names in which you hold bank accounts, stocks, bonds, real estate and other property. This will make things far easier for your attorney-in-fact. If you're including more than one name, enter your full legal name first, followed by "aka" (also known as). Then enter your other names.

Making Your Records Consistent

If you use more than one name and you're up for some extra work, consider settling on one name, entering it on your power of attorney form, and then changing your other documents to conform. This will clean up your records and save your attorney-in-fact some trouble later on. To change your name on official documents and records—for example, bank accounts, deeds or Social Security records—you'll have to contact the appropriate government office or financial institution to find out what documentation they'll need to make the change for you.

In the second blank, enter the city and state where you live. If during the course of a year you live in more than one state, use the address in the state where you vote, register vehicles, own valuable property, have bank accounts or run a business. If you've made your will, healthcare directives or a living trust, be consistent: use the state you declared as your residence in those documents.

In the next blank, after the word "appoint," type in the name and address of the person (or persons) who have agreed to serve as your attorney-in-fact for finances. (A reminder: It's almost always a bad idea to name more than one attorney-in-fact. See Chapter 4, Section A.4.)

You may also, in the next section of the form, name one or two alternate (successor) attorneys-in-fact. You don't have to name an alternate, but it's a good idea. If you named more than one attorney-in-fact, the alternate will serve only if all the people you named first cannot serve. If you name more than one alternate, each will act alone and successively, in the order named.

 Chapter 4, *Your Attorney-in-Fact*, Section A.

Part 2.   Authorization of Attorneys-in-Fact

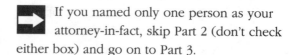 If you named only one person as your attorney-in-fact, skip Part 2 (don't check either box) and go on to Part 3.

If you named more than one person to serve as attorney-in-fact or alternate attorney-in-fact, choose whether or not you want to allow each one to act jointly or independently on your behalf. If you check "jointly," each attorney-in-fact will have to sign all documents and approve all decisions made on your behalf. If you check "independently," each attorney-in-fact may make separate decisions about managing your finances.

 Chapter 4, *Your Attorney-in-Fact*, Section A.4.

Part 3.   Delegation of Authority

If you check the first box here, your attorney-in-fact will be allowed to delegate some or all of his or her authority to someone else. In other words, your attorney-in-fact can name someone else to act as your attorney-in-fact, temporarily or permanently.

 Chapter 5, *Granting Powers to the Attorney-in-Fact*, Section C.

Part 4.   Effective Date

This is the place where you make your power of attorney durable—that is, you state that it won't terminate if you become incapacitated. You do so by checking the second or third box. If you do not check one of these boxes, your plans for making a durable power will fail. You should ignore the first box. That box is for people who want to make a conventional power of attorney—a document that automatically expires if they become incapacitated. (See Chapter 8.)

If you want your durable power of attorney to become effective:

Financial Power of Attorney

WARNING TO PERSON EXECUTING THIS DOCUMENT

THIS IS AN IMPORTANT LEGAL DOCUMENT. IT CREATES A POWER OF ATTORNEY FOR FINANCES. BEFORE EXECUTING THIS DOCUMENT, YOU SHOULD KNOW THESE IMPORTANT FACTS:

THIS DOCUMENT MAY PROVIDE THE PERSON YOU DESIGNATE AS YOUR ATTORNEY-IN-FACT WITH BROAD LEGAL POWERS, INCLUDING THE POWERS TO MANAGE, DISPOSE, SELL AND CONVEY YOUR REAL AND PERSONAL PROPERTY AND TO BORROW MONEY USING YOUR PROPERTY AS SECURITY FOR THE LOAN.

THESE POWERS WILL EXIST UNTIL YOU REVOKE OR TERMINATE THIS POWER OF ATTORNEY. IF YOU SO STATE, THESE POWERS WILL CONTINUE TO EXIST EVEN IF YOU BECOME DISABLED OR INCAPACITATED. YOU HAVE THE RIGHT TO REVOKE OR TERMINATE THIS POWER OF ATTORNEY AT ANY TIME.

THIS DOCUMENT DOES NOT AUTHORIZE ANYONE TO MAKE MEDICAL OR OTHER HEALTHCARE DECISIONS FOR YOU.

IF THERE IS ANYTHING ABOUT THIS FORM THAT YOU DO NOT UNDERSTAND, YOU SHOULD ASK A LAWYER TO EXPLAIN IT TO YOU.

1. Principal and Attorney-in-Fact

I, _Beatrice M. Steiner-Soares_ ,

of _St. Paul, MN_ ,

appoint _Samuel P. Soares, 54 Lakeshore Street, St. Paul MN_

as my attorney-in-fact to act for me in any lawful way with respect to the powers delegated in Part 6 below. If that person (or all of those persons, if I name more than one) is unable or unwilling to serve as attorney-in-fact, I appoint the following alternates, to serve alone in the order named:

First Alternate

Stephanie Soares
Name
390 Harris Street
Address
Minneapolis, MN

Second Alternate

Name

Address

- as soon as you sign it, check the second box, or

- only if you become incapacitated, check the third box.

 Chapter 3, *How Durable Powers of Attorney Work*, Section D.

Part 5. Determination of Incapacity

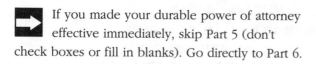 If you made your durable power of attorney effective immediately, skip Part 5 (don't check boxes or fill in blanks). Go directly to Part 6.

If you are creating a springing power of attorney (that is, one that is *not* effective immediately) you must state here who you want to determine, if it becomes necessary, that you have become incapacitated and that the durable power of attorney is in effect. You can have one or two physicians make this determination and sign sworn statements to that effect. (A statement for a physician to sign is included in Appendix B.)

Alaska and New Mexico impose special rules. If you live in Alaska or New Mexico, you should be using the form that is specially designed for your state. Alaska law requires sworn statements from two physicians to make a springing durable power of attorney take effect. New Mexico requires notarized statements from two qualified healthcare professionals, at least one of whom must be a licensed physician.

If you want your attorney-in-fact to choose one or two doctors for you, check the appropriate number of physicians, but don't write any names in the blank lines.

 Chapter 3, *How Durable Powers of Attorney Work*, Section D.2.

Part 6. Powers of the Attorney-in-Fact

This section of the form contains a list of 13 powers; you can give the attorney-in-fact all of them or only some. Either way, you can put specific limitations on the powers that you grant. For example, if you give your attorney-in-fact authority over your real estate, later in the document you can still put in a provision forbidding the attorney-in-fact from selling your residence.

Most people choose to give the broadest possible authority to their attorney-in-fact. As discussed in Chapter 5, generally that's a good strategy, unless you have a particular reason for not granting a certain power.

Scanning the list of powers, you may think that it's not necessary to grant some of them—after all, why give your attorney-in-fact authority over "claims and litigation" when you aren't involved in any lawsuits? What you should keep in mind is that even though you aren't involved in a lawsuit now, you could be later. For example, your power of attorney might spring into effect because you're in the hospital, seriously injured in a car accident, and you can't take care of your financial affairs. Your attorney-in-fact might need authority to settle a claim on your behalf. Each power is discussed in Chapter 5; if you want to see a complete definition of each power, read Part 14 of the form.

- To give your attorney-in-fact all of the listed powers, initial the blank in front of the last item in the list:

  _____ (14) ALL POWERS (1 THROUGH 13) LISTED ABOVE.

- To grant only specific powers to the attorney-in-fact, initial the blank in front of each power you want to grant. Then, cross out the other powers by typing a string of x's through them. (If you initial line 14, however, do *not* cross out any of the powers.)

 Chapter 5, *Granting Powers to the Attorney-in-Fact*, Section A.

2. **Authorization of Attorneys-in-Fact**

    If I have named more than one attorney-in-fact, they are authorized to act:

    ☐ jointly.

    ☐ independently.

3. **Delegation of Authority**

    ☒ My attorney-in-fact may delegate, in writing, any authority granted under this power of attorney to a person he or she selects. Any such delegation shall state the period during which it is valid and specify the extent of the delegation.

    ☐ My attorney-in-fact may not delegate any authority granted under this power of attorney.

4. **Effective Date and Durability**

    ☐ This power of attorney is not durable. It is effective immediately, and shall terminate on

    _____.

    ☒ This power of attorney is durable. It is effective immediately, and shall continue in effect if I become incapacitated or disabled.

    ☐ This power of attorney is durable. It shall take effect only if I become incapacitated or disabled and unable to manage my financial affairs.

5. **Determination of Incapacity**

    If I am creating a springing durable power of attorney under Part 4 of this document, my incapacity or disability shall be determined by written declaration of ☐ one ☐ two licensed physician(s). Each declaration shall be made under penalty of perjury and shall state that in the physician's opinion I am substantially unable to manage my financial affairs. If possible, the declaration(s) shall be made by _____

    _____

    _____.

    No licensed physician shall be liable to me for any actions taken under this part which are done in good faith.

6. **Powers of the Attorney-in-Fact**

    I grant my attorney-in-fact power to act on my behalf in the following matters, as indicated by my initials next to each granted power or on line (14), granting all the listed powers. Powers that are struck through are not granted.

Part 7. Special Instructions to the Attorney-in-Fact

Here, you can qualify the powers you granted in Part 6 with your own instructions or restrictions. The list of possible additions or restrictions is nearly endless; some common examples are discussed in Chapter 5.

- If you don't want to add any powers or restrictions here, type "None" in the space provided.

Because most people don't need to add much to the Nolo form, Part 7 contains room to add only a few extra clauses. If you want to add more, you'll have to retype the form.

 Chapter 5, *Granting Powers to the Attorney-in-Fact*, Section B.

 Not enough room? If you start making too many additions, it's an indication that the Nolo durable power of attorney may not be appropriate in your circumstances. You may want to see a lawyer about drafting a more personalized document. (Chapter 12, *Help Beyond the Book,* discusses how to find and hire a lawyer.)

Part 8. Compensation and Reimbursement of the Attorney-in-Fact

If you decide not to pay your attorney-in-fact, check the first box.

If you want to provide for payment, check one of the last two boxes. It's common to simply give the attorney-in-fact the right to reasonable compensation and let him or her determine an amount. Or you can check the third box and fill in an hourly, monthly or yearly fee. If you want to set an amount, be sure to enter your instructions clearly and carefully. Here are some examples:

- $10 per hour
- $500 per month
- $10,000 per year

- a flat fee of $5,000, payable at the time my document goes into effect.

 Chapter 4, *Your Attorney-in-Fact*, Section C.

Part 9. Personal Benefit by Attorney-in-Fact

Unless you say otherwise, your attorney-in-fact is not permitted to profit or benefit personally from any transaction he or she engages in as your representative. This restriction is designed to protect you, but as explained in Chapter 4, in some instances it's not necessary or desirable.

- If you want to leave the attorney-in-fact free to benefit personally from any acts he or she does as your attorney-in-fact, check the first box.
- If you are not allowing the attorney-in-fact to make gifts to himself or herself under the power of attorney document, and you don't want to allow the attorney-in-fact to benefit personally from any action taken on your behalf, check the second box.
- If, in Part 7 of your form, you have given the attorney-in-fact explicit permission to make gifts of your property to himself or herself, but you don't want the attorney-in-fact to benefit personally from any other transactions under your power of attorney document, check the third box.

 Chapter 4, *Your Attorney-in-Fact*, Section B.1.

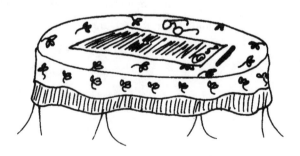

INITIALS

_____ (1) Real estate transactions.

_____ (2) Tangible personal property transactions.

_____ (3) Stock and bond, commodity and option transactions.

_____ (4) Banking and other financial institution transactions.

_____ (5) Business operating transactions.

_____ (6) Insurance and annuity transactions.

_____ (7) Estate, trust, and other beneficiary transactions.

_____ (8) Living trust transactions.

_____ (9) Legal actions.

_____ (10) Personal and family care.

_____ (11) Government benefits.

_____ (12) Retirement plan transactions.

_____ (13) Tax matters.

*BMS* (14) ALL POWERS (1 THROUGH 13) LISTED ABOVE.

These powers are defined in Part 14, below.

7. **Special Instructions to the Attorney-in-Fact**

_____

_____

_____

_____

_____

_____

_____

_____

_____

_____

_____

_____

_____

_____

_____

_____

Part 10. Commingling by the Attorney-in-Fact

Legally, the attorney-in-fact cannot mix (commingle) your monies with his own. But if your attorney-in-fact is your spouse or long-term partner, your funds may have been commingled for a long time. You should authorize this commingling by checking the first box in this part. If you want your attorney-in-fact to keep your property separate, check the second box.

 Chapter 4, *Your Attorney-in-Fact*, Section B.1.

Congratulations! When you've filled in Part 10 of the form, you've completed your power of attorney. The rest of the form is standard language. You should read and understand it, but you don't need to fill in any more blanks.

Part 11. Liability of the Attorney-in-Fact

This clause makes the attorney-in-fact liable for losing your money or other property only if the loss was caused by willful misconduct or gross negligence—that is, intentional wrongdoing or extremely careless behavior. Without this clause, the attorney-in-fact might be liable to you for losses caused by any negligence (unreasonable carelessness) committed while acting as attorney-in-fact. That could make your attorney-in-fact subject to liability for a good-faith mistake—a result you probably don't want, given that you're choosing a close relative or friend to be attorney-in-fact.

 Chapter 4, *Your Attorney-in-Fact*, Section B.

Part 12. Reliance on This Power of Attorney

Banks, brokers and others may be reluctant to accept an attorney-in-fact's authority if they're afraid, for some reason, that the durable power of attorney has been revoked and is no longer valid.

This clause protects people or institutions who rely on the attorney-in-fact's authority when shown the original, signed durable power. Even if the durable power has been revoked, a third party can rely on it unless he or she has actually received notice of a revocation. It can work wonders when it comes to getting bureaucrats and clerks to relax.

⚠ **If you do revoke your power of attorney.** This clause helps your attorney-in-fact get his or her authority accepted, but it also means that if you do revoke the power of attorney, you must give copies of the revocation to anyone you think the attorney-in-fact might try to deal with. It's also wise to record it in the land records office of any county in which you own real estate. If you don't, you could be on the hook for the former attorney-in-fact's actions. (See Chapter 11, *Revoking a Power of Attorney.*)

Part 13. Severability

This is a standard clause in all kinds of legal documents. It ensures that even in the unlikely event that some part of your power of attorney is declared invalid by a court, the rest of the document is still valid.

Part 14. Definition of Powers of the Attorney-in-Fact

This part spells out the details of the attorney-in-fact's powers, which you granted in Part 6. You don't have to check any boxes or fill in any information here.

C. What's Next?

Once you've filled out the power of attorney, you must sign it in front of a notary public and perhaps in front of witnesses as well. Instructions are in the next chapter, *Making Your Durable Power of Attorney Legal.*

8. Compensation and Reimbursement of the Attorney-in-Fact

☒ My attorney-in-fact shall not be compensated for services, but shall be entitled to reimbursement, from my assets, for reasonable expenses. Reasonable expenses include but are not limited to reasonable fees for information or advice from accountants, lawyers or investment experts relating to my attorney-in-fact's responsibilities under this power of attorney.

☐ My attorney-in-fact shall be entitled to reimbursement for reasonable expenses and reasonable compensation for services. What constitutes reasonable compensation shall be determined exclusively by my attorney-in-fact. If more than one attorney-in-fact is named in this document, each shall have the exclusive right to determine what constitutes reasonable compensation for his or her own duties.

☐ My attorney-in-fact shall be entitled to reimbursement for reasonable expenses and compensation for services in the amount of $_____.
If more than one attorney-in-fact is named in this document, each shall be entitled to receive this amount.

9. Personal Benefit to the Attorney-in-Fact

☒ My attorney-in-fact may buy any assets of mine or engage in any transaction he or she deems in good faith to be in my interest, no matter what the interest or benefit to my attorney-in-fact.

☐ My attorney-in-fact may not benefit personally from any transaction engaged in on my behalf.

☐ Although my attorney-in-fact may receive gifts of my property as described in Part 7 of this document, my attorney-in-fact may not benefit personally from any other transaction he or she engages in on my behalf.

10. Commingling by the Attorney-in-Fact

☒ My attorney-in-fact may commingle any of my funds with any funds of his or hers.

☐ My attorney-in-fact may not commingle any of my funds with any funds of his or hers.

11. Liability of the Attorney-in-Fact

My attorney-in-fact shall not incur any liability to me, my estate, my heirs, successors or assigns for acting or refraining from acting under this document, except for willful misconduct or gross negligence. My attorney-in-fact is not required to make my assets produce income, increase the value of my estate, diversify my investments or enter into transactions authorized by this document, as long as my attorney-in-fact believes his or her actions are in my best interests or in the interests of my estate and of those interested in my estate. A successor attorney-in-fact shall not be liable for acts of a prior attorney-in-fact.

(Pages 5-9 of the form are in Appendix B.)

I understand the importance of the powers I delegate to my attorney-in-fact in this document. I recognize that the document gives my attorney-in-fact broad powers over my assets.

Signed this ___10th___ day of ___October___, ___1998___.

State of ___Minnesota___, County of ___Ramsey___.

___Beatrice M. Steiner-Soares___   ___435-22-1071___
Signature   Social Security Number

CERTIFICATE OF ACKNOWLEDGMENT OF NOTARY PUBLIC

State of ___Minnesota___

County of ___Ramsey___ } ss

On ___October 10___, ___1998___, before me, ___Emma Koenig___

___, a notary public in and for said state, personally appeared

___Beatrice M. Steiner-Soares___, personally known to me (or proved on the basis of satisfactory evidence) to be the person whose name is subscribed to the within instrument, and acknowledged to me that he or she executed the same in his or her authorized capacity and that by his or her signature on the instrument the person, or the entity upon behalf of which the person acted, executed the instrument.

WITNESS my hand and official seal.

___Emma Koenig___

Notary Public for the State of ___Minnesota___

[NOTARIAL SEAL]   My commission expires: ___December 31, 2001___

PREPARATION STATEMENT

This document was prepared by:

___Beatrice M. Steiner-Soares___
Name

___54 Lakesore Street___
Address

___St. Paul, MN___

Making Your Durable Power of Attorney Legal

A. Before You Sign 7/2

B. Sign and Notarize the Durable Power of Attorney 7/2

    1. Notarization 7/2

    2. Witnesses 7/2

C. Putting Your Durable Power of Attorney on Public Record 7/4

    1. When You Should Record Your Durable Power of Attorney 7/4

    2. The Preparation Statement 7/4

    3. Where to Record Your Power of Attorney 7/5

    4. How to Record a Document 7/5

D. What to Do With the Signed Document 7/5

E. Making and Distributing Copies 7/5

F. Keeping Your Document Up to Date 7/5

After you've done the hard work of putting together a durable power of attorney, you must carry out a few simple tasks to make sure the document is legally valid. This chapter shows you what to do.

Checklist: Making It Legal

☐ Show the durable power of attorney to banks, brokers, insurers and other financial institutions you expect your attorney-in-fact to deal with.

☐ Sign the durable power of attorney in front of a notary public and, if you wish or state law requires, in the presence of witnesses.

☐ Record (file) the durable power of attorney in the county land records office, if necessary.

☐ Distribute copies of the durable power of attorney to people the attorney-in-fact will deal with.

☐ Store the durable power of attorney where your attorney-in-fact will have quick access to it.

A. Before You Sign

Before you finalize your power of attorney, you may want to show it to the banks, brokers, insurers and other financial institutions you expect your attorney-in-fact to deal with on your behalf.

Discussing your plans with people at these institutions now (and giving them a copy of the durable power of attorney, after you sign it, if you wish), can make your attorney-in-fact's job easier. An institution may ask that you include specific language in your durable power of attorney, authorizing the attorney-in-fact to do certain things on your behalf. You may have to go along if you want cooperation later. If you don't want to change your durable power of attorney, find another bank that will accept the document as it is.

B. Sign and Notarize the Durable Power of Attorney

A durable power of attorney is a serious document, and to make it effective you must observe certain formalities when you sign it. Fortunately, these requirements aren't difficult to meet.

1. Notarization

You must sign your durable power of attorney in the presence of a notary public for your state. In some states, notarization is required by law to make the durable power of attorney valid. But even where law doesn't require it, custom does. A durable power of attorney that isn't notarized may not be accepted by people your attorney-in-fact tries to deal with.

The notary public watches you sign the durable power of attorney and then signs it too and stamps it with an official seal. The notary will want proof of your identity, such as a driver's license that bears your photo and signature. The notary's fee is usually just a few dollars—probably $5 to $10 in most places.

Finding a notary public shouldn't be a problem; many advertise in the Yellow Pages. Or check with your bank, which may provide notarizations as a service to customers. Real estate offices and title companies also have notaries.

If you are gravely ill, you'll need to find a notary who will come to your home or hospital room. To arrange it, call around to notaries listed in the Yellow Pages. Expect to pay a reasonable extra fee for a house call.

2. Witnesses

Most states don't require the durable power of attorney to be signed in front of witnesses. (See the list below.) Nevertheless, it doesn't hurt to have a witness or two watch you sign, and sign the document themselves. Witnesses' signatures may make the power of attorney more acceptable to lawyers, banks, insurance companies and other entities the attorney-in-fact may have to deal with. (Part of the reason is probably that wills, which people are more familiar with, require witnesses.)

Witnesses can serve another function, too. If you're worried that someone may later claim that you weren't of sound mind when you signed your power of attorney, it's prudent to have witnesses. If necessary, they can testify that in their judgment you knew what you were doing when you signed the document.

The witnesses must be present when you sign the document in front of the notary. Witnesses must be mentally competent adults, preferably ones who live nearby and will be easily available if necessary. (Some states impose other requirements; see "States That Require Witnesses," below.) The person who will serve as attorney-in-fact should *not* be a witness. The attorney-in-fact does not have to sign the durable power of attorney.

CROWDS MAKE
ME NERVOUS.

States That Require Witnesses		
State	Number of Witnesses	Other Requirements
Arizona	1	Witness may not be your attorney-in-fact, the spouse or child of your attorney-in-fact, or the notary public who acknowledges your document.
Arkansas	2	The attorney-in-fact may not be a witness.
Connecticut	2	The attorney-in-fact may not be a witness.
District of Columbia	2	Witnesses are necessary only if your power of attorney is to be recorded. (See Section C, below.) The attorney-in-fact may not be a witness.
Florida	2	The attorney-in-fact may not be a witness.
Georgia	2	The attorney-in-fact may not be a witness. In addition, one of your witnesses may not be your spouse or blood relative.
Michigan	2	Witnesses are necessary only if your power of attorney is to be recorded. (See Section C, below.) The attorney-in-fact may not be a witness.
Ohio	2	The attorney-in-fact may not be a witness.
Oklahoma	2	Witnesses may not be your attorney-in-fact, or anyone who is related by blood or marriage to you or your attorney-in-fact.
Pennsylvania	2	The attorney-in-fact may not be a witness.
South Carolina	2	The attorney-in-fact may not be a witness.
Vermont	2	Witnesses are necessary only if your power of attorney is to be recorded. (See Section C, below.) The attorney-in-fact may not be a witness.

⚠️ **Check the last page of your form.** Each of Nolo's tear-out and computer generated forms (except the Power of Attorney for Child Care) has multiple last pages that may, at first glance, appear to be duplicates. Each of these pages is slightly different, however. Choose only the last page that has room for the number of witnesses your state requires—none, one or two. Then, check the page numbers of your documents to make sure everything's in proper order and you aren't missing pages or including any extras.

C. Putting Your Durable Power of Attorney on Public Record

You may need to put a copy of your durable power of attorney on file in the land records office of any counties where you own real estate. This office is called the County Recorder's or Land Registry Office in most states. The process of filing your document is called "recording," or "registration" in some states.

1. When You Should Record Your Durable Power of Attorney

Just two states, North Carolina and South Carolina, require you to record a power of attorney for it to be durable—that is, for it to remain in effect if you become incapacitated.

In other states, you must record the power of attorney only if it gives your attorney-in-fact authority over your real estate. Essentially, this means you must record the document if you granted the real estate power or if you own real estate and have given the attorney-in-fact power to transfer items of your property into a living trust. If the document isn't in the public records, your attorney-in-fact won't be able to sell, mortgage or transfer your real estate.

Recording makes it clear to all interested parties that the attorney-in-fact has power over the property. County land records are checked whenever real estate changes hands (or is mortgaged); if your

attorney-in-fact goes to sell or mortgage your real estate, there must be something in these public records that proves he or she has authority to do so.

There is no time limit on when you must record a durable power of attorney. So if you've created a springing durable power, which may not go into effect for many years (or ever), you may not want to record it immediately. Your attorney-in-fact can always record it later, if the document takes effect.

Even if recording is not legally required, you can go ahead and record your durable power of attorney; officials in some financial institutions may be reassured later on by seeing that you took that step.

Note for North Carolina Readers

In your state, a durable power of attorney must be:
- recorded with the Register of Deeds; and
- filed with the clerk of the superior court within 30 days after recording, *unless* the durable power of attorney waives the requirement that the attorney-in-fact file inventories and accountings with the court. The North Carolina power of attorney form in this book waives that requirement.

2. The Preparation Statement

You may notice something called a "preparation statement" at the very end of your durable power of attorney form. The preparation statement is a simple listing of the name and address of the person who prepared the document. In some states, you cannot record your document without this statement.

In most cases, the name of the principal and the name of the person who prepared the document will be the same—your own. Occasionally, however, someone may use this book to prepare a form for another person—an ailing relative, for example. In that case, the name and address of the person who stepped in to help should appear in the preparation statement.

3. Where to Record Your Power of Attorney

In most states, each county has its own county recorder's (or registry of deeds) office. Take the durable power of attorney to the local office—if you're recording to give the attorney-in-fact authority over real estate—in the county where the real estate is located. If you want your attorney-in-fact to have authority over more than one parcel of real estate, record the power of attorney in each county where you own property.

4. How to Record a Document

Recording a document is easy. You may even be able to do it by mail, but it's safer to go in person. The clerk will make a copy (usually on microfilm these days) for the public records. It will be assigned a reference number, often in terms of books and pages—for example, "Book 14, Page 1932 of the Contra Costa County, California records." In most places, it costs just a few dollars per page to record a document.

D. What to Do With the Signed Document

If the power of attorney is to take effect immediately, give the original, signed and notarized document to the attorney-in-fact. He or she will need it as proof of authority to act on your behalf.

If you named more than one attorney-in-fact, give the original document to one of them. Between them, they will have to work out the best way to prove their authority. For example, they may decide to visit some financial institutions or government offices together to establish themselves as your attorneys-in-fact. Or they may need to take turns with the document. Some agencies, such as the IRS, will accept a copy of the document, rather than the original; flexible policies like this one will make things easier on multiple attorneys-in-fact who need to share one original document.

If the durable power of attorney won't become effective unless you become incapacitated (a springing durable power of attorney), keep the notarized, signed original yourself. Store it in a safe, convenient place that the attorney-in-fact has quick access to. A fireproof box in your home or office is fine. The attorney-in-fact will need the original document to carry out your wishes.

A safe deposit box isn't the best place to store a springing durable power of attorney, unless the attorney-in-fact is a co-tenant with access to the box. It's better just to keep the document wherever you file other important legal papers. Just make sure that the attorney-in-fact knows where it is.

E. Making and Distributing Copies

If you wish, you can give copies of your durable power to the people your attorney-in-fact will need to deal with—banks or government offices, for example. If the durable power is already in their records, it may eliminate hassles for your attorney-in-fact later.

If you're making a springing durable power of attorney, however, it may seem premature to contact people and institutions about a document that may never go into effect. It's up to you.

Be sure to keep a list of everyone to whom you give a copy. If you later revoke your durable power of attorney, you must notify each institution of the revocation. (See Chapter 11.)

F. Keeping Your Document Up to Date

If you make a springing durable power of attorney, it's a good idea to revoke it and create a new one every five to seven years, especially if your circumstances have changed significantly. A durable power of attorney never expires, but if the document was signed many years before it goes into effect, the attorney-in-fact may have more difficulty getting banks, insurance companies or people in government agencies to accept its authority.

What to Do With the Other Documents in This Book

This book contains several additional documents designed to work with your durable power of attorney form. They are discussed throughout the book, but here is a quick summary of what these documents are and what you should do with them. Blank copies of these forms are in Appendix B, or you can print them from the enclosed computer disk.

Information for an Attorney-in-Fact. This sheet is intended to help your attorney-in-fact understand the job. It discusses the attorney-in-fact's duties and responsibilities, including the duty to manage your property honestly and prudently and to keep accurate records. You should give a copy to the person you name in your document, and take some time to talk together about the responsibilities involved. You can find a copy in Chapter 4, Section B.5.

Delegation of Authority. If you allow your attorney-in-fact to delegate tasks to others, he or she may want to use Nolo's "Delegation of Authority" form. Give a copy to your attorney-in-fact. Or, if you've made a springing power of attorney, keep the form with your power of attorney document so your attorney-in-fact will have easy access to it later. For more information and a copy of the form, see Chapter 5, Section C.

Physician's Determination of Incapacity. If you've made a springing power of attorney, the "Physician's Determination of Incapacity" is the form your doctor will fill out to certify that you are incapacitated—and that your durable power of attorney is effective. Your attorney-in-fact will show the certification, along with the power of attorney itself, to prove that he or she is authorized to act on your behalf.

You may need one or two of these forms, depending on the number of physicians you choose. Keep the forms with your completed power of attorney document so your attorney-in-fact will have quick access to them if it's ever necessary to put your document into effect. For more information and a copy of the form, see Chapter 3, Section D.2.

Resignation of Attorney-in-Fact. Your attorney-in-fact can use the "Resignation of Attorney-in-Fact" form to resign from the job. He or she should fill out the form and send it to the alternate attorney-in-fact. (If you name more than one attorney-in-fact, the attorney-in-fact who resigns may send the form to the others.) Give a copy of this form to your attorney-in-fact along with your power of attorney document. Or, if your power of attorney is springing, keep the forms together in a safe place known by your attorney-in-fact; he or she can obtain them if it becomes necessary. For more information and a copy of the form, see Chapter 4, Section B.3.

Notice of Revocation: Unrecorded Power of Attorney. If you ever want to revoke your power of attorney, prepare and sign a Notice of Revocation. You can find this form at the back of the book or on the enclosed computer disk. Keep it on hand in case you ever need it. For more information about revoking your power of attorney, and to see the revocation form, take a look at Chapter 11.

Notice of Revocation: Recorded Power of Attorney. If you record your power of attorney, then change your mind and want to cancel the document, you must also record a Notice of Revocation. To do this, you can use Nolo's "Notice of Revocation of Recorded Power of Attorney" form, contained in Appendix B and on the enclosed disk. Keep a blank copy of the form on file for future use. For more information about revoking your power of attorney, see Chapter 11.

Conventional Powers of Attorney

A. When to Use a Conventional Power of Attorney 8/2

B. How Conventional Powers of Attorney Work 8/3

    1. Who Can Prepare a Conventional Power of Attorney? 8/3

    2. How Much Will It Cost? 8/3

    3. Will Your Power of Attorney Be Accepted? 8/4

    4. When the Power of Attorney Begins and Ends 8/4

C. Choosing Your Attorney-in-Fact 8/5

D. The Attorney-in-Fact's Responsibilities 8/6

E. Granting Powers to the Attorney-in-Fact 8/6

F. Preparing Your Document 8/6

    1. What Forms to Use 8/6

    2. How to Fill Out Your Power of Attorney Form 8/7

    3. Step-by-Step Instructions for the General Power of Attorney Form 8/8

    4. Step-by-Step Instructions for the Limited Power of Attorney Form 8/17

G. Making It Legal 8/20

    1. Before You Sign 8/20

    2. Sign and Notarize the Power of Attorney 8/20

    3. Putting Your Power of Attorney on Public Record 8/23

    4. What to Do With the Signed Document 8/23

    5. Making and Distributing Copies 8/24

H. When to Make a New Power of Attorney 8/24

    1. If You Move to Another State 8/24

    2. After a Divorce 8/24

    3. Keeping Your Document Up to Date 8/24

This book uses the term "conventional" power of attorney to differentiate the document from a "durable" power of attorney. The major difference between the two types of documents is that a conventional power of attorney automatically ends if you become incapacitated and unable to handle your own affairs. A durable power, on the other hand, remains effective if you become incapacitated. (See Chapter 2.) If a power of attorney document does not clearly state that it is durable, it is by definition a conventional power of attorney.

A. When to Use a Conventional Power of Attorney

You should use a conventional power of attorney when you want to authorize someone to handle your finances or property, and you do not want the attorney-in-fact's authority to continue if you ever become incapacitated. Here are some situations when you may want to use the document:

- You are going on vacation and you need someone to handle certain financial matters in your absence,
- You want to authorize an expert, such as an accountant, to make business or financial decisions for you and carry them out, or
- You are in the military or involved in some other activity which regularly takes you away from your business or financial tasks.

You might want someone to handle a single transaction at a set time—for example, signing a certain business contract when you're not available. In that situation, you'll make what's called a limited power of attorney. But if you want your attorney-in-fact to handle all your financial matters for as long as you choose, you'll need a general power of attorney. This book contains both a general and a limited power of attorney form.

> **EXAMPLE 1:** Emily, an investment banker who owns a substantial amount of property, decides to go to Asia on a spiritual quest. However, Emily isn't currently so enlightened (or unen-lightened, depending on your point of view) that she wishes to give away or neglect her property. So Emily authorizes her friend Deb to be her attorney-in-fact, with authority to handle all her financial transactions, pay her bills and take care of her property. Emily puts no time limit on her power of attorney, because she isn't sure when she'll return. Emily has copies of the document placed in her bank records and with her tax accountant, her stockbroker and other people and organizations involved in her finances. When she returns from her journey, she'll formally revoke the power of attorney.

> **EXAMPLE 2:** James is a skilled investor who owns stock in many different companies. He's planning a three-week backpacking trip and is concerned about the fate of certain stocks in his portfolio. To ease his mind, he creates a limited

power of attorney giving his brother Ely the authority to sell those stocks if necessary. James specifies that the document will remain in effect only for the length of his trip, and he gives a copy to his stockbroker.

When to Make a Durable Power of Attorney

If you want to give someone broad powers to handle your financial affairs, and are also concerned that you may become incapacitated while the power of attorney is in effect, you may be better off making a durable power of attorney. (See Chapter 2.) A durable power can give your attorney-in-fact the authority to handle your financial affairs whether or not you are incapacitated. And you can always change your mind and revoke the document, as long as you are of sound mind.

Limited Powers of Attorney for Real Estate or Child Care. If you want someone else to handle a particular real estate transaction for you, or to look after a piece of real estate—and nothing else—use a form specially designed for real estate matters. See Chapter 9, *Powers of Attorney for Real Estate.*

Another reason for making a power of attorney is to arrange for care of children when parents are going out of town. See Chapter 10, *Powers of Attorney for Child Care.*

B. How Conventional Powers of Attorney Work

This section tells you what you need to know to create a legally valid power of attorney document, covering such basics as who can prepare a power of attorney, how much it costs, when the document takes effect and when it ends.

1. Who Can Prepare a Conventional Power of Attorney?

You can create a valid power of attorney if you are an adult (at least 18 years old) and of sound mind. And if you are reading this book, you can consider yourself of sound mind.

2. How Much Will It Cost?

Making a conventional power of attorney shouldn't set you back more than the price of this book and a few dollars for a notary to verify your signature on the document. Occasionally, however, there may be other costs.

a. Up-Front Costs

If you file (record) the power of attorney in the local public land records office, you'll have to pay a small fee—usually a few dollars per page. You'll need to record your power of attorney if you give your attorney-in-fact power over your real estate. Recording your document is a simple process, explained below in Section G.

Although it's not usually necessary, you may decide that you want a lawyer to review or modify your power of attorney. The fee for this service shouldn't be large, at least by lawyers' standards.

b. Ongoing Costs

You may encounter occasional costs as your attorney-in-fact carries out tasks under your power of attorney. Here are a couple of common examples.

Attorney-in-Fact's Payment. You may want to pay your attorney-in-fact. If you're making a general power of attorney, you can include the payment amount in the document itself. (See Chapter 4, Section C.) If you're making a limited document and you want to pay your attorney-in-fact, you and your attorney-in-fact should decide on an amount that's fair and write up a separate agreement.

Fees for Accountants and Experts. If the attorney-in-fact must hire professionals—for example, an accountant or investment counselor—to help with his or her duties, their fees will be paid from your assets.

3. Will Your Power of Attorney Be Accepted?

Powers of attorney are common; financial institutions, insurance companies and government agencies are used to them. Your attorney-in-fact, armed with a signed and notarized power of attorney document, should have no problem getting people to accept his or her authority.

But certain questions may come up when an attorney-in-fact tries to exercise his or her authority.

Is the document still valid? It's reasonable for someone to want to make sure that your power of attorney is still valid and hasn't been changed or revoked. To reassure a third party, your attorney-in-fact can show that person the power of attorney document, which contains language specifically designed to lay these fears to rest. This language clearly states that any person receives a copy of the document may accept it without the risk of legal liability—unless he or she knows that the document has been revoked.

Laws in many states also protect people who rely on apparently valid powers of attorney. For example, an Indiana statute states that a written, signed power of attorney is presumed valid, and a third party may rely on it. Other states have similar laws.

As a last resort, the attorney-in-fact can sign a sworn statement (an affidavit) in front of a notary public, stating that as far as he or she knows, the power of attorney has not been revoked and that you are still alive. Most states have laws that make such a statement conclusive proof that the power of attorney is in fact still valid.

Does the attorney-in-fact have the authority he or she claims? Any third party who relies on a power of attorney must be sure that the attorney-in-fact has the power he or she claims to have. That means the third party must examine the document, to see what power it grants.

Nolo's power of attorney document is very specific about the attorney-in-fact's powers. For example, if you give your attorney-in-fact authority over your banking transactions, the document expressly states that the attorney-in-fact is empowered to write checks on your behalf. Your attorney-in-fact can point to the paragraph that grants that authority, so a doubting bank official can read it in black and white.

An attorney-in-fact who runs into resistance should seek, politely but insistently, someone higher up in the bureaucracy.

4. When the Power of Attorney Begins and Ends

If you are making a general conventional power of attorney that grants broad powers, your document will take effect as soon as you sign it. For limited conventional powers of attorney, you can specify a starting date.

For both kinds of conventional forms, your power of attorney ends on the date you specify in the document. You can revoke it sooner, however. In addition, a power of attorney will end automatically in some circumstances, described below.

a. The Termination Date

When you prepare your document, specify when it will expire. You can enter a specific date, such as the day you will return from a trip abroad. If you don't enter a date, your attorney-in-fact can take care of your financial affairs in an open-ended way until you revoke the document in writing or become incapacitated. Remember, if you want your attorney-in-fact's authority to stay in effect even if you become incapacitated, you need to make a durable power of attorney.

b. You Revoke the Power of Attorney

You can revoke a power of attorney for finances at any time, as long as you are of sound mind. (And if you aren't of sound mind, the document terminates automatically, so you don't have to worry about revoking it.) To revoke your document, all you need to do is fill out a simple form, sign it in front of a notary public, and give copies to the attorney-in-fact and to people or institutions the attorney-in-fact has been dealing with. (Instructions are in Chapter 11; you can find blank tear-out revocation forms in Appendix B and on the enclosed computer disk.) You'll want to keep these forms on hand in case you need them later.

> EXAMPLE: Jeff frequently travels internationally for both business and pleasure. He prepares a conventional power of attorney naming his sister Carla as his attorney-in-fact. He places no time limit on the power of attorney. One year later, Jeff marries Sandy and decides to name her as his attorney-in-fact. Jeff prepares a one-page document that revokes the power of attorney, and gives copies to Carla and each of his financial institutions, letting them know of his new plans. He destroys the old power of attorney document and then prepares a new one, naming Sandy as his attorney-in-fact.

c. After a Divorce

In California, Illinois, Indiana and Missouri, if your spouse is your attorney-in-fact and you divorce, your ex-spouse's authority is immediately terminated. If you name an alternate (successor) attorney-in-fact in your power of attorney, that person takes over as attorney-in-fact.

Regardless of state law, if you get divorced you should revoke your power of attorney and make a new one. (See Chapter 11.)

d. No Attorney-in-Fact Is Available

A power of attorney must end if there's no one to serve as the attorney-in-fact. If you're making a general power of attorney, you can name up to two alternate (successor) attorneys-in-fact, who will serve if your first choice can't. (See Chapter 4, Section A.7.) For a bit of extra insurance, you can also allow the alternate attorney-in-fact to delegate his or her duties to someone else. (See Chapter 5, Section C.)

If you're making a limited power of attorney document—a document that's used for a specific and narrowly defined task—you won't name an alternate. If your first choice can't serve, you will have to make a new power of attorney form and name someone else to represent you.

e. If You Become Incapacitated or Die

A conventional power of attorney always ends when the principal becomes incapacitated or dies. In most states, however, if the attorney-in-fact doesn't know of your incapacity or death and continues to act on your behalf, his or her actions are still valid.

If you want your attorney-in-fact to have any authority over winding up your affairs after your death, you must grant that authority in your will or living trust. (See Chapter 2, Section D.5.)

C. Choosing Your Attorney-in-Fact

The choice of your attorney-in-fact is vitally important. It's crucial to pick someone you trust, both in a business and ethical sense. Choosing an attorney-in-fact is discussed in detail in Chapter 4, Section A.

D. The Attorney-in-Fact's Responsibilities

Your attorney-in-fact has a legal responsibility to represent you honestly and carefully. These legal requirements are discussed in Chapter 4, Section B.

E. Granting Powers to the Attorney-in-Fact

The specific powers you can grant to your attorney-in-fact with Nolo's general power of attorney document include:

- handling transactions with banks and other financial institutions
- buying, selling, maintaining, paying taxes on and mortgaging real estate and other property
- filing and paying your taxes
- investing your money in stocks, bonds and mutual funds
- buying and selling insurance policies and annuities for you
- operating your small business
- claiming or disclaiming property you inherit
- making gifts of your assets to organizations and individuals that you choose
- transferring property to a living trust you've already set up, and
- hiring someone to represent you in court.

These powers are discussed in Chapter 5.

F. Preparing Your Document

Once you've chosen your attorney-in-fact and thought about what authority to give him or her, preparing the actual document is easy.

All you have to do is tear out the appropriate form from the back of the book or print it from the enclosed disk. Then follow the instructions in this section. It probably won't take you more than an hour.

1. What Forms to Use

Which form you use depends on how much authority you want to give your attorney-in-fact. You can find the forms in Appendix B at the back of this book or on the enclosed computer disk.

a. The General Power of Attorney

Use a general power of attorney, called the *Financial Power of Attorney* form in this book, if you want to give your attorney-in-fact a broad range of powers. This basic Nolo form is valid in all states. If you live in one of the states listed below, however, you'll need to use the form designed especially for your state.

Special State Forms
Alaska
Arizona
District of Columbia (use only if you grant power over real estate)
New Mexico
North Carolina
Oklahoma

b. Limited Powers of Attorney

A limited power of attorney grants a much narrower authority to your attorney-in-fact than the general form. This book contains three limited power of attorney forms.

The basic, *Limited Power of Attorney* form is explained in this chapter. This is the form that allows you to give your attorney-in-fact the authority to handle any clearly defined task—for example, selling your car, signing a contract for you or handling your banking transactions while you are on vacation. You fill in the blanks with exactly the powers you want to grant. But if your sole reason for making a power of attorney is to give someone power over your real estate or permission to care for your child, you may find it easier to use the form designed specifically for your situation, described just below.

The *Power of Attorney for Real Estate* is used exclusively for appointing someone to handle a real estate transaction for you. To use this form, skip ahead to Chapter 9, *Powers of Attorney for Real Estate*. It contains the instructions you need.

The *Power of Attorney for Child Care* is a form you can use to name someone to take care of your child in your absence. Chapter 10 explains how to create a power of attorney for child care.

Check With Your Bank

As mentioned earlier, many banks and brokerage houses have their own power of attorney forms. If yours does, we recommend that you use it. If, for example, your bank has its own form, using it will head off any problems for your attorney-in-fact, because the bank will have no need to examine or quibble with the power of attorney. The bank will know exactly what authority its own form grants. If you need to give your attorney-in-fact other authority, you can use one of the power of attorney forms in this book in addition to the bank's limited form.

2. How to Fill Out Your Power of Attorney Form

It's not hard to prepare a power of attorney correctly, but it is important to follow the instructions carefully. If you don't, your attorney-in-fact might not be able to get a bank, title company, insurance company or government agency to accept his or her authority.

Here are some tips to help you get the job done right.

1. **Make copies of the blank form.** Tear out the form you want to use and make a few photocopies. You can use one for a draft and save a clean one for the final document—the one you will sign and have notarized. Or, use the disk at the back of the book to generate a form with your computer.

Check the last page of your form. Each of Nolo's tear-out and computer generated forms (except the Power of Attorney for Child Care) has multiple last pages that may, at first glance, appear to be duplicates. Each of these pages is slightly different, however. Choose only the last page that has room for the number of witnesses your state requires—none, one or two. (You can find the number of witnesses required by your state in Section G.1, below.) Then, check the page numbers of your documents to make sure everything's in proper order and you aren't missing pages or including any extras.

2. **Use a typewriter or word processing program to fill in the blanks.** It's not a legal requirement that a power of attorney be typed, but your attorney-in-fact is much less likely to run into trouble if it is. People expect legal documents to be typed and may be suspicious of handwritten ones.

3. **Don't erase anything.** Your final form should not contain any words that have been erased or whited-out. If the instructions tell you to cross out something, type a string of x's through the words.

⚠️ **Get help if you need it.** A power of attorney can transfer tremendous authority. Even though you can revoke it at any time (as long as you are mentally competent), never create a durable power of attorney unless you thoroughly understand what you're doing. If you have questions, see an expert.

3. Step-by-Step Instructions for the General Power of Attorney Form

Follow the instructions in this section if you're using Nolo's general form, which is titled *Financial Power of Attorney*. (If you're using the limited power of attorney form, skip ahead to Section 4.) You may want to refer to the discussions in earlier chapters as you make the choices necessary to fill out the form. At the end of the instructions for each item, you'll find the name of the chapter that discusses the topic in more detail.

Part 1.   Principal and Attorney-in-Fact

In the blank on the form, fill in your name. Enter your name as it appears on official documents such as your driver's license, bank accounts or real estate deeds. This may or may not be the name on your birth certificate. Enter it first, middle (if you choose), then last.

EXAMPLE: Your birth certificate lists your name as Rose Mary Green. But you've always gone by Mary, and always sign documents as Mary McNee, your married name. You would use Mary McNee on your power of attorney.

Be sure to enter all names in which you hold bank accounts or other property your attorney-in-fact will be dealing with. This will make his or her job far easier.

Making Your Records Consistent

If you use more than one name and you're up for some extra work, consider settling on one name, entering it on your power of attorney form, and then changing your other documents to conform. This will clean up your records and save your attorney-in-fact some trouble later on. To change your name on official documents and records—for example, bank accounts, deeds or Social Security records—you'll have to contact the appropriate government office or financial institution to find out what documentation they'll need to make the change for you.

In the second blank, enter the city and state where you live. If during the course of a year you live in more than one state, use the address in the state where you vote, register vehicles, own valuable property, have bank accounts or run a business. If you've made your will, healthcare directives or a living trust, be consistent: use the state you declared as your residence in those documents.

In the next blank, after the word "appoint," type in the name and address of the person (or persons) who have agreed to serve as your attorney-in-fact for finances. (A reminder: It's almost always a bad idea to name more than one attorney-in-fact. See Chapter 4, Section A.4.)

Financial Power of Attorney

1. **Principal and Attorney-in-Fact**

   I, _Beatrice M. Steiner-Soares_,

   of _St. Paul, MN_,

   appoint _Samuel P. Soares, 54 Lakeshore Street, St. Paul MN_

   as my attorney-in-fact to act for me in any lawful way with respect to the powers delegated in Part 6 below. If that person (or all of those persons, if I name more than one) is unable or unwilling to serve as attorney-in-fact, I appoint the following alternates, to serve alone in the order named:

   First Alternate

   Stephanie Soares
   Name
   390 Harris Street
   Address
   Minneapolis, MN

   Second Alternate

   _____
   Name
   _____
   Address

You may also, in the next section of the form, name one or two alternate (successor) attorneys-in-fact. You don't have to name an alternate, but it's a good idea. If you named more than one attorney-in-fact, the alternate will serve only if all the people you named first cannot serve. If you name more than one alternate, each will act alone and successively, in the order named.

 Chapter 4, *Your Attorney-in-Fact*, Section A.

Part 2. Authorization of Attorneys-in-Fact

 If you named only one person as your attorney-in-fact, skip Part 2 (don't check either box) and go on to Part 3.

If you named more than one person to serve as attorney-in-fact or alternate attorney-in-fact, choose whether or not you want to allow each one to act jointly or independently on your behalf. If you check "jointly," each attorney-in-fact will have to sign all documents and approve all decisions made on your behalf. If you check "independently," each attorney-in-fact may take actions without knowledge or approval of the others.

 Chapter 4, Your *Attorney-in-Fact*, Section A.4.

Part 3. Delegation of Authority

If you check the first box here, your attorney-in-fact will be allowed to delegate some or all of his or her authority to someone else. In other words, your attorney-in-fact can name someone else to act as your attorney-in-fact, temporarily or permanently.

 Chapter 5, *Granting Powers to the Attorney-in-Fact*, Section C.

Part 4. Effective Date

Your conventional power of attorney takes effect as soon as you sign it. You must check the first box in this section. The second and third boxes are only for people who want to make a durable power of attorney.

After you check the first box, you may specify the date on which your power of attorney should expire. You can enter a specific date, such as the date you expect to become available to take care of your own finances again or a date shortly after you expect your financial deal to close. Or you can enter a more general instruction, such as "when I revoke this document in writing." This will allow your attorney-in-fact to take care of your financial affairs indefinitely, as long as you are not incapacitated.

If you leave the line blank, your document will remain in effect unless and until you revoke it or become incapacitated. As a practical matter, you should revoke and re-do an open-ended power of attorney periodically. (See Section H, below.)

Part 5. Determination of Incapacity

 Because you are creating a conventional power of attorney, you should skip Part 5. Go directly to Part 6.

Part 6. Powers of the Attorney-in-Fact

The power of attorney form contains a list of 13 powers; you can give the attorney-in-fact all of them or only some. Either way, you can put specific limitations on the powers that you grant. For example, if you give your attorney-in-fact authority over your real estate, later in the document you can still put in a provision forbidding the attorney-in-fact from selling your residence.

Some people want to give the broadest possible authority to their attorney-in-fact in their conventional power of attorney. This is probably a good

2. **Authorization of Attorneys-in-Fact**

   If I have named more than one attorney-in-fact, they are authorized to act:

   ☐ jointly.

   ☐ independently.

3. **Delegation of Authority**

   ☒ My attorney-in-fact may delegate, in writing, any authority granted under this power of attorney to a person he or she selects. Any such delegation shall state the period during which it is valid and specify the extent of the delegation.

   ☐ My attorney-in-fact may not delegate any authority granted under this power of attorney.

4. **Effective Date and Durability**

   ☒ This power of attorney is not durable. It is effective immediately, and shall terminate ▨▨ when I revoke this document in writing _____.

   ☐ This power of attorney is durable. It is effective immediately, and shall continue in effect if I become incapacitated or disabled.

   ☐ This power of attorney is durable. It shall take effect only if I become incapacitated or disabled and unable to manage my financial affairs.

5. **Determination of Incapacity**

   If I am creating a springing durable power of attorney under Part 4 of this document, my incapacity or disability shall be determined by written declaration of ☐ one ☐ two licensed physician(s). Each declaration shall be made under penalty of perjury and shall state that in the physician's opinion I am substantially unable to manage my financial affairs. If possible, the declaration(s) shall be made by _____ _____ _____.

   No licensed physician shall be liable to me for any actions taken under this part which are done in good faith.

6. **Powers of the Attorney-in-Fact**

   I grant my attorney-in-fact power to act on my behalf in the following matters, as indicated by my initials next to each granted power or on line (14), granting all the listed powers. Powers that are struck through are not granted.

idea if you are going on an extended trip or will be otherwise unavailable to handle your finances and you want your attorney-in-fact to be able to carry out a wide variety of financial tasks. To give your attorney-in-fact all of the listed powers, initial the blank in front of the last item on the list:

    _____   (14) ALL POWERS (1 THROUGH 13) LISTED ABOVE.

On the other hand, you may have just a few powers to grant. In that case, initial only the powers that apply in your situation. Each power is discussed in Chapter 5; if you want to see a complete definition of each one, read Part 14 of the form. To grant only specific powers to the attorney-in-fact, initial the blank in front of each power you choose. Then, cross out any powers you did not grant by typing a string of x's through them. (If you initial line 14, however, do *not* cross out any of the powers.)

   Chapter 5, *Granting Powers to the Attorney-in-Fact*, Section A.

Part 7.   Special Instructions to the Attorney-in-Fact

Here, you can qualify the powers you granted in Part 6 with your own instructions or restrictions. The list of possible additions or restrictions is nearly endless; some common examples are discussed in Chapter 5.

If you don't want to add any powers or restrictions here, type "None" in the space provided.

Because most people don't need to add much to the Nolo form, Part 7 contains room to add only a few extra clauses. If you want to add more, you'll have to retype the form.

   Chapter 5, *Granting Powers to the Attorney-in-Fact*, Section B.

INITIALS

_____ (1) Real estate transactions.

_____ (2) Tangible personal property transactions.

_____ (3) Stock and bond, commodity and option transactions.

_____ (4) Banking and other financial institution transactions.

_____ (5) Business operating transactions.

_____ (6) Insurance and annuity transactions.

_____ (7) Estate, trust, and other beneficiary transactions.

_____ (8) Living trust transactions.

_____ (9) Legal actions.

_____ (10) Personal and family care.

_____ (11) Government benefits.

_____ (12) Retirement plan transactions.

_____ (13) Tax matters.

*BMS* (14) ALL POWERS (1 THROUGH 13) LISTED ABOVE.

These powers are defined in Part 14, below.

7. **Special Instructions to the Attorney-in-Fact**

_____

_____

_____

_____

_____

_____

_____

_____

_____

_____

_____

_____

_____

_____

_____

_____

Part 8. Compensation and Reimbursement of the Attorney-in-Fact

If you decide not to pay your attorney-in-fact, check the first box.

If you want to provide for payment, check one of the last two boxes. It's common to simply give the attorney-in-fact the right to reasonable compensation and let him or her determine an amount. Or you can check the third box and fill in an hourly, monthly or yearly fee. If you want to set an amount, be sure to enter your instructions clearly and carefully. Here are some examples:

- $10 per hour
- $500 per month
- $10,000 per year
- a flat fee of $5,000, payable at the time my document goes into effect.

 Chapter 4, *Your Attorney-in-Fact*, Section C.

Part 9. Personal Benefit by Attorney-in-Fact

Unless you say otherwise, your attorney-in-fact is not permitted to profit or benefit personally from any transaction he or she engages in as your representative. This restriction is designed to protect you, but as explained in Chapter 4, in some instances it's not necessary or desirable.

- If you want to leave the attorney-in-fact free to benefit personally from any acts he or she does as your attorney-in-fact, check the first box.
- If you are not allowing the attorney-in-fact to make gifts to himself or herself under the power of attorney document, and you don't want to allow the attorney-in-fact to benefit personally from any action taken on your behalf, check the second box.
- If, in Part 7 of your form, you have given the attorney-in-fact explicit permission to make gifts of your property to himself or herself, but you don't want the attorney-in-fact to

benefit personally from any other transactions under your power of attorney document, check the third box.

 Chapter 4, *Your Attorney-in-Fact*, Section B.1.

Part 10. Commingling by the Attorney-in-Fact

Legally, the attorney-in-fact cannot mix (commingle) your monies with his own. But if your attorney-in-fact is your spouse or long-term partner, your funds may have been commingled for a long time. You should authorize this commingling by checking the first box in this part. If you want your attorney-in-fact to keep your property separate, check the second box.

 Chapter 4, *Your Attorney-in-Fact*, Section B.1.

Congratulations! When you've filled in Part 10 of the form, you've completed your power of attorney. The rest of the form is standard language. You should read and understand it, but you don't need to fill in any more blanks.

Part 11. Liability of the Attorney-in-Fact

This clause makes the attorney-in-fact liable for losing your money or other property only if the loss was caused by willful misconduct or gross negligence—that is, intentional wrongdoing or extremely careless behavior. Without this clause, the attorney-in-fact might be liable to you for losses caused by any negligence (unreasonable carelessness) committed while acting as attorney-in-fact. That could make your attorney-in-fact subject to liability for a good-faith mistake—a result you probably don't want, given that you're choosing a close relative or friend to be attorney-in-fact.

8. Compensation and Reimbursement of the Attorney-in-Fact

☒ My attorney-in-fact shall not be compensated for services, but shall be entitled to reimbursement, from my assets, for reasonable expenses. Reasonable expenses include but are not limited to reasonable fees for information or advice from accountants, lawyers or investment experts relating to my attorney-in-fact's responsibilities under this power of attorney.

☐ My attorney-in-fact shall be entitled to reimbursement for reasonable expenses and reasonable compensation for services. What constitutes reasonable compensation shall be determined exclusively by my attorney-in-fact. If more than one attorney-in-fact is named in this document, each shall have the exclusive right to determine what constitutes reasonable compensation for his or her own duties.

☐ My attorney-in-fact shall be entitled to reimbursement for reasonable expenses and compensation for services in the amount of $_____.
If more than one attorney-in-fact is named in this document, each shall be entitled to receive this amount.

9. Personal Benefit to the Attorney-in-Fact

☒ My attorney-in-fact may buy any assets of mine or engage in any transaction he or she deems in good faith to be in my interest, no matter what the interest or benefit to my attorney-in-fact.

☐ My attorney-in-fact may not benefit personally from any transaction engaged in on my behalf.

☐ Although my attorney-in-fact may receive gifts of my property as described in Part 7 of this document, my attorney-in-fact may not benefit personally from any other transaction he or she engages in on my behalf.

10. Commingling by the Attorney-in-Fact

☒ My attorney-in-fact may commingle any of my funds with any funds of his or hers.

☐ My attorney-in-fact may not commingle any of my funds with any funds of his or hers.

11. Liability of the Attorney-in-Fact

My attorney-in-fact shall not incur any liability to me, my estate, my heirs, successors or assigns for acting or refraining from acting under this document, except for willful misconduct or gross negligence. My attorney-in-fact is not required to make my assets produce income, increase the value of my estate, diversify my investments or enter into transactions authorized by this document, as long as my attorney-in-fact believes his or her actions are in my best interests or in the interests of my estate and of those interested in my estate. A successor attorney-in-fact shall not be liable for acts of a prior attorney-in-fact.

(Pages 5-9 of the form are in Appendix B)

I understand the importance of the powers I delegate to my attorney-in-fact in this document. I recognize that the document gives my attorney-in-fact broad powers over my assets.

Signed this __10th__ day of __October__, __1998__.

State of __Minnesota__, County of __Ramsey__.

__Beatrice M. Steiner-Soares__   __435-22-1071__
Signature   Social Security Number

CERTIFICATE OF ACKNOWLEDGMENT OF NOTARY PUBLIC

State of __Minnesota__

County of __Ramsey__   } ss

On __October 10__, __1998__, before me, __Emma Koenig__

_____, a notary public in and for said state, personally appeared

__Beatrice M. Steiner-Soares__, personally

known to me (or proved on the basis of satisfactory evidence) to be the person whose name is subscribed to the within instrument, and acknowledged to me that he or she executed the same in his or her authorized capacity and that by his or her signature on the instrument the person, or the entity upon behalf of which the person acted, executed the instrument.

WITNESS my hand and official seal.

__Emma Koenig__

Notary Public for the State of __Minnesota__

[NOTARIAL SEAL]   My commission expires: __December 31, 2001__

PREPARATION STATEMENT

This document was prepared by:

__Beatrice M. Steiner-Soares__
Name

__54 Lakesore Street__
Address

__St. Paul, MN__

Chapter 4, *Your Attorney-in-Fact*, Section B.

Part 12. Reliance on This Power of Attorney

Banks, brokers and others may be reluctant to accept an attorney-in-fact's authority if they're afraid, for some reason, that the power of attorney has been revoked and is no longer valid. This clause protects people or institutions who rely on the attorney-in-fact's authority when shown the original, signed power. Even if the power has been revoked, a third party can rely on it unless he or she has actually received notice of a revocation. It can work wonders when it comes to getting bureaucrats and clerks to relax.

If you do revoke your power of attorney. This clause helps your attorney-in-fact get his or her authority accepted, but it also means that if you do revoke the power of attorney, you must give copies of the revocation to anyone you think the attorney-in-fact might try to deal with. It's also wise to record it in the land records office of any county in which you own real estate. If you don't, you could be on the hook for the former attorney-in-fact's actions. (See Chapter 11, *Revoking a Power of Attorney*.)

Part 13. Severability

This is a standard clause in all kinds of legal documents. It ensures that even in the unlikely event that some part of your power of attorney is declared invalid by a court, the rest of the document is still valid.

Part 14. Definition of Powers of the Attorney-in-Fact

This part spells out the details of the attorney-in-fact's powers, which you granted in Part 6. You

don't have to check any boxes or fill in any information here.

4. Step-by-Step Instructions for the Limited Power of Attorney Form

Here are instructions for filling in the limited power of attorney form, titled simply *Power of Attorney*.

Remember, if you want to create a power of attorney for real estate transactions only, skip to Chapter 9. To make a power of attorney for child care, go to Chapter 10.

Step 1. Principal and Attorney-in-Fact

In the first four blanks on the form, fill in your name and the city, county and state where you live. Enter your name as it appears on official documents such as your driver's license, bank accounts and real estate deeds. This may or may not be the name on your birth certificate. Enter it first, middle (if you choose), then last.

EXAMPLE: Your birth certificate lists your name as Rose Mary Green. But you've always gone by Mary, and always sign documents as Mary McNee, your married name. You would use Mary McNee on your power of attorney.

Be sure to enter all names in which you hold bank accounts or other property your attorney-in-fact will be dealing with. This will make his or her job far easier. If you're including more than one name, enter your full legal name first, followed by "aka" (also known as). Then enter your other names.

Making Your Records Consistent

If you use more than one name and you're up for some extra work, consider settling on one name, entering it on your power of attorney form, and then changing your other documents to conform. This will clean up your records and save your attorney-in-fact some trouble later on. To change your name on official documents and records—for example, bank accounts, deeds or Social Security records—you'll have to contact the appropriate government office or financial institution to find out what documentation they'll need to make the change for you.

If during the course of a year you live in more than one state, use the address in the state where you vote, register vehicles, own valuable property, have bank accounts or run a business. If you've made your will, healthcare directives or a living trust, be consistent: use the state you declared as your residence in those documents.

Next, type in the name of the person who has agreed to serve as your attorney-in-fact. Then enter the city, county and state where your attorney-in-fact lives.

Step 2. Powers of the Attorney-in-Fact

There is a large blank space following the first paragraph of the form. In it, you should type the authority you want to give to your attorney-in-fact. Be as specific as possible when granting powers. For example, include relevant bank account numbers and complete descriptions of any property the attorney-in-fact may deal with.

EXAMPLE 1: You want to give your attorney-in-fact permission to sell your car, so you type the following sentence in the blank space:

handling the sale of my antique Studebaker, license plate number MY CAR, for not less than $50,000 cash.

EXAMPLE 2: You want your attorney-in-fact to sign loan papers for you while you are out of town:

handling all loan transactions, including signing documents on my behalf, between myself and Commercial Bank.

EXAMPLE 3: You want your attorney-in-fact to watch over your investments:

handling all transactions, purchases and sales in my brokerage account, #77-0154, Ace Brokers, Zadoo City, Iowa. My attorney-in-fact may withdraw funds to cover any fees associated with these transactions from my checking account, #0234-478-003, First Zadoo Bank.

If you want to limit the powers you've granted, you should add specific restrictions to your instructions. For example, you might want to forbid your attorney-in-fact from selling certain stock in your brokerage account.

EXAMPLE 4:

handling all transactions, purchases and sales in my brokerage account, #77-0154, Ace Brokers, Zadoo City, Iowa, except that my attorney-in-fact is not permitted to sell my stock in XYZ Company. My attorney-in-fact may withdraw funds to cover any fees associated with these transactions from my checking account, #0234-478-003, First Zadoo Bank.

Step 3. Termination Date

Next, you must specify the termination date for your power of attorney. You can type in a specific

RECORDING REQUESTED BY
AND WHEN RECORDED MAIL TO

_____

_____

_____

Power of Attorney

I, <u>Jay Franklin</u>,
name of principal

of <u>Zadoo</u>, <u>Ames County</u>,
city county

<u>Iowa</u>, appoint <u>Robert Franklin</u>
state name of attorney-in-fact

_____, of <u>Zadoo</u>,
city

<u>Ames</u>, <u>Iowa</u>,
county state

as my attorney-in-fact to act in my place for the purposes of:

<u>handling all transactions, purchases and sales in my brokerage</u>

<u>account #77-0154, Ace Brokers, Zadoo City, Iowa, except that my</u>

<u>attorney-in-fact is not permitted to sell my stock in XYZ Company.</u>

<u>My attorney-in-fact may withdraw funds to cover any fees associated</u>

<u>with these transactions from my checking account, #0234-478-003,</u>

<u>First Zadoo Bank.</u>

_____

_____

_____

_____

_____

_____

This power of attorney takes effect on <u>March 19, 1998</u>, and shall continue

until terminated in writing, or until <u>June 3, 1998</u>, whichever comes first.

I grant my attorney-in-fact full authority to act in any manner both proper and necessary to the exercise of the foregoing powers, and I ratify every act that my attorney-in-fact may lawfully perform in exercising those powers.

date on which you want the power of attorney to expire. Or, if you want the power of attorney to continue indefinitely, type a string of x's through "or until _____ , _____ whichever comes first." If you do so, and you later want to terminate the power of attorney, you must revoke it in writing. (See Chapter 11.)

G. Making It Legal

After you've done the work of preparing a conventional power of attorney, you must carry out a few simple tasks to make sure the document is legally valid. This section shows you what to do.

Checklist: Making It Legal

☐ Show the power of attorney to banks, brokers, insurers and other financial institutions you expect your attorney-in-fact to deal with.

☐ Sign the power of attorney in front of a notary public and, if you wish or state law requires, in the presence of witnesses.

☐ Record (file) the power of attorney in the county land records office, if necessary.

☐ Distribute copies of the power of attorney to people the attorney-in-fact will deal with.

☐ Give the original, signed document to your attorney-in-fact.

---

1. Before You Sign

Before you finalize your power of attorney, you may want to show it to the banks, brokers, insurers and other financial institutions you expect your attorney-in-fact to deal with on your behalf.

Discussing your plans with people at these institutions now (and giving them a copy of the power of attorney, after you sign it, if you wish), can make your attorney-in-fact's job easier. An institution may

ask that you include specific language in your power of attorney, authorizing the attorney-in-fact to do certain things on your behalf. You may have to go along if you want cooperation later. If you don't want to change your power of attorney, find another bank that will accept the document as it is.

2. Sign and Notarize the Power of Attorney

A power of attorney is a serious document, and to make it effective you must observe certain formalities when you sign it. Fortunately, these requirements aren't difficult to meet.

a. Notarization

You must sign your power of attorney in the presence of a notary public for your state. In some states, notarization is required by law to make the power of attorney valid. But even where law doesn't require it, custom does. A power of attorney that isn't notarized may not be accepted by people your attorney-in-fact tries to deal with.

The notary public watches you sign the power of attorney and then signs it too and stamps it with

I agree that any third party who receives a copy of this document may act under it. Revocation of the power of attorney is not effective as to a third party until the third party has actual knowledge of the revocation. I agree to indemnify the third party for any claims that arise against the third party because of reliance on this power of attorney.

Signed this __15th__ day of __March__, __1998__.

State of __Iowa__ County of __Ames__.

__Jay Franklin__   __521-29-2201__
Signature   Social Security Number

CERTIFICATE OF ACKNOWLEDGMENT OF NOTARY PUBLIC

State of __Iowa__

County of __Ames__ } ss

On __March 15__, __1998__, before me, __Melinda Washington__, a notary public in and for said state, personally appeared __Jay Franklin__, personally known to me (or proved on the basis of satisfactory evidence) to be the person whose name is subscribed to the within instrument, and acknowledged to me that he or she executed the same in his or her authorized capacity and that by his or her signature on the instrument the person, or the entity upon behalf of which the person acted, executed the instrument.

WITNESS my hand and official seal.

Melinda Washington

Notary Public for the State of __Iowa__

[NOTARIAL SEAL]   My commission expires: __June 30, 2000__

PREPARATION STATEMENT

This document was prepared by:

__Jay Franklin__
Name
__392 Farm Street__
Address
__Zadoo, Iowa__

an official seal. The notary will want proof of your identity, such as a driver's license that bears your photo and signature. The notary's fee is usually just a few dollars—probably $5 to $10 in most places.

Finding a notary public shouldn't be a problem; many advertise in the Yellow Pages. Or check with your bank, which may provide notarizations as a service to customers. Real estate offices and title companies also have notaries.

b. Witnesses

Most states don't require the power of attorney to be signed in front of witnesses. (See the list below.) Nevertheless, it doesn't hurt to have a witness or two watch you sign, and sign the document themselves. Witnesses' signatures may make the power of attorney more acceptable to lawyers, banks, insurance companies and other entities the attorney-in-fact may have to deal with. (Part of the reason is probably that wills, which people are more familiar with, require witnesses.)

The witnesses must be present when you sign the document in front of the notary. Witnesses must be mentally competent adults, preferably ones who live nearby and will be easily available if necessary. (A few states impose other requirements; see "States That Require Witnesses," below.) The person who will serve as attorney-in-fact should *not* be a witness. The attorney-in-fact does not have to sign the power of attorney.

⚠ **Check the last page of your form.** Each of Nolo's tear-out and computer generated forms (except the Power of Attorney for Child Care) has multiple last pages that may, at first glance, appear to be duplicates. Each of these pages is slightly different, however. Choose only the last page that has room for the number of witnesses your state requires—none, one or two. Then, check the page numbers of your documents to make sure everything's in proper order and you aren't missing pages or including any extras.

States That Require Witnesses

State	Number of Witnesses	Other Requirements
Arizona	1	Witness may not be your attorney-in-fact, the spouse or child of your attorney-in-fact, or the notary public who acknowledges your document.
Arkansas	2	The attorney-in-fact may not be a witness.
Connecticut	2	The attorney-in-fact may not be a witness.
District of Columbia	2	Witnesses are necessary only if your power of attorney is to be recorded. (See Section 3, below.) The attorney-in-fact may not be a witness.
Florida	2	The attorney-in-fact may not be a witness.
Georgia	2	The attorney-in-fact may not be a witness. In addition, one of your witnesses may not be your spouse or blood relative.
Michigan	2	Witnesses are necessary only if your power of attorney is to be recorded. (See Section 3, below.) The attorney-in-fact may not be a witness.
Ohio	2	The attorney-in-fact may not be a witness.
Oklahoma	2	Witnesses may not be your attorney-in-fact, or anyone who is related by blood or marriage to you or your attorney-in-fact.
Pennsylvania	2	The attorney-in-fact may not be a witness.
South Carolina	2	The attorney-in-fact may not be a witness.
Vermont	2	Witnesses are necessary only if your power of attorney is to be recorded. (See Section 3, below.) The attorney-in-fact may not be a witness.

3. Putting Your Power of Attorney on Public Record

You may need to put a copy of your power of attorney on file in the land records office of any counties where you own real estate. This office is called the County Recorder's or Land Registry Office in most states. The process of filing your document is called "recording," or "registration" in some states.

a. When You Should Record Your Power of Attorney

You must record your power of attorney only if it gives your attorney-in-fact authority over your real estate. Essentially, this means you must record the document if you granted a real estate power or if you own real estate and have given the attorney-in-fact power to transfer items of your property into a living trust. If your document isn't in the public records, your attorney-in-fact won't be able to sell, mortgage or transfer your real estate.

Recording makes it clear to all interested parties that the attorney-in-fact has power over the property. County land records are checked whenever real estate changes hands or is mortgaged; if your attorney-in-fact goes to sell or mortgage your real estate, there must be something in these public records that proves he or she has authority to do so.

Even if recording is not legally required, you can go ahead and record your power of attorney; officials in some financial institutions may be reassured by seeing that you took that extra step to formalize your document.

b. The Preparation Statement

You may notice something called a "preparation statement" at the very end of your power of attorney form. The preparation statement is a simple listing of the name and address of the person who prepared the document. In some states, you cannot record your document without this statement.

In most cases, the name of the principal and the name of the person who prepared the document will be the same—your own. But if it's not, the person who filled out the form should include his or her name and address in the preparation statement.

c. Where to Record Your Power of Attorney

In most states, each county has its own county recorder's (or registry of deeds) office. Take the power of attorney to the local office—if you're recording to give the attorney-in-fact authority over real estate—in the county where the real estate is located. If you want your attorney-in-fact to have authority over more than one parcel of real estate, record the power of attorney in each county where you own property.

d. How to Record a Document

Recording a document is easy. You may even be able to do it by mail, but it's safer to go in person. The clerk will make a copy (usually on microfilm these days) for the public records. It will be assigned a reference number, often in terms of books and pages—for example, "Book 14, Page 1932 of the Contra Costa County, California records." In most places, it costs just a few dollars per page to record a document.

4. What to Do With the Signed Document

Give the original, signed and notarized document to the attorney-in-fact. He or she will need it as proof of authority to act on your behalf.

If you named more than one attorney-in-fact, give the original document to one of them. Between them, they will have to work out the best way to prove their authority. For example, they may decide to visit some financial institutions or government offices together to establish themselves as your attorneys-in-fact. Or they may need to take turns with the document. Some agencies, such as the IRS, will accept a copy of the document, rather than the original; flexible policies like this one will make things easier on multiple attorneys-in-fact who need to share one original document.

5. Making and Distributing Copies

If you wish, you can give copies of your power to the people your attorney-in-fact will need to deal with—banks or government offices, for example. If your financial power of attorney is already in their records, it may eliminate hassles for your attorney-in-fact later.

Be sure to keep a list of everyone to whom you give a copy. If you later revoke your power of attorney, you must notify each institution of the revocation. (See Chapter 11.)

H. When to Make a New Power of Attorney

There are a few situations in which you should revoke your conventional power of attorney and make a new one. Revocation is explained in Chapter 11.

1. If You Move to Another State

If you move to another state, it's best to revoke your old power of attorney and create a new one, complying with all regulations of your new state. This is true even though your old power of attorney may be acceptable under your new state's laws.

Making a new document will ensure that things will go smoothly for your attorney-in-fact. Otherwise, your attorney-in-fact may run into problems that are more practical than legal. For example, the document may need to be recorded (put on file) with the local land records office in the new state. If the document does not meet certain requirements, the recorder's office in the new state may not accept it.

2. After a Divorce

If your spouse is your attorney-in-fact and you get divorced, you should revoke your power of attorney and make a new one. In a few states, an ex-spouse's authority under a power of attorney is automatically terminated after a divorce. In any state, however, third parties may question the validity of a document created before a divorce that names the ex-spouse as attorney-in-fact. You'll head off problems by making a new document.

3. Keeping Your Document Up to Date

Banks and other financial institutions are often reluctant to accept conventional powers of attorney that are fairly old, even if the document states that it is open-ended. For this reason, it is a good idea to re-do a conventional power of attorney every year or so if you want it to remain effective. Old copies should be destroyed, and the people and institutions with old copies should be notified that you have revoked your old power of attorney and made a new one. (See Chapter 11.) ■

Powers of Attorney for Real Estate

A. When to Use a Power of Attorney for Real Estate 9/2

B. How Powers of Attorney for Real Estate Work 9/3

    1. Who Can Prepare a Power of Attorney for Real Estate? 9/3

    2. How Much Will It Cost? 9/3

    3. Making Sure Your Power of Attorney Is Accepted 9/3

    4. When the Power of Attorney Begins and Ends 9/4

C. Choosing Your Attorney-in-Fact 9/4

D. The Attorney-in-Fact's Authority 9/5

E. Preparing Your Document 9/5

F. Making It Legal 9/10

    1. Before You Sign 9/10

    2. Sign and Notarize the Power of Attorney 9/10

    3. Putting Your Power of Attorney on Public Record 9/12

    4. What to Do With the Signed Document 9/13

    5. Making and Distributing Copies 9/13

    6. Keeping Your Document Up to Date 9/13

A power of attorney for real estate is a useful, but limited, legal document. It allows you to give someone the authority to buy or sell a piece of real estate for you, or to conduct any other business concerning real estate that you own. A power of attorney for real estate is a "conventional" power of attorney (see Chapter 8), meaning that it automatically expires if you become incapacitated and unable to manage your own financial affairs. (If you want a document that will stay in effect even if you become incapacitated, you need a "durable" power of attorney. See Chapter 2.)

A. When to Use a Power of Attorney for Real Estate

A power of attorney for real estate may be useful in a number of situations. Here are a few common ones:

- you will be out of town or otherwise unavailable when important real estate documents need to be signed,
- you will not be available to look after your real estate for a limited period of time, or
- you live far away from property that you own and you want to authorize someone to manage it in your absence.

EXAMPLE 1: Alan is purchasing a condominium. Escrow has been opened at a title company, but the closing is delayed for several weeks. Because of the delay, the closing is now scheduled for the middle of Alan's long-planned trip to Greece. To solve this problem, Alan prepares a power of attorney for real estate, authorizing his sister Jennifer to sign any documents necessary to complete the closing and to withdraw any amounts of money (from an identified bank account) necessary to pay expenses and costs incurred because of the closing. Alan specifies that Jennifer's authority expires on the date he is to return from Greece.

Alan discusses his plans with his bank and the title company before he leaves, to be sure they'll accept the power of attorney and the authority of his attorney-in-fact. Both organizations assure him they'll accept a valid power of attorney for real estate. He has copies of his power of attorney placed in the bank's records and in his file at the title company. He leaves the original document with Jennifer, his attorney-in-fact.

EXAMPLE 2: Ann owns a summer cottage. Her friend Ellen lives in the next cottage as her permanent home. Ann and Ellen agree that because Ellen is on the spot she'll take care of renting Ann's cottage, collecting rent and paying all house bills and costs. Ann prepares a power of attorney for real estate giving Ellen authority to represent Ann for all transactions concerning her property at 20 Heron Lake Road. Ann specifies that the power of attorney will continue indefinitely. She also provides that Ellen has no authority to sell the cottage nor to

represent her in any transaction that doesn't concern the cottage.

If you know that you need an attorney-in-fact for real estate transactions and nothing else, it makes good sense to use the limited real estate power rather than a general power of attorney that encompasses real estate transactions. (See Chapter 8.) Even though the general power of attorney is just as legal, you don't need most of the language it contains. And it's not wise to clutter your document with lots of unnecessary legal language and a list of powers that you don't want to grant. The power of attorney for real estate is a short, straightforward document that allows you to clearly describe the powers and the property at issue—something that most financial institutions will want to see. Mortgage lenders and title companies are likely to be much more comfortable accepting a document that's narrowly tailored to your purposes.

⚠️ **Talk with your financial institutions.** After you decide to make a power of attorney for real estate, it's important to talk with the financial institutions that are involved in your real estate transactions and give them copies of your document. Doing so will ensure that these institutions will honor your document. For more information, see Section B.3, *Making Sure Your Power of Attorney Is Accepted.*

B. How Powers of Attorney for Real Estate Work

This section tells you what you need to know to create a legally valid power of attorney for real estate.

1. Who Can Prepare a Power of Attorney for Real Estate?

You can create a valid power of attorney for real estate if you are an adult (at least 18 years old) and of sound mind. If you are reading this book, you can consider yourself of sound mind.

2. How Much Will It Cost?

Making a power of attorney for real estate shouldn't set you back more than the price of this book and a few dollars for having your document notarized and recorded in your local public land records office. (Notarization and recording are required to make your document legal; you will learn more about these requirements in Section F, below.)

Occasionally, however, you may encounter costs as your attorney-in-fact carries out tasks under your power of attorney. Here are a couple of common examples.

Attorney-in-fact's payment. The power of attorney document doesn't require that you pay your attorney-in-fact, but you may wish to do so. If so, you and your attorney-in-fact should decide on an amount that's fair, and write up a separate agreement.

Expert's fees. If complications crop up during a real estate transaction, your attorney-in-fact may need to hire someone—a lawyer, for example—to help out. Your attorney-in-fact is allowed to seek whatever assistance is reasonably necessary under the circumstances, and you'll be required to pay for it.

3. Making Sure Your Power of Attorney Is Accepted

Powers of attorney are common, and financial institutions are used to them. Your attorney-in-fact, armed with a properly executed power of attorney document, should have no problem getting people to accept his or her authority.

The most important thing you can do to ensure that financial institutions, such as your mortgage lender or title company, will accept your power of attorney is talk with them in advance. Be sure that they're willing to accept the document and the authority of your attorney in fact. Your financial institution may ask you to include certain language in your form or even to use its own power of attorney form. If so, you should comply with its wishes. (If you're working with more than one financial institution, you may end up using more than one form.) Even though you can make a perfectly valid, legal document with this book, your financial institution may balk at accepting any form other than its own. Following your financial institutions' recommendations will save time and trouble for you and your attorney-in-fact.

4. When the Power of Attorney Begins and Ends

Your power of attorney for real estate takes effect on a date you specify in your document. It ends when you revoke it in writing, or on a date that you specify in the power of attorney document. In addition, the document will end automatically in some circumstances, described below.

a. The Termination Date

When you prepare your document, you can specify the date on which it will expire. You can enter a specific day, such as the day you expect to return from a trip. Or, you can make an open-ended document. If you don't specify an ending date, your attorney-in-fact is legally permitted to act for you until you revoke the power of attorney in writing.

b. You Revoke the Power of Attorney

You can revoke your power of attorney for real estate at any time, as long as you are of sound mind. (And if you aren't of sound mind, the document terminates automatically, so you don't have to worry about revoking it.) To revoke your document, all you need to do is fill out a simple form, sign it in front of a notary public, and give copies to the attorney-in-fact and to people or institutions the attorney-in-fact has been dealing with. This book contains revocation forms you can use. (Sample forms are in Chapter 11; you can find blank forms in Appendix B and on the enclosed disk.) You'll want to keep these forms on hand in case you need them later.

c. After a Divorce

In California, Illinois, Indiana and Missouri, if your spouse is your attorney-in-fact and you divorce, your ex-spouse's authority is immediately terminated. Regardless of state law, however, if you've named your spouse as attorney-in-fact and you get divorced, you should revoke your power of attorney and make a new one.

d. No Attorney-in-Fact Is Available

Your power of attorney will automatically end if your attorney-in-fact dies, resigns or becomes unable to represent you for any other reason.

e. If You Become Incapacitated or Die

Your power of attorney for real estate will automatically end if you become incapacitated or die. In most states, however, if the attorney-in-fact doesn't know of your incapacity or death and continues to act on your behalf, his or her actions are still valid.

C. Choosing Your Attorney-in-Fact

The choice of your attorney-in-fact is vitally important. You must pick someone you trust, both in a business and ethical sense. How to choose an attorney-in-fact is discussed in detail in Chapter 4 of this book.

D. The Attorney-in-Fact's Authority

The Nolo power of attorney for real estate form gives your attorney-in-fact the authority to act for you in all matters concerning real estate, including the following:

- buying or leasing real estate,
- selling, mortgaging, partitioning or leasing real estate,
- paying your mortgage and taxes (with your assets),
- arranging for necessary repairs and maintenance,
- refinancing your mortgage to get a better interest rate,
- paying off liens (legal claims) on your property,
- buying insurance for your property,
- building, remodeling or removing structures on your property,
- granting easements over your property, and
- bringing or defending lawsuits over real estate.

No matter what the attorney-in-fact does, however, he or she has a legal obligation to take only those actions that are in your best interests, and to represent you honestly and carefully. (These legal requirements are discussed in detail in Chapter 4, Section B.)

In your power of attorney document, you may limit the powers listed above in any way you choose. For example, if you are creating a power of attorney to give your attorney-in-fact the power to manage real estate for you, you can state in the document that your attorney in fact is not allowed, under any circumstances, to sell or mortgage the property.

You may also add additional powers to your document, if they are related to the real estate matters. For example, your attorney-in-fact may need access to your bank account to pay the costs of managing your property or handling a real estate deal. Grant that access in your document and specify the bank account from which your attorney-in-fact may withdraw funds.

SAMPLE CLAUSE:

I further grant to my attorney-in-fact full authority to act in any manner both proper and necessary to the exercise of the foregoing powers, including <u>withdrawing funds from my checking account, #4482 478 880, Anderson Valley Savings and Loan, Booneville, CA,</u> and I ratify every act that my attorney-in-fact may lawfully perform in exercising those powers.

E. Preparing Your Document

Once you've chosen your attorney-in-fact and thought about what authority to give him or her, preparing the actual document is easy.

All you have to do is tear out the *Power of Attorney for Real Estate* form from the back of the book or print it from the enclosed disk. Then follow the instructions in this section. It probably won't take you more than an hour.

It's not hard to prepare a power of attorney correctly, but it is important to follow the instructions carefully. If you don't, a bank, title company or other financial institution might not accept the document.

- **Make copies of the blank form.** Tear out the *Power of Attorney for Real Estate* and make a few photocopies. You can use one for a draft and save a clean one for the final document—the one you will sign and have notarized. Or, use the disk at the back of the book to generate a form with your computer.

- **Check the last page of your form.** The *Power of Attorney for Real Estate* has multiple last pages that may, at first glance, appear to be duplicates. Each of these pages is slightly different, however. Choose only the last page that has room for the number of witnesses your state requires—none, one or two. (You can find the number of witnesses required by your state in Section F.3, below.) Then, check the page numbers of your document to make sure everything's in proper order and you aren't missing pages or including any extras.

- **Use a typewriter or word processing program to fill in the blanks.** It's not a legal requirement that a power of attorney be typed, but your attorney-in-fact is much less likely to run into trouble if it is. People expect legal documents to be typed and may be suspicious of hand-written ones.
- **Don't erase anything.** Your final form should not contain any words that have been erased or whited-out. If the instructions tell you to cross out something, type a string of x's through the words.

⚠ **Get help if you need it.** A power of attorney can transfer tremendous power. Even though you can revoke it at any time (as long as you are mentally competent), never create a power of attorney unless you thoroughly understand the authority you plan to transfer. If you have questions, see an expert.

Here are instructions for filling in the *Power of Attorney for Real Estate* form.

Step 1. Principal and Attorney-in-Fact

In the first four blanks on the form, fill in your name and the city, county and state where you live. Enter your name as it appears on official documents such as your driver's license, bank accounts and real estate deeds. This may or may not be the name on your birth certificate. Enter it first, middle (if you choose), then last.

> **EXAMPLE:** Your birth certificate lists your name as Rose Mary Green. But you've always gone by Mary, and always sign documents as Mary McNee, your married name. You would use Mary McNee on your power of attorney.

Be sure to enter all names in which you hold bank accounts or other property your attorney-in-fact will be dealing with. This will make his or her

job far easier. If you're including more than one name, enter your full legal name first, followed by "aka" (also known as). Then enter your other names.

Making Your Records Consistent

If you use more than one name and you're up for some extra work, you may also consider settling on one name, entering it on your power of attorney form, and then changing your other documents to conform. This will clean up your records and save your attorney-in-fact some trouble later on. To change your name on official documents and records—for example, bank accounts, deeds or Social Security records—you'll have to contact the appropriate government office or financial institution to find out what documentation they'll need to make the change for you.

If during the course of a year you live in more than one state, use the address in the state where you vote, register vehicles, own valuable property, have bank accounts or run a business. If you've made your will, healthcare directives or a living trust, be consistent: use the address in the state you declared as your residence in those documents.

Next, type in the name of the person who has agreed to serve as your attorney-in-fact. (Remember: It's best to name just one person. The pitfalls of naming multiple attorneys-in-fact are discussed in Chapter 4.) Then enter the city, county and state where your attorney-in-fact lives.

Step 2. Description of Your Real Property

There is a large blank space following the first paragraph of the form. In it, you should type a description of the real estate your power of attorney will govern. Enter the exact street address, if your property has one. Then, attach a copy of the deed to your power of attorney form to avoid the trouble of retyping the lengthy and often confusing legal description contained in the deed.

RECORDING REQUESTED BY
AND WHEN RECORDED MAIL TO

Alice Hodge

41 East Avenue

Oakland, CA 94601

Power of Attorney for Real Estate

I, __Alice Hodge_____,
name of principal

of __Oakland_____, __Alameda County_____,
city   county

__California_____, appoint __Darcy Davis_____
state   name of attorney-in-fact

_____, of __Oakland_____,
city

__Alameda County_____, __California_____,
county   state

to act in my place with respect to the real property described as follows:

216 40th Street, Oakland, California 94609 (see attached deed.)

EXAMPLE:

9 Lotus Lane, Danville, CA 94558, Contra Costa County, California, as further described in the attached deed.

If you're up for it, you can type in the legal description instead. But be sure to type the entire description, exactly as it appears on the deed.

EXAMPLE:

LOT 195, as shown upon that certain map entitled, "Map of Greenbrae Sub. No. One, Marin Co. Calif.", filed May 2, 1946 in Book 6 of Maps, at Page 7, Marin County Records.

Step 3. Limiting the Powers Granted to the Attorney-in-Fact

Read through the powers described in the second paragraph of the document. If you don't want to grant one or more of the numbered powers, you can type a string of x's through those that you don't need. If you just want to limit the numbered powers in some way, type your instructions in the blank space following the list of powers. For example, you might want to forbid your attorney-in-fact from selling your property; you can type that limitation in the blank space.

If you don't want to limit the powers in any way, type a string of x's through the phrase "However, my attorney-in-fact shall not have the power to:"

Step 4. Additional Powers

In the fourth paragraph of the form, you can authorize your attorney-in-fact to carry out any additional powers related to the real estate powers you've granted. For example, you may want to authorize your attorney-in-fact to withdraw funds from a named bank account to cover any costs that arise in relation to his or her duties.

If you don't want to add any powers to the document, type a string of x's through the word "including."

Step 5. Termination Date

In the last paragraph of the form, you can type in a specific date on which you want the power of attorney to expire.

If you want the power of attorney to continue indefinitely, type a string of x's through "or until _____, _____, whichever comes first." If you do so, and you later want to terminate the power of attorney, you must revoke it in writing. (See Chapter 11.)

My attorney-in-fact may act for me in any manner to deal with all or any part of any interest in the real property described in this document, under such terms, conditions and covenants as my attorney-in-fact deems proper. My attorney-in-fact's powers include but are not limited to the power to:

1. Accept as a gift, or as security for a loan, reject, demand, buy, lease, receive or otherwise acquire ownership of possession of any estate or interest in real property.

2. Sell, exchange, convey with or without covenants, quitclaim, release, surrender, mortgage, encumber, partition or consent to the partitioning of, grant options concerning, lease, sublet or otherwise dispose of any interest in the real property described in this document.

3. Maintain, repair, improve, insure, rent, lease, and pay or contest taxes or assessments on any estate or interest in the real property described in this document.

4. Prosecute, defend, intervene in, submit to arbitration, settle and propose or accept a compromise with respect to any claim in favor of or against me based on or involving the real property described in this document.

However, my attorney in fact shall not have the power to:

sell, exchange, convey, quitclaim, release or surrender the property.

I further grant to my attorney-in-fact full authority to act in any manner both proper and necessary to the exercise of the foregoing powers, including withdrawing funds from my checking account #0125 073 640, Great Western Savings,

and I ratify every act that my attorney-in-fact may lawfully perform in exercising those powers.

F. Making It Legal

After you've filled out the power of attorney, you must sign it in front of a notary public and perhaps in front of witnesses as well. Then you must record the document in your local land records office. These simple steps will ensure that the document is legally valid and will be accepted by the people your attorney-in-fact will have to deal with. This section shows you what to do.

Checklist: Making It Legal

- ☐ Show the power of attorney to banks, brokers, insurers and other financial institutions you expect your attorney-in-fact to deal with.
- ☐ Sign the power of attorney in front of a notary public and, if you wish or state law requires, in the presence of witnesses.
- ☐ Record the power of attorney in the county land records office.
- ☐ Distribute copies of the power of attorney to people the attorney-in-fact will deal with.
- ☐ Give the original, signed document to your attorney-in-fact.

---

1. Before You Sign

Before you finalize your power of attorney, you should show it to the banks, title companies, real estate agents, insurers and others you expect your attorney-in-fact to deal with on your behalf.

Discussing your plans with people at these institutions now (and giving them a copy of the power of attorney, after you sign it, if you wish), will make your attorney-in-fact's job easier.

2. Sign and Notarize the Power of Attorney

A power of attorney is a serious document, and to make it effective you must observe certain formalities when you sign it. Fortunately, these requirements aren't difficult to meet.

a. Notarization

You must sign your power of attorney in the presence of a notary public for your state. The notary public watches you sign the power of attorney and then signs it too and stamps it with an official seal. The notary will want proof of your identity, such as a driver's license that bears your photo and signature. The notary's fee is usually just a few dollars—probably $5 to $10 in most places.

Finding a notary public shouldn't be a problem; many advertise in the Yellow Pages. Or check with your bank, which may provide notarizations as a service to customers. Real estate offices and title companies also have notaries.

b. Witnesses

Most states don't require the power of attorney to be signed in front of witnesses. (See the list below.) Nevertheless, it doesn't hurt to have a witness or two watch you sign, and sign the document themselves. Witnesses' signatures may make the power of attorney more acceptable to lawyers, banks, insurance companies and other entities the attorney-in-fact may have to deal with.

If you're giving your attorney-in-fact authority to handle real estate in a state other than the state where you live, be sure the document has at least the number of witnesses required by the state where the real property is located. Otherwise, you may not be able to record the power of attorney in that state.

This power of attorney takes effect on _____July 15, 1998_____, and shall continue until terminated in writing, or until _____December 1, 1999_____, whichever comes first.

I agree that any third party who receives a copy of this document may act under it. Revocation of the power of attorney is not effective as to a third party until the third party has actual knowledge of the revocation. I agree to indemnify the third party for any claims that arise against the third party because of reliance on this power of attorney.

Signed this ___10th___ day of ___July___, ___1998___.

State of ___California___, County of ___Alameda___.

___Alice Hodge___   ___573-21-0665___
Signature   Social Security Number

CERTIFICATE OF ACKNOWLEDGMENT OF NOTARY PUBLIC

State of ___California___ }
County of ___Alameda___ } ss

On ___July 10___, ___1998___, before me, ___Justin Smith___ _____, a notary public in and for said state, personally appeared ___Alice Hodge___ _____, personally known to me (or proved on the basis of satisfactory evidence) to be the person whose name is subscribed to the within instrument, and acknowledged to me that he or she executed the same in his or her authorized capacity and that by his or her signature on the instrument the person, or the entity upon behalf of which the person acted, executed the instrument.

WITNESS my hand and official seal.

___Justin Smith___

Notary Public for the State of ___California___

[NOTARIAL SEAL]   My commission expires: ___February 28, 2001___

PREPARATION STATEMENT

This document was prepared by:

___Alice Hodge___
Name
___216 40th Street___
Address
___Oakland, California___

The witnesses must be present when you sign the document before the notary. Witnesses must be mentally competent adults, preferably ones who live nearby and will be easily available if necessary. The person who will serve as attorney-in-fact should *not* be a witness. (Some states have additional requirements as well. See the chart below.) The attorney-in-fact does not have to sign the power of attorney document.

⚠ **Check the last page of your form.** The *Power of Attorney for Real Estate* has multiple last pages that may, at first glance, appear to be duplicates. Each of these pages is slightly different, however. Choose only the last page that has room for the number of witnesses your state requires—none, one or two. Then, check the page numbers of your document to make sure everything's in proper order and you aren't missing pages or including any extras.

3. Putting Your Power of Attorney on Public Record

You must put a copy of your power of attorney on file in the county land records office, called the county recorder's or land registry office in most states. This is called "recording," or "registration" in some states. If you don't record the power of attorney, your attorney-in-fact may not be permitted to handle certain real estate transactions for you.

Recording makes it clear to all interested parties that the attorney-in-fact has power over the property at issue. County land records are checked whenever real estate changes hands or is mortgaged. If, for example, your attorney-in-fact is supposed to sell or mortgage a piece of property for you, there must be something in the public records that proves he or she has authority to do so.

a. The Preparation Statement

You will notice something called a "preparation statement" at the very end of the power of attorney

States That Require Witnesses

State	Number of Witnesses	Other Requirements
Arizona	1	Witness may not be your attorney-in-fact, the spouse or child of your attorney-in-fact, or the notary public who acknowledges your document.
Arkansas	2	The attorney-in-fact may not be a witness.
Connecticut	2	The attorney-in-fact may not be a witness.
District of Columbia	2	Witnesses are necessary only if your power of attorney is to be recorded. (See Section 3, above.) The attorney-in-fact may not be a witness.
Florida	2	The attorney-in-fact may not be a witness.
Georgia	2	The attorney-in-fact may not be a witness. In addition, one of your witnesses may not be your spouse or blood relative.
Michigan	2	Witnesses are necessary only if your power of attorney is to be recorded. (See Section 3, above.) The attorney-in-fact may not be a witness.
Ohio	2	The attorney-in-fact may not be a witness.
Oklahoma	2	Witnesses may not be your attorney-in-fact, or anyone who is related by blood or marriage to you or your attorney-in-fact.
Pennsylvania	2	The attorney-in-fact may not be a witness.
South Carolina	2	The attorney-in-fact may not be a witness.
Vermont	2	Witnesses are necessary only if your power of attorney is to be recorded. (See Section 3, above.) The attorney-in-fact may not be a witness.

form. The preparation statement is a simple listing of the name and address of the person who prepared the document. In some states, you cannot record your document without this statement.

In most cases, the name of the principal and the name of the person who prepared the document will be the same—your own. But if it's not, the person who filled out the form should include his or her name and address in the preparation statement.

b. Where to Record Your Power of Attorney

In most states, each county has its own county recorder's (or registry of deeds) office. Take the power of attorney to the office in the county where the real estate is located. If you are granting your attorney-in-fact authority over more than one parcel of real estate, record the power of attorney in each county where you own property.

c. How to Record a Document

Recording a document is easy. You may even be able to do it by mail, but it's safer to go in person. The clerk will make a copy (usually on microfilm these days) for the public records. It will be assigned a reference number, often in terms of books and pages—for example, "Book 14, Page 1932 of the Contra Costa County, California records." In most places, it costs just a few dollars per page to record a document.

4. What to Do With the Signed Document

Give the original, signed and notarized document to the attorney-in-fact. He or she will need it as proof of authority to act on your behalf.

5. Making and Distributing Copies

You should give copies of your power of attorney to the people your attorney-in-fact will need to deal with—banks or title companies, for example. If your power of attorney is in their records, it may eliminate hassles for your attorney-in-fact later.

Be sure to keep a list of everyone to whom you give a copy. If you later revoke your power of attorney, notify each institution of the revocation. (See Chapter 11.)

6. Keeping Your Document Up to Date

If you've made a power of attorney without a specific termination date, you should redo it every year or so. Banks and other financial institutions may be reluctant to accept a power of attorney that's more than a couple of years old, even though the document is still technically valid. You should destroy any copies of the old power of attorney document and notify the people and institutions with copies of the former document that you have revoked your old power of attorney and made a new one. (See Chapter 11.) ∎

10

Powers of Attorney for Child Care

A. When to Use a Power of Attorney for Child Care 10/2

B. How Powers of Attorney for Child Care Work 10/3

    1. Who Can Prepare a Power of Attorney for Child Care? 10/3

    2. The Expense of a Power of Attorney for Child Care 10/3

    3. Making Sure Your Power of Attorney Is Accepted 10/4

    4. When the Power of Attorney Begins and Ends 10/4

C. The Attorney-in-Fact's Authority 10/5

D. Preparing Your Document 10/5

    1. Which Form to Use 10/5

    2. How to Fill Out the Form 10/6

E. Making It Legal 10/8

    1. Before You Sign 10/8

    2. Sign and Notarize the Power of Attorney 10/8

    3. What to Do With the Signed Document 10/8

    4. Making and Distributing Copies 10/10

A power of attorney for child care authorizes someone to care for your child in your absence—for example, if you go out of town. With the document in hand, your attorney-in-fact should be able to pay your child's bills and day-to-day expenses, authorize needed medical care and take care of any school-related matters. However, it is important to realize that the power of attorney document doesn't make anyone your child's legal "guardian." Only a court can do that. A guardianship is a court proceeding that gives someone full custody of and authority over a child, just as a parent would have.

A power of attorney does not have the legal force of a court-ordered guardianship. Strictly speaking, the power of attorney can give your attorney-in-fact full legal authority only to pay for your child's expenses. But in practice, many people and organizations, such as doctors and schools, will accept a power of attorney for child care and allow your attorney-in-fact to authorize emergency medical decisions and take care of any school-related matters. If you are going to be away from your child for just a few weeks or months, you probably won't want to go to the trouble of setting up a formal guardianship. A power of attorney allows you to name someone you trust to take care of your child, without the expense and hassles of going to court.

A. When to Use a Power of Attorney for Child Care

Consider making a power of attorney for child care whenever you will be away from your child and unable to make important decisions for him or her. This may occur for any number of reasons, for example:

- you will be out of town for an extended period of time,
- you are seriously ill and sometimes unable to take care of the child,
- your child will be staying with friends or relatives for an extended period of time, or
- your child will be living with someone else in order to attend a particular school.

EXAMPLE 1: Doug and Missy, a married couple with two teen-aged children, are planning a six-month business and pleasure trip to Europe. Neither child wants to go, so Doug's sister Margaret will care for the children during the trip. Doug and Missy prepare a power of attorney for child care authorizing Margaret to pay all the bills and reasonable expenses of the children, including their private school tuition, from an identified bank account. The power of attorney document also authorizes Margaret to make medical and school-related decisions for the children. Doug and Missy transfer enough money into the bank account to cover what they estimate the expenses will be. Finally, they give copies of the power of attorney to their bank, as well as to the children's school and doctors.

EXAMPLE 2: Colette, a single parent with a nine-year-old daughter, Alice, must go to another state to care for her sick father. She doesn't want to disrupt Alice's schooling, so she completes a power of attorney for child care authorizing her best friend Nancy to look after her daughter. Because she doesn't know how long she'll be gone, Colette doesn't put an ending date on her power of attorney. Colette gives copies of the document to her bank and also to Alice's school, doctor and orthodontist. When she returns, she will revoke the power of attorney and inform the people and institutions to whom she's given copies.

A power of attorney for child care may not be needed in every situation. For example, emergency medical care is normally administered without written consent.

It's also possible that the form won't satisfy all institutions in all circumstances. If someone will be taking your child across the U.S. border, for example, that person would need a signed letter from you that specifically authorizes travel to another country.

A power of attorney should be only temporary. Use the power of attorney only as a temporary measure, not as an attempt to transfer custody of your child to someone else. You cannot give someone legal custody of your child without a court guardianship or adoption order.

B. How Powers of Attorney for Child Care Work

This section tells you what you need to know to create a valid power of attorney for child care; it covers issues such as who can prepare the document, how much it costs, how to make sure the document is accepted, and when the document begins and ends.

1. Who Can Prepare a Power of Attorney for Child Care?

You can create a valid power of attorney for any child over whom you have legal custody, as long as you are of sound mind. (If you are reading this book, you can consider yourself to be of sound mind.) If you have joint custody of a child, you can use a power of attorney to delegate only as much authority as you have over the child. In other words, you can't use a power of attorney to take away any authority from a parent with whom you share custody.

This book contains two *Power of Attorney for Child Care* forms. One of these is for single parents; the other should be used by a couple who wants to jointly transfer authority to care for their child.

2. The Expense of a Power of Attorney for Child Care

Making a power of attorney for child care shouldn't set you back more than the price of this book and a few dollars for having your document notarized. (Notarization is required to make your document legal; it is discussed in Section E.2, below.)

In addition, you may wish to pay your attorney-in-fact for taking care of your child. The power of attorney document doesn't require it, so the decision is yours to make. If you do want to pay your attorney-in-fact, you and your attorney-in-fact should decide on an amount that's fair, and write up a separate agreement.

3. Making Sure Your Power of Attorney Is Accepted

Powers of attorney are common, and most institutions are used to them. Your attorney-in-fact, armed with a signed and notarized power of attorney document that specifies clearly his or her authority, shouldn't have any trouble getting your bank to accept his or her authority to withdraw money for the purpose of caring for your child. Your child's caretakers may have their own rules about accepting powers of attorney, however, and it pays to take steps to be sure they will honor your document.

The most important thing you can do to ensure that your bank, as well as your child's doctors, schools or other caretakers will accept your power of attorney is talk with these people and institutions in advance. Be sure that everyone is willing to accept the document and the authority of your attorney-in-fact. An individual or institution may ask you to include certain language in your form—or even to use its own power of attorney form in addition to the form contained in this book. If so, you should comply with these wishes. It will save time and trouble for you and your attorney-in-fact—and will ensure that your child gets the right care.

4. When the Power of Attorney Begins and Ends

Your power of attorney for child care takes effect on a date you specify in the document. It ends when you revoke it in writing, or on a date that you specify in the power of attorney document. In addition, the document will end automatically under certain circumstances.

a. The Termination Date

When you prepare your document, you can specify the date on which it should expire. You can enter a specific day, such as the day you expect to return from an out-of-town trip. Or, you can make an open-ended document that allows your attorney-in-fact to take care of your child's needs until you revoke the power of attorney in writing.

b. You Revoke the Power of Attorney

You can revoke your power of attorney for child care at any time, as long as you are of sound mind. (And if you aren't of sound mind, the document terminates automatically.) To revoke your document, all you need to do is fill out a simple form, sign it in front of a notary public, and give copies to the attorney-in-fact and to people or institutions the attorney-in-fact has been dealing with. This book contains revocation you can use. (Sample forms are shown in Chapter 11; you can find blank forms in Appendix B or on the enclosed computer disk.) You'll want to keep these forms on hand in case you need them later.

c. No Attorney-in-Fact Is Available

Your power of attorney will automatically end if your attorney-in-fact dies or becomes unable to represent you for any reason. Obviously, you'll need to make arrangements for someone to take over caring for your child if your attorney-in-fact becomes unavailable.

d. If You Become Incapacitated or Die

A power of attorney for child care will automatically end if you become incapacitated or die. If you want to name a guardian—the person who would care for your child if you were to die—you must do so in your will.

Make Your Will

There are lots of good reasons to make a will. But one of the best is to name someone to care for your child in the event of your death.

If both parents of a child die while the child is still a minor, a "personal guardian" must step in to care for him or her. You and the child's other parent can use your wills to nominate someone to fill this position. To avert conflicts, you should each name the same person. If a guardian is needed, a judge will appoint your nominee as long as he or she agrees that it is in the best interest of your children.

If one parent dies, the other usually takes responsibility for raising the child. But if you feel strongly that the other parent is incapable of caring for your child properly, or simply won't assume the responsibility, you should write a letter explaining why, and attach it to your will. The judge will take it into account, and may appoint the person you choose instead of the other parent.

For more information about making a will, take a look at one of these books or software programs from Nolo Press:

- *WillMaker* (software for Windows or Macintosh) lets you create a valid will, healthcare directive and final arrangements document using your computer.
- *Nolo's Will Book*, by Denis Clifford, contains a detailed discussion of wills and all the forms you need to create one.
- *The Quick and Legal Will Book*, by Denis Clifford, contains forms and instructions for creating a basic will.
- *Nolo's Law Form Kit: Wills*, contains a simple fill-in-the-blanks will.

C. The Attorney-in-Fact's Authority

The Nolo power of attorney for child care gives your attorney-in-fact the authority to act for you in all matters relating to the care, custody and control of your child, including the following:

- enrolling or withdrawing your child from school,
- consenting to necessary medical treatment (including surgery, medication, therapy and hospitalization), and
- hiring someone to care for or counsel your child.

You can also use your power of attorney to authorize your attorney-in-fact to pay your child's bills and day-to-day expenses from a bank account you specify.

No matter what the attorney-in-fact does, however, he or she has a legal obligation to take only those actions that are in your best interests, and to act with care.

D. Preparing Your Document

It's not hard to make a power of attorney for child care. All you have to do is tear out the correct *Power of Attorney for Child Care* form from the back of the book or print it from the enclosed disk. Then follow the instructions in this section. It probably won't take you more than half an hour.

1. Which Form to Use

There are two *Power of Attorney for Child Care* forms in this book. One is a joint form that you should use if both parents are available to transfer authority to the attorney-in-fact. The other is for single parents; you should use it if you are caring for a child on your own and need to delegate your authority to someone else.

2. How to Fill Out the Form

It's not hard to prepare a power of attorney correctly, but it is important to follow the instructions carefully. If you don't, your attorney-in-fact might have trouble getting the document accepted.

- **Make copies of the blank form.** Tear out your *Power of Attorney for Child Care* and make a few photocopies. You can use one for a draft and save a clean one for the final document —the one you will sign and have notarized. Or, use the disk at the back of the book to generate a form with your computer.
- **Use a typewriter or word processing program to fill in the blanks.** It's not a legal requirement that a power of attorney be typed, but your attorney-in-fact is much less likely to run into trouble if it is. People expect legal documents to be typed and may be suspicious of handwritten ones.
- **Don't erase anything.** Your final form should not contain any words that have been erased or whited-out. If the instructions tell you to cross out something, type a string of x's through the words.

⚠ Get help if you need it. A power of attorney can transfer tremendous power. Even though you can revoke it at any time (as long as you are mentally competent), never create a power of attorney unless you thoroughly understand the authority you plan to transfer. If you have questions, see an expert.

Here are instructions for filling in the *Power of Attorney for Child Care* form.

Step 1. Principal, Children and Attorney-in-Fact

In the first four blanks on the form, fill in your name and the city, county and state where you live. Enter your name as it appears on official documents such as your driver's license, bank accounts and real estate deeds. This may or may not be the name on your birth certificate. Enter it first, middle (if you choose), then last.

EXAMPLE: Your birth certificate lists your name as Rose Mary Green. But you've always gone by Mary, and always sign documents as Mary McNee, your married name. You would use Mary McNee on your power of attorney.

If during the course of a year you live in more than one state, use the address in the state where you vote, register vehicles, own valuable property, have bank accounts or run a business.

If you've made your will, healthcare directives or a living trust, be consistent: use the address in the state you declared as your residence in those documents.

Next, type in the full name of your child. If you have more than one child, you don't need to make a separate form for each. Simply list all of their names in this blank.

Finally, type in the name of the person who has agreed to serve as your attorney-in-fact. (You should name only one person.) Then enter the city, county and state where your attorney-in-fact lives.

Step 2. Granting the Power to Withdraw Money from a Bank Account

In the second paragraph of the form, you can authorize your attorney-in-fact to carry out any additional powers related to the general child care powers listed in the form. This is the place to authorize your attorney-in-fact to withdraw funds from a named bank account to cover any costs that arise while taking care of your child. If you want to do so, type your instructions, the name of your bank and the bank account number on the blank lines.

If you don't want to add this or any other specific powers to the document, type a string of x's through the word "including."

SAMPLE CLAUSE:

I further grant to my attorney-in-fact full authority to act in any manner both proper and necessary to the exercise of the foregoing powers, including withdrawing funds from my checking account, #4482 478 880, Anderson Valley

Power of Attorney for Child Care

We, __Zoe Shryne__

name of principal

and __Ted Shryne__ ,

name of principal

of __Plymouth__ , __Cook County__ ,

city   county

__Illinois__ , are the parents of and have legal custody of

state

__Karyn Shryne__ .

name of child

We appoint __Rebecca Linwood__ ,

name of attorney-in-fact

of __Plymouth__ , __Cook County__ ,

city   county

__Illinois__ , as our attorney-in-fact to take any of the actions

state

with respect to the care of our child. Our attorney-in-fact's powers include, but are not limited to, the following:

1. Enroll or withdraw our child from school or any similar institution.

2. Hire, retain or fire a third person to care for, counsel, treat or otherwise assist our child.

3. Consent to any necessary medical treatment, surgery, medication, therapy, hospitalization or similar care for our child.

4. Exercise the same parental rights we may exercise with respect to the care, custody and control of our child.

We further grant our attorney-in-fact full authority to act in any manner both proper and necessary to the exercise of the foregoing powers, including __withdrawing funds from our__

__checking account #2201-175-631, Charter Bank and Trust,__

and we ratify every act that our attorney-in-fact may lawfully perform in exercising those powers.

This power of attorney takes effect on __September 1, 1998__ , and shall continue until terminated in writing, or until __December 15, 1998__ , whichever comes first.

We agree that any third party who receives a copy of this document may act under it. Revocation of the power of attorney is not effective as to a third party until the third party has actual knowledge of the revocation. We agree to indemnify the third party for any claims that arise against the third party because of reliance on this power of attorney.

Savings and Loan, Booneville, CA, and I ratify every act that my attorney-in-fact may lawfully perform in exercising those powers.

Step 3. Termination Date

In the third paragraph of the form, you can type in a specific date on which you want the power of attorney to expire.

If you want the power of attorney to continue indefinitely, type a string of x's through "or until _____, _____, whichever comes first." If you do so, your power of attorney will remain valid until you sign and distribute a notice of revocation, as discussed in Chapter 11.

E. Making It Legal

After you've done all the work of putting together your power of attorney for child care, you must take just a couple of steps to make sure the document is legally valid. This section shows you what to do.

Checklist: Making It Legal

After you've completed your power of attorney, follow these steps:

☐ Show the power of attorney to the people and institutions you expect your attorney-in-fact might deal with while caring for your child.

☐ Sign the power of attorney in front of a notary public.

☐ Distribute copies of the power of attorney to people and institutions involved in your child's care.

☐ Give the original, signed document to your attorney-in-fact.

---

1. Before You Sign

Before you finalize your power of attorney, you should show it to the people and institutions you expect your attorney-in-fact to deal with on your behalf.

Discussing your plans with people at these institutions now (and giving them a copy of the power of attorney, after you sign it, if you wish), will make your attorney-in-fact's job much easier.

2. Sign and Notarize the Power of Attorney

You must sign your power of attorney in the presence of a notary public for your state. In some states, notarization is required by law to make the power of attorney valid. But even where law doesn't require it, custom does. A power of attorney that isn't notarized may not be accepted by people your attorney-in-fact tries to deal with.

The notary public watches you sign the power of attorney and then signs it, too and stamps it with an official seal. The notary will want proof of your identity, such as a driver's license that bears your photo and signature. The notary's fee is usually just a few dollars—probably $5 to $10 in most places.

Finding a notary public shouldn't be a problem; many advertise in the Yellow Pages. Or check with your bank, which may provide notarizations as a service to customers. Real estate offices and title companies also have notaries.

3. What to Do With the Signed Document

Give the original, signed and notarized document to the attorney-in-fact. He or she will need it as proof of authority to act on your behalf.

Signed this _____ 26th _____ day of ___ August _____, 1998 ___.

State of ___ Illinois _____, County of ___ Cook _____.

_Zoe Shryne_____   671-21-7276_____
Signature   Social Security Number

_Ted Shryne_____   639-21-3325_____
Signature   Social Security Number

CERTIFICATE OF ACKNOWLEDGMENT OF NOTARY PUBLIC

State of __ Illinois _____ ⎫
                                             ⎬ ss
County of __ Cook _____ ⎭

On __ August 26 _____, __ 1998 __, before me, __ Pamela Blue _____
_____, a notary public in and for said state, personally appeared

Zoe Shryne _____ and

Ted Shryne _____, personally

known to me (or proved on the basis of satisfactory evidence) to be the persons whose names are

subscribed to the within instrument, and acknowledged to me that he or she executed the same in

their authorized capacities and that by their signatures on the instrument the persons, or the entity

upon behalf of which the persons acted, executed the instrument.

WITNESS my hand and official seal.

_Pamela Blue_____

Notary Public for the State of ___ Illinois _____

[NOTARIAL SEAL]   My commission expires: __ December 31, 1999 _____

4. Making and Distributing Copies

You should give copies of your power to the people your attorney-in-fact will need to deal with—your bank and your child's doctors and school, for example. If your power of attorney is in their records, it may eliminate hassles for your attorney-in-fact later.

Be sure to keep a list of everyone to whom you give a copy. If you later revoke your power of attorney, notify each person and institution of the revocation. ∎

11

Revoking a Power of Attorney

A. Special Considerations for Durable Powers of Attorney 11/2

   1. When You Can Revoke Your Document 11/2

   2. If a Conservator or Guardian Is Appointed 11/3

B. When to Revoke a Power of Attorney 11/3

   1. You Want to Change the Terms of the Power of Attorney 11/3

   2. You Move to Another State 11/3

   3. You Lose the Power of Attorney Document 11/5

   4. You Get Married or Divorced 11/5

   5. Your Durable Power Is Old 11/5

C. How to Revoke a Power of Attorney 11/5

   1. Prepare a Notice of Revocation 11/5

   2. Sign and Notarize the Revocation 11/8

   3. Record the Notice of Revocation 11/8

   4. Notify Anyone Who Deals With the Former Attorney-in-Fact 11/8

After you grant a power of attorney—whether it is durable, conventional or limited—you can revoke it at any time, as long as you are of sound mind and physically able to do so. Of course, if it's a conventional or limited power, the document will be automatically revoked if you become incapacitated. Durable powers will remain effective during your incapacity.

If you decide you want to revoke your power of attorney document, you should carefully follow all the procedures set out in this chapter.

Checklist: Revoking a Power of Attorney

☐ Prepare a Notice of Revocation.

☐ Sign the Notice of Revocation in front of a notary public (and in the presence of witnesses, if you wish).

☐ Record the Notice of Revocation at the county land records office, if necessary.

☐ Deliver a copy of the Notice of Revocation to the attorney-in-fact and each institution and person who has dealt or might deal with the former attorney-in-fact.

A. Special Considerations for Durable Powers of Attorney

If you've made a durable power of attorney, special questions may arise when you decide to revoke it. If you've made another type of document—a general or limited conventional power of attorney, power of attorney for real estate or power of attorney for child care—skip ahead to Section B.

1. When You Can Revoke Your Document

As mentioned just above, you can revoke your power of attorney as long as you are of sound mind

and physically able to do so. The sound mind requirement is not difficult to satisfy. If someone challenged the revocation, a court would look only at whether or not you understood, when you signed it, the consequences of your act. (It's the same standard that is applied to creation of a valid power of attorney in the first place; see Chapter 3, Section A.)

If you revoke a durable power of attorney that hasn't taken effect yet (remember, it's called a "springing" power), you shouldn't run into any problems. You simply sign the Notice of Revocation (explained later in this chapter), and it's as if you had never prepared the original power of attorney.

If, however, your springing durable power of attorney has already taken effect, it means that one or two physicians (as required by your power of attorney document) have stated, in writing, that you are incapacitated and unable to handle your financial affairs. Your attorney-in-fact may feel that you do not have the capacity to revoke the durable power of attorney. If the attorney-in-fact doesn't accept the validity of the revocation, and keeps control over your financial matters, there may have to be court proceedings to resolve the conflict.

> **EXAMPLE:** In a springing durable power of attorney, Arthur authorizes Jim to be his attorney-in-fact. Two years later, Arthur has a stroke. A doctor signs a statement saying that Arthur cannot manage his financial affairs, and Jim begins to act as Arthur's attorney-in-fact for finances.
>
> Arthur slowly recovers and eventually feels able to handle his own affairs again. But Jim thinks that Arthur is irrational and shouldn't be allowed to make his own decisions. He continues acting for Arthur, concluding that his authority is unchanged because Arthur isn't of sound mind and so can't revoke the durable power of attorney.
>
> If Arthur insists, Jim will have to accede to his wishes, or one of them will have to request a court proceeding, where a judge will determine whether or not Arthur is competent to revoke the durable power of attorney and manage his own affairs.

An attorney-in-fact who refuses to accept a revocation can create serious problems. If you get into such a dispute with your attorney-in-fact, consult a lawyer.

2. If a Conservator or Guardian Is Appointed

If your attorney-in-fact is satisfactorily handling your financial affairs while you can't, it's very unlikely that a court will need to appoint a conservator for you. After all, your affairs are being handled—the attorney-in-fact is depositing your checks, paying your bills and looking after your property. (Conservators are discussed in Chapter 2, Section A.)

If, however, you or a family member objected to the attorney-in-fact's actions, a court might appoint a conservator. In a few states, appointment of a conservator automatically revokes a durable power of attorney. In that case, the conservator would become solely responsible for your property and financial matters.

In many states, the conservator would have the legal authority to revoke your durable power of attorney. Someone appointed to take physical care of you (usually called a "guardian" or "guardian of the person"), not your property, may also, depending on state law, have the power to revoke a financial power of attorney. Each state's rules are listed below.

Don't spend much time worrying about this. (Five or ten minutes should do it.) Again, keep in mind that a conservator will probably never be appointed.

B. When to Revoke a Power of Attorney

Here are the most common situations in which you should revoke a power of attorney and start over.

1. You Want to Change the Terms of the Power of Attorney

There is no accepted way to amend a power of attorney. If you want to change or amend a power of attorney, the safe course is to revoke the existing document and prepare a new one. Don't go back and modify your old document with pen, typewriter or correction fluid—you could throw doubt on the authenticity of the whole thing.

> **EXAMPLE:** Tom signed a durable power of attorney several years ago. Now he is in declining health and wants to add to the authority he gave his attorney-in-fact, Sarah, giving her the specific power to sell Tom's real estate if necessary.
>
> Tom should revoke his old durable power of attorney and create a new one, granting the additional authority.

Similarly, you should revoke your power of attorney if you change your mind about whom you want to name as attorney-in-fact. If you create a springing durable power of attorney, the person you named to be your attorney-in-fact may become unavailable before he or she is needed. Or you may simply change your mind. If that's the case, you can revoke the durable power of attorney before it ever takes effect.

2. You Move to Another State

If you move to a different state, your attorney-in-fact may run into some trouble getting others to accept the validity of a power of attorney signed in your old state. It's best to revoke your power of attorney and prepare a new one.

Power of Conservator or Guardian to Revoke Power of Attorney

Alabama	Curator or guardian of the estate can revoke power of attorney	**Mississippi**	Conservator or guardian of the estate can revoke power of attorney
Alaska	Conservator can revoke power of attorney	**Missouri**	Conservator can revoke power of attorney only with court approval
Arizona	Conservator can revoke power of attorney		
Arkansas	Conservator or guardian of the estate can revoke power of attorney	**Montana**	Conservator can revoke power of attorney
		Nebraska	Conservator or guardian of the estate can revoke power of attorney
California	Conservator can revoke power of attorney only if authorized by court	**Nevada**	Guardian can revoke power of attorney
Colorado	Conservator can revoke power of attorney	**New Hampshire**	Guardian or conservator can revoke power of attorney
Connecticut	Power of attorney automatically revoked if conservator of the estate appointed	**New Jersey**	Guardian can revoke power of attorney
Delaware	Power of attorney revoked to the extent that the attorney-in-fact's powers are specifically granted to the guardian of the person or of the estate. Guardian can revoke power of attorney only if authorized by court.	**New Mexico**	Conservator can revoke power of attorney
		New York	Committee or conservator can revoke power of attorney
		North Carolina	Conservator, guardian of the estate or guardian of the person can revoke power of attorney
Dist. of Columbia	Conservator or guardian of the estate can revoke power of attorney		
		North Dakota	Conservator or guardian of the estate can revoke power of attorney
Florida	Power of attorney automatically suspended if a guardianship proceeding begun; revoked if guardian appointed	**Ohio**	Guardian can revoke power of attorney
		Oklahoma	Conservator or guardian of the estate can revoke power of attorney
Georgia	Power of attorney automatically revoked if guardian or receiver appointed	**Oregon**	Conservator can revoke power of attorney
Hawaii	Guardian of the property can revoke power of attorney	**Pennsylvania**	Guardian can revoke power of attorney
Idaho	Conservator or guardian of the estate can revoke power of attorney	**Rhode Island**	Conservator or guardian can revoke power of attorney
Illinois	Guardian can revoke power of attorney only if ordered by court	**South Carolina**	Attorney-in-fact's powers revoked as to matters within scope of the guardianship or conservatorship, unless the power of attorney provides otherwise
Indiana	Guardian can revoke power of attorney only if ordered by court		
Iowa	Conservator can revoke power of attorney	**South Dakota**	Guardian of the estate can revoke power of attorney
Kansas	Conservator or guardian of the estate can revoke power of attorney	**Tennessee**	Conservator or guardian of the estate can revoke power of attorney
Kentucky	Power of attorney automatically revoked if fiduciary appointed	**Texas**	Power of attorney automatically revoked when guardian appointed
Louisiana	Power of attorney automatically terminated if curator qualified	**Utah**	Conservator can revoke power of attorney
		Vermont	Guardian can revoke power of attorney
Maine	Conservator or guardian can revoke power of attorney	**Virginia**	Guardian or committee can revoke power of attorney only if authorized by court
Maryland	Guardian can revoke power of attorney	**Washington**	Guardian can revoke power of attorney
Massachusetts	Conservator or guardian of the estate can revoke power of attorney	**West Virginia**	Conservator or guardian of the estate can revoke power of attorney
Michigan	Conservator can revoke power of attorney	**Wisconsin**	Conservator or guardian of the estate can revoke power of attorney
Minnesota	Conservator or guardian can revoke power of attorney	**Wyoming**	Conservator can revoke power of attorney

3. You Lose the Power of Attorney Document

If you conclude that you've really lost your signed power of attorney document, it's wise to formally revoke it, destroy any copies and create a new one. Very few people are likely to accept your attorney-in-fact's authority if they can't look at the document it's based on. By officially revoking the lost version, you minimize chances that the old power of attorney might someday appear and confuse matters.

4. You Get Married or Divorced

If you get married after signing a power of attorney, you'll probably want to designate your new spouse to be your attorney-in-fact, if he or she wasn't the person you named originally.

If you name your spouse as your attorney-in-fact and later divorce, you should revoke the power of attorney and create a new one, naming someone else as the attorney-in-fact.

In California, Illinois, Indiana and Missouri, the designation is automatically ended if you divorce the attorney-in-fact. In that case, the alternate you named (if any) would serve as attorney-in-fact. You still may want to create a new power of attorney, one that doesn't mention your former spouse and lets you name another alternate attorney-in-fact.

5. Your Durable Power Is Old

If you make a springing durable power of attorney, it's a good idea to review it every five to seven years. A durable power of attorney never expires, but if the document was signed many years before it goes into effect, the attorney-in-fact may have trouble getting banks, insurance companies or people in government agencies to accept its authority, just because people don't trust documents that are 15 years old. You may want to revoke it and sign a new one.

It's especially important to review your durable power of attorney if significant changes occur in your life. For example, if the person you named as your attorney-in-fact moves far away, becomes ill or is no longer closely involved with your life, you should appoint someone else to serve. To do that, revoke the old power of attorney and prepare a new one.

C. How to Revoke a Power of Attorney

There are two ways to revoke your power of attorney:
- Prepare and sign a document called a Notice of Revocation.
- Destroy *all* existing copies of the power of attorney document.

The first method is always preferable, because it creates proof that you really revoked the power of attorney.

Note for Alaska Readers. Alaska law allows you to revoke your power of attorney by preparing a new one. It's still advisable, however, to prepare a separate notice of revocation and notify everyone who needs to know about the revocation.

1. Prepare a Notice of Revocation

The "Notice of Revocation" is called that because its purpose is to notify the attorney-in-fact, and those he or she may have been dealing with, that you have revoked the durable power of attorney.

This book contains two kinds of Notice of Revocation forms for you to use. If you didn't record your power of attorney in the county land records office, use the standard form. If you did record the original power of attorney, you must also record the revocation; use the Notice of Revocation for a recorded power of attorney. Sample forms are shown below; you can find the blank tear-out forms in Appendix B and on the enclosed computer disk.

Notice of Revocation of Durable Power of Attorney

I, __Ramona Ellsworth__,

of the City of ___Hartford___, County of ___Hartford___,

State of __Connecticut__, revoke the power of attorney dated

__September 15, 1999__, empowering __Bill Piersall__

to act as my attorney-in-fact. I revoke and withdraw all power and authority granted under that power of attorney. Power of Attorney for Child Care

Dated: __February 5, 2000__

Ramona Ellsworth
Signature of Principal

Ramona Ellsworth
_____, Principal

CERTIFICATE OF ACKNOWLEDGMENT OF NOTARY PUBLIC

State of ___Connecticut___

County of ___Hartford___ } ss

On __February 5__, __2000__, before me, __Daniel Sweeny__

_____, a notary public in and for said state, personally appeared

__Ramona Ellsworth__, personally known to me (or proved on the basis of satisfactory evidence) to be the person whose name is subscribed to the within instrument, and acknowledged to me that he or she executed the same in his or her authorized capacity and that by his or her signature on the instrument the person, or the entity upon behalf of which the person acted, executed the instrument.

WITNESS my hand and official seal.

Daniel Sweeney

Notary Public for the State of __Connecticut__

[NOTARIAL SEAL]   My commission expires: __April 1, 2003__

RECORDING REQUESTED BY

AND WHEN RECORDED MAIL TO

David L. Hernandez

463 Arlington St., N.E.

Portland, OR 97510

Notice of Revocation of Durable Power of Attorney

I, David L. Hernandez ,

of the City of Portland , County of Multnomah ,

State of Oregon , revoke the power of attorney dated

May 26, 1998 , empowering Francis M. Rowland

to act as my attorney-in-fact. I revoke and withdraw all power and authority granted under that

power of attorney.

That power of attorney was recorded on May 30 , 1998 , in Book

421 , at Page 2436 of the Official Records, County of Multnomah ,

State of Oregon .

Dated: November 2, 1999

David L. Hernandez

Signature of Principal

David L. Hernandez , Principal

CERTIFICATE OF ACKNOWLEDGMENT OF NOTARY PUBLIC

State of Oregon

County of Multnomah } ss

On November 3 , 1999 , before me, Evelyn Kramer

, a notary public in and for said state, personally appeared

David L. Hernandez , personally

known to me (or proved on the basis of satisfactory evidence) to be the person whose name is

subscribed to the within instrument, and acknowledged to me that he or she executed the same in

his or her authorized capacity and that by his or her signature on the instrument the person, or the

entity upon behalf of which the person acted, executed the instrument.

WITNESS my hand and official seal.

Evelyn Kramer

Notary Public for the State of Oregon

[NOTARIAL SEAL]   My commission expires: August 1, 2000

2. Sign and Notarize the Revocation

You must sign and date the Notice of Revocation. It needn't be witnessed, but having witnesses watch you sign may be a prudent idea, especially if you have reason to believe that someone might later raise questions regarding your mental state at the time you signed the revocation. If you want witnesses' signatures, you'll have to retype the Notice of Revocation. Add a witness statement like the one that follows.

Sign the Notice of Revocation in front of a notary public. Finding a notary shouldn't be a problem; many advertise in the Yellow Pages. Or check with a bank, real estate office or attorney's office. (For more on notarization, see Chapter 7, Section B.1.)

3. Record the Notice of Revocation

If you recorded the original power of attorney at your local recorder of deeds office, you must also record the revocation. (How to record documents is explained in Chapter 7, Section C.)

But even if the original power of attorney was not recorded, you can record a revocation if you fear that the former attorney-in-fact might try to act without authorization. If the revocation is part of the public records, people who check those records (as anyone should if real estate is involved) will know that the former attorney-in-fact is no longer authorized to act on your behalf.

Note for North Carolina Readers. When you register a revocation in the Register of Deeds Office, it must be accompanied by a document stating that a copy of the revocation notice has been served on (delivered to) the former attorney-in-fact. This document is called a "proof of service." The revocation must be served on the attorney-in-fact by the county sheriff or someone else authorized by law to serve legal papers.

4. Notify Anyone Who Deals With the Former Attorney-in-Fact

It's not enough to sign a revocation, or even to record it, for it to take effect; there's one more crucial step. You must notify the former attorney-in-fact and all institutions and people who have dealt or might deal with the former attorney-in-fact. Each

---

WITNESSES

On the date written above, the principal declared to me that this instrument is his or her financial power of attorney, and that he or she willingly executed it as a free and voluntary act. The principal signed this instrument in my presence.

_____   _____
Name   Name

_____   _____
Address   Address

_____   _____
County   County

of them must receive a copy of the Notice of Revocation.

If you don't give this written notification, people or institutions who don't know the power of attorney has been revoked might still enter into transactions with the (former) attorney-in-fact. If they do this in good faith, they are legally protected. You may well be held legally liable for the acts of your attorney-in-fact, even though you have revoked his or her authority. In other words, once you create a power of attorney, the legal burden is on you to be sure everyone knows you have revoked it.

EXAMPLE: When Michael undergoes a serious operation, his springing durable power of attorney goes into effect. After his convalescence, Michael revokes the power of attorney, in writing. He sends a copy of the revocation to Colette, his attorney-in-fact, but neglects to send a copy to his bank. Colette, fraudulently acting as Michael's attorney-in-fact, removes money from Michael's accounts and spends it. The bank isn't responsible to Michael for his loss.

When you're ready to send out revocation notices, try to think of everyone with whom the attorney-in-fact has had, or may have, dealings. Here are some examples:

- banks
- mortgage companies
- title companies
- stockbrokers
- insurance companies
- credit card companies
- Social Security offices
- Medicare or Medicaid offices
- military or civil service offices
- IRS
- pension fund administrators
- post offices
- hospitals
- doctors
- schools
- relatives
- business partners
- landlords
- lawyers
- accountants
- real estate agents
- maintenance and repair persons. ■

Help Beyond the Book

A. Legal Typing Services 12/2

B. Finding a Lawyer 12/2

    1. Look for a Group Legal Plan 12/2

    2. Check Out a Prepaid Legal Plan 12/3

    3. Ask Businesspeople and Friends 12/3

    4. Consult a Legal Clinic 12/3

    5. Call an Attorney Referral Service 12/4

C. Working With a Lawyer 12/4

D. Lawyers' Fees 12/4

E. Doing Your Own Legal Research 12/5

    1. Going to the Law Library 12/5

    2. Online Legal Research 12/7

If you prepare your own financial power of attorney with this book, you probably won't need to see a lawyer. If, however, you have specific questions or unusual circumstances—a very large amount of property, potential family squabbles, or special worries about the attorney-in-fact's powers, for example—you may need legal advice.

If you do need more legal information or advice, you can hire a lawyer or look for your answers yourself, either by going to a law library or by using your computer to hunt for information online. If you need clerical help typing your document, you may want to get help from a legal typing service.

A. Legal Typing Services

Even if you need "legal" help, you may not need a lawyer. People who operate legal typing services, also known as independent paralegals or legal technicians, are experts at preparing legal documents. They are not lawyers and do not give legal advice. But if you know what you want, a typing service can help you prepare the legal paperwork at an affordable price. For example, if you need to retype one of the forms in this book (for example, you need more room for special instructions in your durable power of attorney or you want to add a witness statement to a notice of revocation) and you're concerned about getting everything in the right place, a typing service might be able to help.

Here are some things to look for when choosing a typing service.

- **An established or recommended service.** Few typing services stay in business unless they provide honest and competent services. A recommendation from a social service agency, friend, court clerk or lawyer is probably a good place to take your business.
- **Reasonable fees.** About $10 a page or $20 an hour.
- **Trained staff.** One indication of whether or not people are committed to providing good services is if they have undertaken skills training through independent paralegal associations and continuing education seminars.

B. Finding a Lawyer

If you decide that you want to talk about your situation face to face with a lawyer, do a little shopping around. The trick isn't just finding (or being found by) any lawyer, but finding one who is trustworthy, competent and charges fairly.

Look for a lawyer who has experience with estate planning and preparing financial powers of attorney. Lawyers who concentrate on other kinds of law—divorce, tax or insurance, for example—may not know nearly as much as you do about the intelligent use of financial powers of attorney. A specialist's fee may be 10% to 30% higher than that of a general practitioner, but a good specialist will probably produce results more efficiently and save you money in the long run.

Here are some suggestions on how to go about finding a good lawyer.

1. Look for a Group Legal Plan

Some unions, employers and consumer organizations offer group legal plans to their members or employees. Good group plans offer comprehensive legal assistance for free or at low rates. If you are a member of such a plan, check with it first. Your problem may be covered free of charge. If it is, and you are satisfied that the lawyer you are referred to is knowledgeable about estate planning and powers of attorney, this route is probably a good choice.

Some plans, however, give you only a slight reduction in a lawyer's fee. In that case, you may be referred to a lawyer whose main virtue is the willingness to reduce fees in exchange for a high volume of referrals. Be wary. There's a better way to pick a good lawyer.

2. Check Out a Prepaid Legal Plan

For basic advice, you may want to consider joining a prepaid legal "insurance" plan that offers advice, by phone or in person, at no extra charge. It's a misnomer to refer to these programs as legal insurance. The programs provide an initial level of service for a low fee—usually $75 to $150—and then charge for additional or extra work. Thus, most prepaid plans are more a marketing device for the participating lawyers than they are an insurance plan. Your initial membership fee, however, may be worth the initial consultation you receive, even if you use it only once. Most plans have renewal fees; it's common to join a plan for a specific service and then not renew.

These plans aren't as easy to find as they once were; many providers have ceased offering them. Even if you find one, there's no guarantee that the lawyers available through these plans are of the best caliber. As with anything you buy, you should check out the plan—and the lawyer you'll be seeing—carefully before you sign up.

The American Association of Retired Persons (AARP) Legal Plan

If you're a member of AARP, you may be able to participate in its new prepaid legal service plan. Under this plan, you're entitled to a half-hour of free legal advice, then 20% off your assigned lawyer's standard fee. You're also entitled to low fixed rates for basic services, such as having your will drafted. Currently, the program is available in only a few states, but is expected to grow. For more information, contact AARP at 800-424-3410.

Whenever you avail yourself of a service offered by a prepaid legal plan, be forewarned: The lawyer is probably getting only $2 to $5 per month for dealing with you—obviously, not enough to cover costs. In most prepaid plans, lawyers agree to work for this minimal amount in the hope of finding clients who will pay for extra legal services not covered by the monthly premium. This set-up gives the lawyers a financial incentive to complicate, rather than simplify, your problem. So if a plan lawyer recommends an expensive legal procedure, get a second opinion.

3. Ask Businesspeople and Friends

Personal contacts are the traditional, and probably the best, means for locating a good lawyer. Ask people you know in any social or other organization in which you are involved. They may well know of a good lawyer whose attitudes are similar to yours. Senior citizens' centers and other groups that advise and assist older people may have a list of well regarded local lawyers who specialize in estate planning.

Anyone who owns a small business probably has an ongoing relationship with a lawyer. Ask around to find someone you know who is a satisfied client. If that lawyer does not handle estate planning, he or she will likely know someone who does. And because of the continuing relationship with your friend, the lawyer has an incentive to recommend someone who is competent.

4. Consult a Legal Clinic

Law firms with lots of small offices across the country, such as Hyatt Legal Services, trumpet their low initial consultation fees. It's true that a basic consultation is cheap, but anything beyond that isn't cheap at all. Rates average about the same as those charged by other lawyers in general practice.

If you do consult a legal clinic, often the trick is to quickly extract the information you need and resist attempts to convince you that you need more services. If the lawyer you talk to is experienced in estate planning, however, and you're comfortable with the person and the service, it may be worthwhile. Unfortunately, most of these offices have extremely high lawyer turnover, so you may see a different one every time you visit.

5. Call an Attorney Referral Service

A lawyer referral service will give you the name of an attorney who practices in your area. Usually, you can get a referral to an attorney who claims to specialize in estate planning and will give you an initial consultation for a low fee.

Most county bar associations have referral services. In some states, independent referral services, run by or for groups of lawyers, also operate.

Never assume a bar association referral is a seal of approval. Few referral services thoroughly screen the attorneys they list, which means those who participate may not be the most experienced or competent. Often, lawyers who sign up with referral services simply need clients, because they are just starting out or for some other reason. (Experienced lawyers with good reputations usually get plenty of new clients from recommendations of their current ones.) It may be possible to find a skilled lawyer through a referral service, but be sure to take the time to check out the credentials and experience of the person to whom you're referred.

C. Working With a Lawyer

Before you talk to a lawyer, decide what kind of help you really need. Do you want someone to review your durable power of attorney to make sure it looks all right? Or do you want advice on a complete estate plan? If you don't clearly tell the lawyer what you want, you may find yourself agreeing to more than you'd planned.

If you just want a lawyer to review your power of attorney to reassure you that it looks fine, you may have a hard time finding a willing lawyer.

Although you may think it's perfectly reasonable for the lawyer to take a quick glance and charge you a half-hour's fee, from the lawyer's point of view there are several problems. First, a conscientious lawyer may feel that it's impossible to give an intelligent opinion about the wisdom of your power of attorney without first talking to you about your finances and family.

A related factor is the fear of a malpractice lawsuit sometime down the road. A lawyer doesn't want to give you a bit of advice now, for a small fee, and get a phone call from you years later saying that something has gone wrong. Economically, the risk isn't worth it.

Before you see the lawyer, a good strategy is to write down your questions as specifically as you can. If the lawyer doesn't give you clear, concise answers, say thank you and try someone else. Preparing a valid power of attorney isn't an overly complicated job in most instances; a knowledgeable lawyer should be able to give you satisfactory answers on the spot.

If the lawyer acts wise but says little except to ask that the problem be placed in his or her hands—with a substantial fee, of course—watch out. You're either dealing with someone who doesn't know the answer and won't admit it (common) or someone who finds it impossible to let go of the "me expert, you plebeian" philosophy (even more common).

D. Lawyers' Fees

Most lawyers charge $100 to $300 per hour. It depends on where you live, but generally, fees of $100 to $200 per hour are reasonable in urban areas, given the lawyer's overhead expense. In rural areas and smaller cities, $80 to $150 is more like it.

Price is not always related to quality. A fancy office, corporate clothes and solemn face are no guarantee (or even any indication) that a lawyer is competent, but they do guarantee a high price tag. Fortunately, many good lawyers operate more modestly and pass the savings on to their clients.

Whatever the fee arrangement, be sure you've settled it—preferably in writing—at the start of your relationship. In addition to the hourly fee, you should get a clear, written commitment from the lawyer about how many hours your problem should take to handle.

E. Doing Your Own Legal Research

If you're willing to learn how to do your own legal research, the benefits are substantial. Not only will you save some money, you'll gain a sense of mastery over an area of law and a confidence that will spill over into your other dealings with legal matters.

Fortunately, the law governing durable powers of attorney is not particularly difficult to research. But first, of course, you've got to find a law library or a computer with online access.

1. Going to the Law Library

There are several kinds of law libraries available to you:
- a public law library (usually located in or near the county courthouse)
- a public library with a good law collection, or
- a library at a public (or even private, if you ask permission) law school.

When you get to the library, you'll probably need the help of a good legal research guidebook (see *Finding the Law*, below) and a kind reference librarian. Thankfully, law librarians are almost always helpful and courteous to non-lawyers who try to do their own legal research.

Statutes. The first thing to do is to ask a librarian where to find the state statutes, which are called "codes," "laws" or "statutes," depending on the state. If you can, get an "annotated version," which contains both your state's statutes and excerpts from any relevant court cases and references to related articles.

Once you've found your state's statutes, you can look up the laws that govern powers of attorney.

The citation for each state's laws is given in the chart below.

Each state groups its power of attorney laws together. Statutes are numbered, so once you get to the correct number, it should be easy to find the provision you need. If you have trouble, ask the law librarian for help. When you find what you're looking for, make sure you're reading the most recent version of the statute by checking the back of the statute book to see if there's a "pocket part" (supplement) inserted inside the back cover. Pocket parts contain statutory changes (and summaries of related court decisions) made since the hardback book was printed.

Be warned that statutes are rarely easy to read. Commonly, they are written in dense prose, full of incredibly long sentences, obscure legal terms and cross-references to other statutes. Wade through them as best you can, and expect to read any section you're interested in several times.

Power of Attorney Statutes

Alabama	Ala. Code §§ 26-1-2 to 26-1-2.1	Missouri	Mo. Ann. Stat. §§ 404.700 to 404.735
Alaska	Alaska Stat. §§ 13.26.332 to 13.26.358	Montana	Mont. Code Ann. §§ 72-5-501 to 72-5-502 and 72-31-201 to 72-31-238
Arizona	Ariz. Rev. Stat. Ann. §§ 14-5501 to 14-5503	Nebraska	Neb. Rev. Stat. §§ 30-2664 to 30-2672
Arkansas	Ark. Code Ann. §§ 28-68-101, 28-68-201 and 28-68-301 to -313	Nevada	Nev. Rev. Stat. Ann. §§ 11.450 to 11.470
California	Cal. Probate Code §§ 4000 to 4465	New Hampshire	N.H. Rev. Stat. Ann. §§ 506:6 to 506:7
Colorado	Colo. Rev. Stat. §§ 15-1-1301 to 15-1-1320	New Jersey	N.J. Stat. Ann. §§ 46:2B-8 to 46:2B-19
Connecticut	Conn. Gen. Stat. Ann. §§ 45a-562 and 1-42 to 1-56b	New Mexico	N.M. Stat. Ann. §§ 45-5-501 to 45-5-617
Delaware	Del. Code Ann. tit. 12, §§ 4901 to 4905	New York	N.Y. Gen. Obligations Law §§ 3-501 and 5-1501 to 5-1602
District of Columbia	D.C. Code Ann. §§ 21-2081 to 21-2085	North Carolina	N.C. Gen. Stat. §§ 32A-1 to 32A-14
Florida	Fla. Stat. Ann. §§ 709.08 to 709.11	North Dakota	N.D. Cent. Code §§ 30.1-30-01 to 30.1-30-05
Georgia	Ga. Code Ann. §§ 10-6-36 to 10-6-142	Ohio	Ohio Rev. Code Ann. §§ 1337.09 to 1337.10
Hawaii	Haw. Rev. Stat. §§ 551D-1 to 551D-7	Oklahoma	Okla. Stat. tit. 58, §§ 1071 to 1077
Idaho	Idaho Code §§ 15-5-501 to 15-5-507	Oregon	Or. Rev. Stat. §§ 127.005 and 127.015
Illinois	755 ILCS 45/1-1 to 45/3-4	Pennsylvania	Pa. Stat. Ann. tit. 20, §§ 5601 to 5607
Indiana	Ind. Code Ann. §§ 30-5-1-1 to 30-5-10-4	Rhode Island	R.I. Gen. Laws § 34-22-6.1
Iowa	Iowa Code Ann. §§ 633.705 to 633.706	South Carolina	S.C. Code Ann. §§ 62-5-501 to 62-5-503
Kansas	Kan. Stat. Ann. §§ 58-610 to 58-617	South Dakota	S.D. Codified Laws Ann. §§ 59-7-2.1 to 59-7-2.4
Kentucky	Ky. Rev. Stat. Ann. § 386.093	Tennessee	Tenn. Code Ann. §§ 34-6-101 to 34-6-109
Louisiana	La. Rev. Stat. Ann. § 2985-3034	Texas	Tex. Probate Code Ann. §§ 481 to 506
Maine	Me. Rev. Stat. Ann. tit. 18-A, §§ 5-501 to 5-505	Utah	Utah Code Ann. §§ 75-5-501 to 75-5-502
Maryland	Md. Code Ann., Estates and Trusts §§ 13-601 to 13-603	Vermont	Vt. Stat. Ann. tit. 14, §§ 3051 to 3052
Massachusetts	Mass. Gen. Laws Ann. ch. 210B §§ 1 to 7	Virginia	Va. Code Ann. §§ 11-9.1 to 11-9.5
Michigan	Mich. Comp. Laws Ann. §§ 700.495 and 700.497	Washington	Wash. Rev. Code Ann. §§ 11.94.010 to 11.94.900
Minnesota	Minn. Stat. Ann. §§ 523.01 to 523.09	West Virginia	W. Va. Code §§ 39-4-1 to 39-4-7
Mississippi	Miss. Code Ann. §§ 87-3-1 to 87-3-17	Wisconsin	Wis. Stat. Ann. §§ 243.07 to 243.10
		Wyoming	Wyo. Stat. §§ 3-5-101 to 3-5-103

After you've looked at the basic law, you'll probably want to check any recent court decisions mentioned in the "Annotation" section of the code immediately following the law itself.

Form books. Form books, which are how-to-do-it books written primarily for lawyers, can also be very helpful. You may find a form book that contains sample power of attorney forms valid in your state. Ask a law librarian to help you find a form book.

Finding the Law. *Legal Research: How to Find and Understand the Law,* by Stephen Elias and Susan Levinkind (Nolo Press), is a hands-on guide to the law library. It addresses research methods in detail and should answer most questions that arise in the course of your research. It also contains a good discussion of how to read and analyze statutes.

Legal Research Made Easy (Nolo Press) is an entertaining videotape in which renowned legal research professor Robert Berring explains how to do effective legal research in the law library.

Gilbert's Legal Research, by Peter Honigsberg (Harcourt Brace Legal and Professional Publications), is a no-nonsense guide to commonly-used law library resources.

2. Online Legal Research

Another way to approach legal research is to use a computer. If you want information about a recent court decision, a federal or state statute or a current legal issue, you'll probably be able to find it somewhere on the Internet.

You may want to start by visiting Nolo's site on the World Wide Web (www.nolo.com). Nolo offers extensive information on estate planning and related matters, as well as more information about doing your own legal research—on paper and online.

How to Get to the World Wide Web

Getting onto the Web requires a computer, a modem, specially designed software and an account with an Internet service provider ("ISP"). If you are using a law library with a connection to the Web, all this will be taken care of for you. Just look on the screen for the icon or name that tells you that the computer is loaded with a Web browser. Or ask for help.

If you want to get onto the Internet on your own, you can buy a modem from any computer store and sign up with an ISP in your area. The ISP will usually provide you with the software you need. Or, you may wish to join an online service such as America Online or CompuServe, which will also supply you with a connection to the Web.

Many online sites offer state-specific information about powers of attorney, particularly durable powers of attorney for finances. If you want to search for your state's statutes or answers to frequently asked questions about powers of attorney in your state, you can use an online search engine to hunt for a site that will help you. A search engine asks you to type in one or more key words or phrases in a text entry box, and then produces a list of materials that contain them. For example, if you live in Arizona and you're looking for information about durable powers of attorney in your state, you could type in "durable power of attorney" and "Arizona." Your query would produce a list of every online site, in the database checked by that search engine, that contains those words.

A search may turn up hundreds of entries, which you can view in successive lists of ten or 20. Because the entries are usually listed according to the frequency with which the words in your query appear, items at the top of the list tend to be most helpful.

Useful Search Engines

Here's a handful of search engines you may want to try.

Findlaw	http://www.findlaw.com
The World Wide Web Virtual Law Library	http://www.law.indiana.edu/law/v-lib/lawindex.html
The U.S. House of Representatives Internet Law Library	http:/www.law.house.gov
The Meta-Index for U.S. Legal Research	http://www.gsulaw.gsu.edu/metaindex/
Yahoo	http://www.yahoo.com/law/

Finding the Law Online. *Law on the Net,* by James Evans (Nolo Press), is the definitive guide to legal resources on the Internet. It contains listings for thousands of helpful online sites. ■

How to Use the Forms Disk

1. Copying the Disk Files Onto Your Computer ....Appendix A/2

    a. Windows 95 Users ....Appendix A/2

    b. Windows 3.1 Users ....Appendix A/2

    c. Macintosh Users ....Appendix A/3

    d. DOS Users ....Appendix A/3

2. Creating Your Documents With the Forms Disk Files ....Appendix A/3

    a. Opening a File..Appendix A/3

    b. Editing Your Document ....Appendix A/4

    c. Printing Out the Form ....Appendix A/4

    d. Saving Your Document ....Appendix A/4

All of the forms in this book can be found in Appendix B and on the 3½" floppy disk in the back of the book. This forms disk is formatted for the PC (MS-DOS), and can be used by any PC running Windows or DOS. If you use a Mac, you must have a super disk drive and Apple File Exchange, or a similar utility, to use this disk. These files can be opened, filled in and printed out with your word processing program or text editor.

 The disk does not contain software and you do not need to install any files.

The forms disk contains only files that can be opened and edited using a word processor. This is not a software program. See the README.TXT file included on the disk for additional instructions on how to use these files.

How to View the README File

If you do not know how to view the file README.TXT, insert the forms disk into your computer's floppy disk drive and follow these instructions:

- **Windows 95:** (1) On your PC's Desktop, double-click the icon for the floppy disk drive into which the forms disk was inserted; (2) double-click the file README.TXT.
- **Windows 3.1:** (1) Open File Manager; (2) double-click the icon for the floppy disk drive into which the forms disk was inserted; (3) double-click the file README.TXT.
- **Macintosh:** (1) On your Mac Desktop, double-click the icon for the floppy disk that you inserted; (2) double-click on the file README.TXT.
- **DOS:** At the DOS prompt, type EDIT A:README.TXT and press the Enter key.

While the ReadMe is open, print it out by using the Print command in the File menu.

---

1. Copying the Disk Files Onto Your Computer

Before you do anything else, copy the files from the forms disk onto your hard disk. Then work on these copies *only*. This way the original files and instructions will be untouched and can be used again. Instructions on how to copy files are provided below.

In accordance with U.S. copyright laws, remember that copies of the disk and its files are for your personal use only.

Insert the forms disk and do the following:

a. Windows 95 Users

(These instructions assume that the A: drive is the source you want to copy from and that the C: drive is the location you want to copy the files to.)

Step 1: Double-click the My Computer icon on your desktop.

Step 2: Double-click the C: drive icon in the My Computer window to open the C:\ drive window.

Step 3: Open the File menu, click on New, then click on Folder. This will create an untitled folder on the C: drive

Step 4: Type "FPOA Forms " to rename the untitled folder.

Step 5: Go back to the My Computer window and double-click the 3½ Floppy (A:) icon .

Step 6: Choose Select All from the Edit menu .

Step 7: Drag and drop the selected contents of the A:\ window into the "FPOA Forms" folder

b. Windows 3.1 Users

(These instructions assume that the A: drive is the source you want to copy from and that the C: drive is the location you want to copy the files to.)

Step 1: Open File Manager.

Step 2: Choose Create Directory from the File menu.

Step 3: In the dialog box, type C:\FPOAFORM
         then click the OK button.
Step 4: Choose Copy from the File menu to open
         the Copy dialog box.
Step 5: In the From box, type A:*.*
Step 6: In the To box, type C:\FPOAFORM
Step 7: Click the OK button.

c. Macintosh Users

Step 1: If the FPOAFORM folder is open, close it .
Step 2: Click on the FPOAFORM disk icon and
         drag in it onto the icon of your hard disk.
Step 3: Read the message to make sure you want
         to go ahead, then click OK.

d. DOS Users

(These instructions assume that the A: drive is the
source you want to copy from and that the C: drive
is the location you want to copy the files to.)

Step 1: To create a directory named "FPOAFORM"
         on your C: hard disk drive, type the
         following at the DOS prompt:

             C: <ENTER>

             CD\ <ENTER>

             MD FPOAFORM<ENTER>

Step 2: Change to the FPOAFORM directory by
         typing:

             CD FPOAFORM <ENTER>

Step 3: Copy all the files on the forms disk (in
         your A: drive) to the current disk or
         directory by typing:

             COPY A:*.* <ENTER>

All of the files on the distribution disk will be
copied into the FPOAFORM directory on your C:
drive.

2. Creating Your Documents With the Forms Disk Files

This disk contains all forms in two file types (or
formats):

   • the standard ASCII text format (TXT), and
   • rich text format (RTF).

ASCII files can be read by every word processor
or text editor including DOS Edit, all flavors of MS
Word and WordPerfect (including Macintosh),
Windows Notepad and WordPad and Macintosh
SimpleText or TeachText.

RTF files have the same text as the ASCII files,
but have additional formatting. They can be read by
most recent word processing programs including all
version of MS Word for Windows and Macintosh
and recent versions of WordPerfect for Windows
and Macintosh.

To use a form on the disk to create your documents you must: (1) open a file in your word processor or text editor; (2) edit the form by filling in
the required information; (3) print it out; (4) save
your revised file.

The following are general instructions on how to
do this. However, each word processor uses different commands to open, format, save and print documents. Please read your word processor's manual
for specific instructions on performing these tasks.

Do not call Nolo's technical support if you
have questions on how to use your word
processor.

a. Opening a File

To open a file in your word processor, you need to
start your word processing program and open the
file from within the program. This process usually
entails going to the File menu and choosing the
Open command. This opens a dialog box where
you will tell the program (1) the type of file you
want to open (either *.TXT or *.RTF) and (2) the
location and name of the file (you will need to
navigate through the directory tree to get to the

folder/directory on your hard disk that you created and copied the disk's files to). If these directions are unclear you will need to look through the manual for your word processing program—Nolo's technical support department will NOT be able to help you with the use of your word processing program.

Which File Format Should You Use?

If you are not sure which file format to use with your word processor, try opening the RTF files first. Rich text files (RTF) contain most of the formatting included in the sample forms found in this book and in Appendix B. Most current Windows and Macintosh word processing programs, such as Microsoft Word or WordPerfect, can read RTF files.

   If you are unable to open the RTF file in your word processor, or a bunch of "garbage" characters appear on screen when you do, then use the TXT files instead . All word processors and text editors can read TXT files, which contain only text, tabs and carriage returns; all other formatting and special characters have been stripped.

Windows and Mac users can also open a file more directly by double-clicking on it. Use File Manager (Windows 3.1), My Computer or Windows Explorer (Windows 95) or the Finder (Macintosh) go to the folder/directory you created and copied the disk's files to. Then, double-click on the specific file you want to open. If you click on a RTF file and you have a program installed that "understands" RTF, your word processor should launch and load the file that you double-clicked on. If the file isn't loaded, or it contains a bunch of garbage characters, use your word processor's Open command, as described above, to open the TXT file instead. If you directly double-click on a TXT file, it will load into a basic text editor like Notepad or SimpleText rather than your word processor.

b. Editing Your Document

Fill in the appropriate information according to the instructions and sample agreements in the book. Underlines are used to indicate where you need to enter your information, frequently followed by instructions in brackets. If you do not know how to use your word processor to edit a document, you will need to look through the manual for your word processing program—Nolo's technical support department will NOT be able to help you with the use of your word processing program.

c. Printing Out the Form

Use your word processor's or text editor's Print command to print out your document. If you do not know how to use your word processor to print a document, you will need to look through the manual for your word processing program—Nolo's technical support department will NOT be able to help you with the use of your word processing program.

d. Saving Your Document

After filling in the form, do a "save as" and give the file a new name.

⚠️ If you do not rename the file, the underlines that indicate where you need to enter your information will be lost and you will not be able to create a new document with this file without re-copying the original file from the floppy disk. Never edit the original file on your floppy.

   If you do not know how to use your word processor to save a document, you will need to look through the manual for your word processing program—Nolo's technical support department will NOT be able to help you with the use of your word processing program. ■

APPENDIX

B

Power of Attorney Forms

⚠ **Check the last page of your form.** Each of the power of attorney forms (except the *Power of Attorney for Child Care)* has multiple last pages that may, at first glance, appear to be duplicates. Each of these pages is slightly different, however. Choose only the last page that has room for the number of witnesses your state requires—none, one or two. Then, check the page numbers of your documents to make sure everything's in proper order and you aren't missing pages or including any extras.

GENERAL POWERS OF ATTORNEY (DURABLE OR CONVENTIONAL)

Form	Title	File Name
1	Financial Power of Attorney	FORM1
2	Financial Power of Attorney: Alaska	FORM2
3	Financial Power of Attorney: Arizona	FORM3
4	Financial Power of Attorney: District of Columbia	FORM4
5	Financial Power of Attorney: New Mexico	FORM5
6	Financial Power of Attorney: North Carolina	FOM6
7	Financial Power of Attorney: Oklahoma	FORM7

LIMITED POWERS OF ATTORNEY

Form	Title	File Name
8	Limited Power of Attorney	FORM8
9	Power of Attorney for Real Estate	FORM9
10	Power of Attorney for Child Care: Single Parent	FORM10
11	Power of Attorney for Child Care: Two Parents	FORM11

OTHER FORMS

Form	Title	File Name
12	Information for an Attorney-in-Fact	FORM12
13	Physician's Determination of Incapacity (All States Except New Mexico)	FORM13
14	Healthcare Professional's Determination of Incapacity (New Mexico)	FORM14
15	Delegation of Authority	FORM15
16	Resignation of Attorney-in-Fact	FORM16
17	Notice of Revocation: Unrecorded	FORM17
18	Notice of Revocation: Recorded	FORM18

Financial Power of Attorney: ALASKA

1. Principal and Attorney-in-Fact

I, _____,

of _____,

appoint _____

_____

_____

as my attorney-in-fact to act for me in any lawful way with respect to the powers delegated in Part 6 below. If that person (or all of those persons, if I name more than one) is unable or unwilling to serve as attorney-in-fact, I appoint the following alternates, to serve alone in the order named:

First Alternate

_____
Name

_____
Address

_____

Second Alternate

_____
Name

_____
Address

_____

2. Authorization of Attorneys-in-Fact

If I have named more than one attorney-in-fact, they are authorized to act:

☐ jointly.

☐ independently.

3. Delegation of Authority

☐ My attorney-in-fact may delegate, in writing, any authority granted under this power of attorney to a person he or she selects. Any such delegation shall state the period during which it is valid and specify the extent of the delegation.

☐ My attorney-in-fact may not delegate any authority granted under this power of attorney.

4. Effective Date and Durability

☐ This power of attorney is not durable. It is effective immediately, and shall terminate on

_____.

☐ This power of attorney is durable. It is effective immediately, and shall continue in effect if I become incapacitated or disabled.

☐ This power of attorney is durable. It shall take effect only if I become incapacitated or disabled and unable to manage my financial affairs.

5. Determination of Incapacity

If I am creating a springing durable power of attorney under Part 4 of this document, my incapacity or disability shall be determined by written declaration of two licensed physicians. Each declaration shall be made under penalty of perjury and shall state that in the physician's opinion I am substantially unable to manage my financial affairs. If possible, the declarations shall be made by _____

_____

_____.

No licensed physician shall be liable to me for any actions taken under this part which are done in good faith.

One physician's declaration is acceptable if only one physician is available and the declaration so states.

6. Powers of the Attorney-in-Fact

I grant my attorney-in-fact power to act on my behalf in the following matters, as indicated by my initials next to each granted power or on line (14), granting all the listed powers. Powers that are struck through are not granted.

INITIALS

_____ (1) Real estate transactions.

_____ (2) Tangible personal property transactions.

_____ (3) Stock and bond, commodity and option transactions.

_____ (4) Banking and other financial institution transactions.

_____ (5) Business operating transactions.

_____ (6) Insurance and annuity transactions.

_____ (7) Estate, trust, and other beneficiary transactions.

_____ (8) Living trust transactions.

_____ (9) Legal actions.

_____ (10) Personal and family care.

_____ (11) Government benefits.

_____ (12) Retirement plan transactions.

_____ (13) Tax matters.

_____ (14) ALL POWERS (1 THROUGH 13) LISTED ABOVE.

These powers are defined in Part 14, below.

7. **Special Instructions to the Attorney-in-Fact**

_____

_____

_____

_____

_____

_____

_____

_____

_____

_____

_____

_____

_____

_____

_____

_____

8. Compensation and Reimbursement of the Attorney-in-Fact

☐ My attorney-in-fact shall not be compensated for services, but shall be entitled to reimbursement, from my assets, for reasonable expenses. Reasonable expenses include but are not limited to reasonable fees for information or advice from accountants, lawyers or investment experts relating to my attorney-in-fact's responsibilities under this power of attorney.

☐ My attorney-in-fact shall be entitled to reimbursement for reasonable expenses and reasonable compensation for services. What constitutes reasonable compensation shall be determined exclusively by my attorney-in-fact. If more than one attorney-in-fact is named in this document, each shall have the exclusive right to determine what constitutes reasonable compensation for his or her own duties.

☐ My attorney-in-fact shall be entitled to reimbursement for reasonable expenses and compensation for services in the amount of $_____.

If more than one attorney-in-fact is named in this document, each shall be entitled to receive this amount.

9. Personal Benefit to the Attorney-in-Fact

☐ My attorney-in-fact may buy any assets of mine or engage in any transaction he or she deems in good faith to be in my interest, no matter what the interest or benefit to my attorney-in-fact.

☐ My attorney-in-fact may not benefit personally from any transaction engaged in on my behalf.

☐ Although my attorney-in-fact may receive gifts of my property as described in Part 7 of this document, my attorney-in-fact may not benefit personally from any other transaction he or she engages in on my behalf.

10. Commingling by the Attorney-in-Fact

☐ My attorney-in-fact may commingle any of my funds with any funds of his or hers.

☐ My attorney-in-fact may not commingle any of my funds with any funds of his or hers.

11. Liability of the Attorney-in-Fact

My attorney-in-fact shall not incur any liability to me, my estate, my heirs, successors or assigns for acting or refraining from acting under this document, except for willful misconduct or gross negligence. My attorney-in-fact is not required to make my assets produce income, increase the value of my estate, diversify my investments or enter into transactions authorized by this document, as long as my attorney-in-fact believes his or her actions are in my best interests or in the interests of my estate and of those interested in my estate. A successor attorney-in-fact shall not be liable for acts of a prior attorney-in-fact.

12. Reliance on This Power of Attorney

Any third party who receives a copy of this document may rely on and act under it. Revocation of the power of attorney is not effective as to a third party until the third party has actual knowledge of the revocation. I agree to indemnify the third party for any claims that arise against the third party because of reliance on this power of attorney.

13. Severability

If any provision of this document is ruled unenforceable, the remaining provisions shall stay in effect.

14. Definition of Powers Granted to the Attorney-in-Fact

The powers granted in Part 6 of this document authorize my attorney-in-fact to do the following.

(1) Real estate transactions

Act for me in any manner to deal with all or any part of any interest in real property that I own at the time of execution of this document or later acquire, under such terms, conditions and covenants as my attorney-in-fact deems proper. My attorney-in-fact's powers include but are not limited to the power to:

(a) Accept as a gift, or as security for a loan, reject, demand, buy, lease, receive or otherwise acquire ownership of possession of any estate or interest in real property.

(b) Sell, exchange, convey with or without covenants, quitclaim, release, surrender, mortgage, encumber, partition or consent to the partitioning of, grant options concerning, lease, sublet or otherwise dispose of any interest in real property.

(c) Maintain, repair, improve, insure, rent, lease, and pay or contest taxes or assessments on any estate or interest in real property I own or claim to own.

(d) Prosecute, defend, intervene in, submit to arbitration, settle and propose or accept a compromise with respect to any claim in favor of or against me based on or involving any real estate transaction.

(2) Tangible personal property transactions

Act for me in any manner to deal with all or any part of any interest in personal property that I own at the time of execution of this document or later acquire, under such terms as my attorney-in-fact deems proper. My attorney-in-fact's powers include but are not limited to the power to lease, buy, exchange, accept as a gift or as security for a loan, acquire, possess, maintain, repair, improve, insure, rent, convey, mortgage, pledge, and pay or contest taxes and assessments on any tangible personal property.

(3) Stock and bond, commodity, option and other securities transactions

Do any act which I can do through an agent, with respect to any interest in a bond, share, other instrument of similar character or commodity. My attorney-in-fact's powers include but are not limited to the power to:

(a) Accept as a gift or as security for a loan, reject, demand, buy, receive or otherwise acquire ownership or possession of any bond, share, instrument of similar character, commodity interest or any investment with respect thereto, together with the interest, dividends, proceeds or other distributions connected with it.

(b) Sell (including short sales), exchange, transfer, release, surrender, pledge, trade in or otherwise dispose of any bond, share, instrument of similar character or commodity interest.

(c) Demand, receive and obtain any money or other thing of value to which I am or may become or may claim to be entitled as the proceeds of any interest in a bond, share, other instrument of similar character or commodity interest.

(d) Agree and contract, in any manner, and with any broker or other person and on any terms, for the accomplishment of any purpose listed in this section.

(e) Execute, acknowledge, seal and deliver any instrument my attorney-in-fact thinks useful to accomplish a purpose listed in this section, or any report or certificate required by law or regulation.

(4) Banking and other financial institution transactions

Do any act that I can do through an agent in connection with any banking transaction that might affect my financial or other interests. My attorney-in-fact's powers include but are not limited to the power to:

(a) Continue, modify and terminate any deposit account or other banking arrangement, or open either in the name of the agent alone or my name alone or in both our names jointly, a deposit account of any type in any financial institution, rent a safe deposit box or vault space, have access to a safe deposit box or vault to which I would have access, and make other contracts with the institution.

(b) Make, sign and deliver checks or drafts, and withdraw my funds or property from any financial institution by check, order or otherwise.

(c) Prepare financial statements concerning my assets and liabilities or income and expenses and deliver them to any financial institution, and receive statements, notices or other documents from any financial institution.

(d) Borrow money from a financial institution on terms my attorney-in-fact deems acceptable, give security out of my assets, and pay, renew or extend the time of payment of any note given by or on my behalf.

(5) Business operating transactions

Do any act that I can do through an agent in connection with any business operated by me that my attorney-in-fact deems desirable. My attorney-in-fact's powers include but are not limited to the power to:

(a) Perform any duty and exercise any right, privilege or option which I have or claim to have under any contract of partnership, enforce the terms of any partnership agreement, and defend, submit to arbitration or settle any legal proceeding to which I am a party because of membership in a partnership.

(b) Exercise in person or by proxy and enforce any right, privilege or option which I have as the holder of any bond, share or instrument of similar character and defend, submit to arbitration or settle a legal proceeding to which I am a party because of any such bond, share or instrument of similar character.

(c) With respect to a business owned solely by me, continue, modify, extend or terminate any contract on my behalf, demand and receive all money that is due or claimed by me and use such funds in the operation of the business, engage in banking transactions my attorney-in-fact deems desirable, determine the location of the operation, the nature of the business it undertakes, its name, methods of manufacturing, selling, marketing, financing, accounting, form of organization and insurance, and hiring and paying employees and independent contractors.

(d) Execute, acknowledge, seal and deliver any instrument of any kind that my attorney-in-fact thinks useful to accomplish any purpose listed in this section.

(e) Pay, compromise or contest business taxes or assessments.

(f) Demand and receive money or other things of value to which I am or claim to be entitled as the proceeds of any business operation, and conserve, invest, disburse or use anything so received for purposes listed in this section.

(6) Insurance and annuity transactions

Do any act that I can do through an agent, in connection with any insurance or annuity policy, that my attorney-in-fact deems desirable. My attorney-in-fact's powers include but are not limited to the power to:

(a) Continue, pay the premium on, modify, rescind or terminate any annuity or policy of life, accident, health, disability or liability insurance procured by me or on my behalf before the execution of this power of attorney. My attorney-in-fact cannot name himself or herself as beneficiary of a renewal, extension or substitute for such a policy unless he or she was already the beneficiary before I signed the power of attorney.

(b) Procure new, different or additional contracts of health, disability, accident or liability insurance on my life, modify, rescind or terminate any such contract and designate the beneficiary of any such contract.

(c) Sell, assign, borrow on, pledge, or surrender and receive the cash surrender value of any policy.

(7) Estate, trust and other beneficiary transactions

Act for me in all matters that affect a trust, probate estate, guardianship, conservatorship, escrow, custodianship or other fund from which I am, may become or claim to be entitled, as a beneficiary, to a share or payment. My attorney-in-fact's authority includes the power to disclaim any assets which I am, may become or claim to be entitled, as a beneficiary, to a share or payment.

(8) Living trust transactions

Transfer any of my interests in real property, stocks, bonds, accounts with financial institutions, insurance or other property to the trustee of a revocable trust I have created as settlor.

(9) Legal actions

Act for me in all matters that affect claims in favor of or against me and proceedings in any court or administrative body. My attorney-in-fact's powers include but are not limited to the power to:

(a) Hire an attorney to assert any claim or defense before any court, administrative board or other tribunal.

(b) Submit to arbitration or mediation or settle any claim in favor of or against me or any litigation to which I am a party, pay any judgment or settlement and receive any money or other things of value paid in settlement.

(10) Personal and family maintenance

Do all acts necessary to maintain my customary standard of living, and that of my spouse and children and other persons customarily supported by or legally entitled to be supported by me. My attorney-in-fact's powers include but are not limited to the power to:

(a) Pay for medical, dental and surgical care, living quarters, usual vacations and travel expenses, shelter, clothing, food, appropriate education and other living costs.

(b) Continue arrangements with respect to automobiles or other means of transportation, charge accounts, discharge of any services or duties assumed by me to any parent, relative or friend, contributions or payments incidental to membership or affiliation in any church, club, society or other organization.

(11) Government benefits

Act for me in all matters that affect my right to government benefits, including Social Security, Medicare, Medicaid, or other governmental programs, or civil or military service. My attorney-in-fact's powers include but are not limited to the power to:

(a) Prepare, execute, file, prosecute, defend, submit to arbitration or settle a claim on my behalf to benefits or assistance, financial or otherwise.

(b) Receive the proceeds of such a claim and conserve, invest, disburse or use them on my behalf.

(12) Retirement plan transactions

Act for me in all matters that affect my retirement plans. My attorney-in-fact's powers include but are not limited to the power to select payment options under any retirement plan in which I participate, make contributions to those plans, exercise investment options, receive payment from a plan, roll over plan benefits into other retirement plans, designate beneficiaries under those plans and change existing beneficiary designations.

(13) Tax matters

Act for me in all matters that affect my local, state and federal taxes. My attorney-in-fact's powers include but are not limited to the power to:

(a) Prepare, sign and file federal, state, local and foreign income, gift, payroll, Federal Insurance Contributions Act returns and other tax returns, claims for refunds, requests for extension of time, petitions, any power of attorney required by the Internal Revenue Service or other taxing authority, and other documents.

(b) Pay taxes due, collect refunds, post bonds, receive confidential information, exercise any election available to me and contest deficiencies determined by a taxing authority.

I understand the importance of the powers I delegate to my attorney-in-fact in this document. I recognize that the document gives my attorney-in-fact broad powers over my assets.

Signed this _____ day of _____, _____.

State of Alaska, County of _____.

_____   _____
Signature   Social Security Number

CERTIFICATE OF ACKNOWLEDGMENT OF NOTARY PUBLIC

Subscribed and sworn to or affirmed before me at _____

_____

on _____.

_____
Signataure of Officer or Notary

[NOTARIAL SEAL]   My commission expires: _____

WARNING TO PERSON EXECUTING THIS DOCUMENT

THIS IS AN IMPORTANT LEGAL DOCUMENT. IT CREATES A POWER OF ATTORNEY FOR FINANCES. BEFORE EXECUTING THIS DOCUMENT, YOU SHOULD KNOW THESE IMPORTANT FACTS:

THIS DOCUMENT MAY PROVIDE THE PERSON YOU DESIGNATE AS YOUR ATTORNEY-IN-FACT WITH BROAD LEGAL POWERS, INCLUDING THE POWERS TO MANAGE, DISPOSE, SELL AND CONVEY YOUR REAL AND PERSONAL PROPERTY AND TO BORROW MONEY USING YOUR PROPERTY AS SECURITY FOR THE LOAN.

THESE POWERS WILL EXIST UNTIL YOU REVOKE OR TERMINATE THIS POWER OF ATTORNEY. IF YOU SO STATE, THESE POWERS WILL CONTINUE TO EXIST EVEN IF YOU BECOME DISABLED OR INCAPACITATED. YOU HAVE THE RIGHT TO REVOKE OR TERMINATE THIS POWER OF ATTORNEY AT ANY TIME.

THIS DOCUMENT DOES NOT AUTHORIZE ANYONE TO MAKE MEDICAL OR OTHER HEALTHCARE DECISIONS FOR YOU.

IF THERE IS ANYTHING ABOUT THIS FORM THAT YOU DO NOT UNDERSTAND, YOU SHOULD ASK A LAWYER TO EXPLAIN IT TO YOU.

---

1. Principal and Attorney-in-Fact

I, _____,

of _____,

appoint _____

_____

_____

as my attorney-in-fact to act for me in any lawful way with respect to the powers delegated in Part 6 below. If that person (or all of those persons, if I name more than one) is unable or unwilling to serve as attorney-in-fact, I appoint the following alternates, to serve alone in the order named:

First Alternate

_____
Name

_____
Address

_____

Second Alternate

_____
Name

_____
Address

_____

2. **Authorization of Attorneys-in-Fact**

   If I have named more than one attorney-in-fact, they are authorized to act:

   ☐ jointly.

   ☐ independently.

3. **Delegation of Authority**

   ☐ My attorney-in-fact may delegate, in writing, any authority granted under this power of attorney to a person he or she selects. Any such delegation shall state the period during which it is valid and specify the extent of the delegation.

   ☐ My attorney-in-fact may not delegate any authority granted under this power of attorney.

4. **Effective Date and Durability**

   ☐ This power of attorney is not durable. It is effective immediately, and shall terminate on

   _____.

   ☐ This power of attorney is durable. It is effective immediately, and shall continue in effect if I become incapacitated or disabled.

   ☐ This power of attorney is durable. It shall take effect only if I become incapacitated or disabled and unable to manage my financial affairs.

5. **Determination of Incapacity**

   If I am creating a springing durable power of attorney under Part 4 of this document, my incapacity or disability shall be determined by written declaration of ☐ one ☐ two licensed physician(s). Each declaration shall be made under penalty of perjury and shall state that in the physician's opinion I am substantially unable to manage my financial affairs. If possible, the declaration(s) shall be made by _____

   _____

   _____.

   No licensed physician shall be liable to me for any actions taken under this part which are done in good faith.

6. **Powers of the Attorney-in-Fact**

   I grant my attorney-in-fact power to act on my behalf in the following matters, as indicated by my initials next to each granted power or on line (14), granting all the listed powers. Powers that are struck through are not granted.

INITIALS

_____ (1) Real estate transactions.

_____ (2) Tangible personal property transactions.

_____ (3) Stock and bond, commodity and option transactions.

_____ (4) Banking and other financial institution transactions.

_____ (5) Business operating transactions.

_____ (6) Insurance and annuity transactions.

_____ (7) Estate, trust, and other beneficiary transactions.

_____ (8) Living trust transactions.

_____ (9) Legal actions.

_____ (10) Personal and family care.

_____ (11) Government benefits.

_____ (12) Retirement plan transactions.

_____ (13) Tax matters.

_____ (14) ALL POWERS (1 THROUGH 13) LISTED ABOVE.

These powers are defined in Part 14, below.

7. **Special Instructions to the Attorney-in-Fact**

_____

_____

_____

_____

_____

_____

_____

_____

_____

_____

_____

_____

_____

_____

_____

8. Compensation and Reimbursement of the Attorney-in-Fact

☐ My attorney-in-fact shall not be compensated for services, but shall be entitled to reimbursement, from my assets, for reasonable expenses. Reasonable expenses include but are not limited to reasonable fees for information or advice from accountants, lawyers or investment experts relating to my attorney-in-fact's responsibilities under this power of attorney.

☐ My attorney-in-fact shall be entitled to reimbursement for reasonable expenses and reasonable compensation for services. What constitutes reasonable compensation shall be determined exclusively by my attorney-in-fact. If more than one attorney-in-fact is named in this document, each shall have the exclusive right to determine what constitutes reasonable compensation for his or her own duties.

☐ My attorney-in-fact shall be entitled to reimbursement for reasonable expenses and compensation for services in the amount of $_____.
If more than one attorney-in-fact is named in this document, each shall be entitled to receive this amount.

9. Personal Benefit to the Attorney-in-Fact

☐ My attorney-in-fact may buy any assets of mine or engage in any transaction he or she deems in good faith to be in my interest, no matter what the interest or benefit to my attorney-in-fact.

☐ My attorney-in-fact may not benefit personally from any transaction engaged in on my behalf.

☐ Although my attorney-in-fact may receive gifts of my property as described in Part 7 of this document, my attorney-in-fact may not benefit personally from any other transaction he or she engages in on my behalf.

10. Commingling by the Attorney-in-Fact

☐ My attorney-in-fact may commingle any of my funds with any funds of his or hers.

☐ My attorney-in-fact may not commingle any of my funds with any funds of his or hers.

11. Liability of the Attorney-in-Fact

My attorney-in-fact shall not incur any liability to me, my estate, my heirs, successors or assigns for acting or refraining from acting under this document, except for willful misconduct or gross negligence. My attorney-in-fact is not required to make my assets produce income, increase the value of my estate, diversify my investments or enter into transactions authorized by this document, as long as my attorney-in-fact believes his or her actions are in my best interests or in the interests of my estate and of those interested in my estate. A successor attorney-in-fact shall not be liable for acts of a prior attorney-in-fact.

12. Reliance on This Power of Attorney

Any third party who receives a copy of this document may rely on and act under it. Revocation of the power of attorney is not effective as to a third party until the third party has actual knowledge of the revocation. I agree to indemnify the third party for any claims that arise against the third party because of reliance on this power of attorney.

13. Severability

If any provision of this document is ruled unenforceable, the remaining provisions shall stay in effect.

14. Definition of Powers Granted to the Attorney-in-Fact

The powers granted in Part 6 of this document authorize my attorney-in-fact to do the following.

(1) Real estate transactions

Act for me in any manner to deal with all or any part of any interest in real property that I own at the time of execution of this document or later acquire, under such terms, conditions and covenants as my attorney-in-fact deems proper. My attorney-in-fact's powers include but are not limited to the power to:

(a) Accept as a gift, or as security for a loan, reject, demand, buy, lease, receive or otherwise acquire ownership of possession of any estate or interest in real property.

(b) Sell, exchange, convey with or without covenants, quitclaim, release, surrender, mortgage, encumber, partition or consent to the partitioning of, grant options concerning, lease, sublet or otherwise dispose of any interest in real property.

(c) Maintain, repair, improve, insure, rent, lease, and pay or contest taxes or assessments on any estate or interest in real property I own or claim to own.

(d) Prosecute, defend, intervene in, submit to arbitration, settle and propose or accept a compromise with respect to any claim in favor of or against me based on or involving any real estate transaction.

(2) Tangible personal property transactions

Act for me in any manner to deal with all or any part of any interest in personal property that I own at the time of execution of this document or later acquire, under such terms as my attorney-in-fact deems proper. My attorney-in-fact's powers include but are not limited to the power to lease, buy, exchange, accept as a gift or as security for a loan, acquire, possess, maintain, repair, improve, insure, rent, convey, mortgage, pledge, and pay or contest taxes and assessments on any tangible personal property.

(3) Stock and bond, commodity, option and other securities transactions

Do any act which I can do through an agent, with respect to any interest in a bond, share, other instrument of similar character or commodity. My attorney-in-fact's powers include but are not limited to the power to:

(a) Accept as a gift or as security for a loan, reject, demand, buy, receive or otherwise acquire ownership or possession of any bond, share, instrument of similar character, commodity interest or any investment with respect thereto, together with the interest, dividends, proceeds or other distributions connected with it.

(b) Sell (including short sales), exchange, transfer, release, surrender, pledge, trade in or otherwise dispose of any bond, share, instrument of similar character or commodity interest.

(c) Demand, receive and obtain any money or other thing of value to which I am or may become or may claim to be entitled as the proceeds of any interest in a bond, share, other instrument of similar character or commodity interest.

(d) Agree and contract, in any manner, and with any broker or other person and on any terms, for the accomplishment of any purpose listed in this section.

(e) Execute, acknowledge, seal and deliver any instrument my attorney-in-fact thinks useful to accomplish a purpose listed in this section, or any report or certificate required by law or regulation.

(4) Banking and other financial institution transactions

Do any act that I can do through an agent in connection with any banking transaction that might affect my financial or other interests. My attorney-in-fact's powers include but are not limited to the power to:

(a) Continue, modify and terminate any deposit account or other banking arrangement, or open either in the name of the agent alone or my name alone or in both our names jointly, a deposit account of any type in any financial institution, rent a safe deposit box or vault space, have access to a safe deposit box or vault to which I would have access, and make other contracts with the institution.

(b) Make, sign and deliver checks or drafts, and withdraw my funds or property from any financial institution by check, order or otherwise.

(c) Prepare financial statements concerning my assets and liabilities or income and expenses and deliver them to any financial institution, and receive statements, notices or other documents from any financial institution.

(d) Borrow money from a financial institution on terms my attorney-in-fact deems acceptable, give security out of my assets, and pay, renew or extend the time of payment of any note given by or on my behalf.

(5) Business operating transactions

Do any act that I can do through an agent in connection with any business operated by me that my attorney-in-fact deems desirable. My attorney-in-fact's powers include but are not limited to the power to:

(a) Perform any duty and exercise any right, privilege or option which I have or claim to have under any contract of partnership, enforce the terms of any partnership agreement, and defend, submit to arbitration or settle any legal proceeding to which I am a party because of membership in a partnership.

(b) Exercise in person or by proxy and enforce any right, privilege or option which I have as the holder of any bond, share or instrument of similar character and defend, submit to arbitration or settle a legal proceeding to which I am a party because of any such bond, share or instrument of similar character.

(c) With respect to a business owned solely by me, continue, modify, extend or terminate any contract on my behalf, demand and receive all money that is due or claimed by me and use such funds in the operation of the business, engage in banking transactions my attorney-in-fact deems desirable, determine the location of the operation, the nature of the business it undertakes, its name, methods of manufacturing, selling, marketing, financing, accounting, form of organization and insurance, and hiring and paying employees and independent contractors.

(d) Execute, acknowledge, seal and deliver any instrument of any kind that my attorney-in-fact thinks useful to accomplish any purpose listed in this section.

(e) Pay, compromise or contest business taxes or assessments.

(f) Demand and receive money or other things of value to which I am or claim to be entitled as the proceeds of any business operation, and conserve, invest, disburse or use anything so received for purposes listed in this section.

(6) Insurance and annuity transactions

Do any act that I can do through an agent, in connection with any insurance or annuity policy, that my attorney-in-fact deems desirable. My attorney-in-fact's powers include but are not limited to the power to:

(a) Continue, pay the premium on, modify, rescind or terminate any annuity or policy of life, accident, health, disability or liability insurance procured by me or on my behalf before the execution of this power of attorney. My attorney-in-fact cannot name himself or herself as beneficiary of a renewal, extension or substitute for such a policy unless he or she was already the beneficiary before I signed the power of attorney.

(b) Procure new, different or additional contracts of health, disability, accident or liability insurance on my life, modify, rescind or terminate any such contract and designate the beneficiary of any such contract.

(c) Sell, assign, borrow on, pledge, or surrender and receive the cash surrender value of any policy.

(7) Estate, trust and other beneficiary transactions

Act for me in all matters that affect a trust, probate estate, guardianship, conservatorship, escrow, custodianship or other fund from which I am, may become or claim to be entitled, as a beneficiary, to a share or payment. My attorney-in-fact's authority includes the power to disclaim any assets which I am, may become or claim to be entitled, as a beneficiary, to a share or payment.

(8) Living trust transactions

Transfer any of my interests in real property, stocks, bonds, accounts with financial institutions, insurance or other property to the trustee of a revocable trust I have created as settlor.

(9) Legal actions

Act for me in all matters that affect claims in favor of or against me and proceedings in any court or administrative body. My attorney-in-fact's powers include but are not limited to the power to:

(a) Hire an attorney to assert any claim or defense before any court, administrative board or other tribunal.

(b) Submit to arbitration or mediation or settle any claim in favor of or against me or any litigation to which I am a party, pay any judgment or settlement and receive any money or other things of value paid in settlement.

(10) Personal and family maintenance

Do all acts necessary to maintain my customary standard of living, and that of my spouse and children and other persons customarily supported by or legally entitled to be supported by me. My attorney-in-fact's powers include but are not limited to the power to:

(a) Pay for medical, dental and surgical care, living quarters, usual vacations and travel expenses, shelter, clothing, food, appropriate education and other living costs.

(b) Continue arrangements with respect to automobiles or other means of transportation, charge accounts, discharge of any services or duties assumed by me to any parent, relative or friend, contributions or payments incidental to membership or affiliation in any church, club, society or other organization.

(11) Government benefits

Act for me in all matters that affect my right to government benefits, including Social Security, Medicare, Medicaid, or other governmental programs, or civil or military service. My attorney-in-fact's powers include but are not limited to the power to:

(a) Prepare, execute, file, prosecute, defend, submit to arbitration or settle a claim on my behalf to benefits or assistance, financial or otherwise.

(b) Receive the proceeds of such a claim and conserve, invest, disburse or use them on my behalf.

(12) Retirement plan transactions

Act for me in all matters that affect my retirement plans. My attorney-in-fact's powers include but are not limited to the power to select payment options under any retirement plan in which I participate, make contributions to those plans, exercise investment options, receive payment from a plan, roll over plan benefits into other retirement plans, designate beneficiaries under those plans and change existing beneficiary designations.

(13) Tax matters

Act for me in all matters that affect my local, state and federal taxes. My attorney-in-fact's powers include but are not limited to the power to:

(a) Prepare, sign and file federal, state, local and foreign income, gift, payroll, Federal Insurance Contributions Act returns and other tax returns, claims for refunds, requests for extension of time, petitions, any power of attorney required by the Internal Revenue Service or other taxing authority, and other documents.

(b) Pay taxes due, collect refunds, post bonds, receive confidential information, exercise any election available to me and contest deficiencies determined by a taxing authority.

I understand the importance of the powers I delegate to my attorney-in-fact in this document. I recognize that the document gives my attorney-in-fact broad powers over my assets.

Signed this _____ day of _____, _____.

State of Arizona, County of _____.

_____   _____
Signature   Social Security Number

WITNESSES

I state that I am not the attorney-in-fact named in this document, nor am I the spouse or child of the attorney-in-fact. I further state that I am not the notary public who acknowledged this document.

    On the date written above, the principal declared to me that this instrument is his or her power of attorney, and that he or she willingly executed it as a free and voluntary act. The principal signed this instrument in my presence.

_____
Name

_____
Address

_____
County

CERTIFICATE OF ACKNOWLEDGMENT OF NOTARY PUBLIC

State of Arizona

County of _____ } ss

On _____, _____, before me, _____

_____, a notary public, personally appeared _____

_____ , known

to me or proved on the basis of satisfactory evidence to be the person whose name is subscribed to this instrument as principal and acknowledged and executed the same.

_____
Signature of Notary Public

[NOTARIAL SEAL]   My commission expires: _____

Financial Power of Attorney: DISTRICT OF COLUMBIA

<table>
<tr><td>

NOTICE

THIS POWER OF ATTORNEY AUTHORIZES THE PERSON NAMED BELOW AS MY ATTORNEY-IN-FACT TO DO ONE OR MORE OF THE FOLLOWING: TO SELL, LEASE, GRANT, ENCUMBER, RELEASE OR OTHERWISE CONVEY ANY INTEREST IN MY REAL PROPERTY AND TO EXECUTE DEEDS AND ALL OTHER INSTRUMENTS ON MY BEHALF, UNLESS THIS POWER IS OTHERWISE LIMITED HEREIN TO SPECIFIC REAL PROPERTY.

</td></tr>
</table>

<table>
<tr><td>

WARNING TO PERSON EXECUTING THIS DOCUMENT

THIS IS AN IMPORTANT LEGAL DOCUMENT. IT CREATES A POWER OF ATTORNEY FOR FINANCES. BEFORE EXECUTING THIS DOCUMENT, YOU SHOULD KNOW THESE IMPORTANT FACTS:

THIS DOCUMENT PROVIDES THE PERSON YOU DESIGNATE AS YOUR ATTORNEY-IN-FACT WITH BROAD LEGAL POWERS, INCLUDING ONE OR MORE OF THOSE ENUMERATED IN THE NOTICE ABOVE.

THESE POWERS WILL EXIST UNTIL YOU REVOKE OR TERMINATE THIS POWER OF ATTORNEY. IF YOU SO STATE, THESE POWERS WILL CONTINUE TO EXIST EVEN IF YOU BECOME DISABLED OR INCAPACITATED. YOU HAVE THE RIGHT TO REVOKE OR TERMINATE THIS POWER OF ATTORNEY AT ANY TIME.

THIS DOCUMENT DOES NOT AUTHORIZE ANYONE TO MAKE MEDICAL OR OTHER HEALTHCARE DECISIONS FOR YOU.

IF THERE IS ANYTHING ABOUT THIS FORM THAT YOU DO NOT UNDERSTAND, YOU SHOULD ASK A LAWYER TO EXPLAIN IT TO YOU.

</td></tr>
</table>

1. Principal and Attorney-in-Fact

I, _____,

of _____,

appoint _____

_____

as my attorney-in-fact to act for me in any lawful way with respect to the powers delegated in Part 6 below. If that person (or all of those persons, if I name more than one) is unable or unwilling to serve as attorney-in-fact, I appoint the following alternates, to serve alone in the order named:

First Alternate

_____
Name

_____
Address

Second Alternate

_____

Name

_____

Address

_____

2. Authorization of Attorneys-in-Fact

If I have named more than one attorney-in-fact, they are authorized to act:

☐ jointly.

☐ independently.

3. Delegation of Authority

☐ My attorney-in-fact may delegate, in writing, any authority granted under this power of attorney to a person he or she selects. Any such delegation shall state the period during which it is valid and specify the extent of the delegation.

☐ My attorney-in-fact may not delegate any authority granted under this power of attorney.

4. Effective Date and Durability

☐ This power of attorney is not durable. It is effective immediately, and shall terminate on

_____.

☐ This power of attorney is durable. It is effective immediately, and shall continue in effect if I become incapacitated or disabled.

☐ This power of attorney is durable. It shall take effect only if I become incapacitated or disabled and unable to manage my financial affairs.

5. Determination of Incapacity

If I am creating a springing durable power of attorney under Part 4 of this document, my incapacity or disability shall be determined by written declaration of ☐ one ☐ two licensed physician(s). Each declaration shall be made under penalty of perjury and shall state that in the physician's opinion I am substantially unable to manage my financial affairs. If possible, the declaration(s) shall be made by _____

_____. No licensed physician shall be liable to me for any actions taken under this part which are done in good faith.

6. Powers of the Attorney-in-Fact

I grant my attorney-in-fact power to act on my behalf in the following matters, as indicated by my initials next to each granted power or on line (14), granting all the listed powers. Powers that are struck through are not granted.

INITIALS

_____ (1) Real estate transactions.

_____ (2) Tangible personal property transactions.

_____ (3) Stock and bond, commodity and option transactions.

_____ (4) Banking and other financial institution transactions.

_____ (5) Business operating transactions.

_____ (6) Insurance and annuity transactions.

_____ (7) Estate, trust, and other beneficiary transactions.

_____ (8) Living trust transactions.

_____ (9) Legal actions.

_____ (10) Personal and family care.

_____ (11) Government benefits.

_____ (12) Retirement plan transactions.

_____ (13) Tax matters.

_____ (14) ALL POWERS (1 THROUGH 13) LISTED ABOVE.

These powers are defined in Part 14, below.

7. **Special Instructions to the Attorney-in-Fact**

_____

_____

_____

_____

_____

_____

_____

_____

_____

_____

_____

_____

_____

_____

_____

8. Compensation and Reimbursement of the Attorney-in-Fact

☐ My attorney-in-fact shall not be compensated for services, but shall be entitled to reimbursement, from my assets, for reasonable expenses. Reasonable expenses include but are not limited to reasonable fees for information or advice from accountants, lawyers or investment experts relating to my attorney-in-fact's responsibilities under this power of attorney.

☐ My attorney-in-fact shall be entitled to reimbursement for reasonable expenses and reasonable compensation for services. What constitutes reasonable compensation shall be determined exclusively by my attorney-in-fact. If more than one attorney-in-fact is named in this document, each shall have the exclusive right to determine what constitutes reasonable compensation for his or her own duties.

☐ My attorney-in-fact shall be entitled to reimbursement for reasonable expenses and compensation for services in the amount of $_____.
If more than one attorney-in-fact is named in this document, each shall be entitled to receive this amount.

9. Personal Benefit to the Attorney-in-Fact

☐ My attorney-in-fact may buy any assets of mine or engage in any transaction he or she deems in good faith to be in my interest, no matter what the interest or benefit to my attorney-in-fact.

☐ My attorney-in-fact may not benefit personally from any transaction engaged in on my behalf.

☐ Although my attorney-in-fact may receive gifts of my property as described in Part 7 of this document, my attorney-in-fact may not benefit personally from any other transaction he or she engages in on my behalf.

10. Commingling by the Attorney-in-Fact

☐ My attorney-in-fact may commingle any of my funds with any funds of his or hers.

☐ My attorney-in-fact may not commingle any of my funds with any funds of his or hers.

11. Liability of the Attorney-in-Fact

My attorney-in-fact shall not incur any liability to me, my estate, my heirs, successors or assigns for acting or refraining from acting under this document, except for willful misconduct or gross negligence. My attorney-in-fact is not required to make my assets produce income, increase the value of my estate, diversify my investments or enter into transactions authorized by this document, as long as my attorney-in-fact believes his or her actions are in my best interests or in the interests of my estate and of those interested in my estate. A successor attorney-in-fact shall not be liable for acts of a prior attorney-in-fact.

12. Reliance on This Power of Attorney

Any third party who receives a copy of this document may rely on and act under it. Revocation of the power of attorney is not effective as to a third party until the third party has actual knowledge of the revocation. I agree to indemnify the third party for any claims that arise against the third party because of reliance on this power of attorney.

13. Severability

If any provision of this document is ruled unenforceable, the remaining provisions shall stay in effect.

14. Definition of Powers Granted to the Attorney-in-Fact

The powers granted in Part 6 of this document authorize my attorney-in-fact to do the following.

(1) Real estate transactions

Act for me in any manner to deal with all or any part of any interest in real property that I own at the time of execution of this document or later acquire, under such terms, conditions and covenants as my attorney-in-fact deems proper. My attorney-in-fact's powers include but are not limited to the power to:

(a) Accept as a gift, or as security for a loan, reject, demand, buy, lease, receive or otherwise acquire ownership of possession of any estate or interest in real property.

(b) Sell, exchange, convey with or without covenants, quitclaim, release, surrender, mortgage, encumber, partition or consent to the partitioning of, grant options concerning, lease, sublet or otherwise dispose of any interest in real property.

(c) Maintain, repair, improve, insure, rent, lease, and pay or contest taxes or assessments on any estate or interest in real property I own or claim to own.

(d) Prosecute, defend, intervene in, submit to arbitration, settle and propose or accept a compromise with respect to any claim in favor of or against me based on or involving any real estate transaction.

(2) Tangible personal property transactions

Act for me in any manner to deal with all or any part of any interest in personal property that I own at the time of execution of this document or later acquire, under such terms as my attorney-in-fact deems proper. My attorney-in-fact's powers include but are not limited to the power to lease, buy, exchange, accept as a gift or as security for a loan, acquire, possess, maintain, repair, improve, insure, rent, convey, mortgage, pledge, and pay or contest taxes and assessments on any tangible personal property.

(3) Stock and bond, commodity, option and other securities transactions

Do any act which I can do through an agent, with respect to any interest in a bond, share, other instrument of similar character or commodity. My attorney-in-fact's powers include but are not limited to the power to:

(a) Accept as a gift or as security for a loan, reject, demand, buy, receive or otherwise acquire ownership or possession of any bond, share, instrument of similar character, commodity interest or any investment with respect thereto, together with the interest, dividends, proceeds or other distributions connected with it.

(b) Sell (including short sales), exchange, transfer, release, surrender, pledge, trade in or otherwise dispose of any bond, share, instrument of similar character or commodity interest.

(c) Demand, receive and obtain any money or other thing of value to which I am or may become or may claim to be entitled as the proceeds of any interest in a bond, share, other instrument of similar character or commodity interest.

(d) Agree and contract, in any manner, and with any broker or other person and on any terms, for the accomplishment of any purpose listed in this section.

(e) Execute, acknowledge, seal and deliver any instrument my attorney-in-fact thinks useful to accomplish a purpose listed in this section, or any report or certificate required by law or regulation.

(4) Banking and other financial institution transactions

Do any act that I can do through an agent in connection with any banking transaction that might affect my financial or other interests. My attorney-in-fact's powers include but are not limited to the power to:

(a) Continue, modify and terminate any deposit account or other banking arrangement, or open either in the name of the agent alone or my name alone or in both our names jointly, a deposit account of any type in any financial institution, rent a safe deposit box or vault space, have access to a safe deposit box or vault to which I would have access, and make other contracts with the institution.

(b) Make, sign and deliver checks or drafts, and withdraw my funds or property from any financial institution by check, order or otherwise.

(c) Prepare financial statements concerning my assets and liabilities or income and expenses and deliver them to any financial institution, and receive statements, notices or other documents from any financial institution.

(d) Borrow money from a financial institution on terms my attorney-in-fact deems acceptable, give security out of my assets, and pay, renew or extend the time of payment of any note given by or on my behalf.

(5) Business operating transactions

Do any act that I can do through an agent in connection with any business operated by me that my attorney-in-fact deems desirable. My attorney-in-fact's powers include but are not limited to the power to:

(a) Perform any duty and exercise any right, privilege or option which I have or claim to have under any contract of partnership, enforce the terms of any partnership agreement, and defend, submit to arbitration or settle any legal proceeding to which I am a party because of membership in a partnership.

(b) Exercise in person or by proxy and enforce any right, privilege or option which I have as the holder of any bond, share or instrument of similar character and defend, submit to arbitration or settle a legal proceeding to which I am a party because of any such bond, share or instrument of similar character.

(c) With respect to a business owned solely by me, continue, modify, extend or terminate any contract on my behalf, demand and receive all money that is due or claimed by me and use such funds in the operation of the business, engage in banking transactions my attorney-in-fact deems desirable, determine the location of the operation, the nature of the business it undertakes, its name, methods of manufacturing, selling, marketing, financing, accounting, form of organization and insurance, and hiring and paying employees and independent contractors.

(d) Execute, acknowledge, seal and deliver any instrument of any kind that my attorney-in-fact thinks useful to accomplish any purpose listed in this section.

(e) Pay, compromise or contest business taxes or assessments.

(f) Demand and receive money or other things of value to which I am or claim to be entitled as the proceeds of any business operation, and conserve, invest, disburse or use anything so received for purposes listed in this section.

(6) Insurance and annuity transactions

Do any act that I can do through an agent, in connection with any insurance or annuity policy, that my attorney-in-fact deems desirable. My attorney-in-fact's powers include but are not limited to the power to:

(a) Continue, pay the premium on, modify, rescind or terminate any annuity or policy of life, accident, health, disability or liability insurance procured by me or on my behalf before the execution of this power of attorney. My attorney-in-fact cannot name himself or herself as beneficiary of a renewal, extension or substitute for such a policy unless he or she was already the beneficiary before I signed the power of attorney.

(b) Procure new, different or additional contracts of health, disability, accident or liability insurance on my life, modify, rescind or terminate any such contract and designate the beneficiary of any such contract.

(c) Sell, assign, borrow on, pledge, or surrender and receive the cash surrender value of any policy.

(7) Estate, trust and other beneficiary transactions

Act for me in all matters that affect a trust, probate estate, guardianship, conservatorship, escrow, custodianship or other fund from which I am, may become or claim to be entitled, as a beneficiary, to a share or payment. My attorney-in-fact's authority includes the power to disclaim any assets which I am, may become or claim to be entitled, as a beneficiary, to a share or payment.

(8) Living trust transactions

Transfer any of my interests in real property, stocks, bonds, accounts with financial institutions, insurance or other property to the trustee of a revocable trust I have created as settlor.

(9) Legal actions

Act for me in all matters that affect claims in favor of or against me and proceedings in any court or administrative body. My attorney-in-fact's powers include but are not limited to the power to:

(a) Hire an attorney to assert any claim or defense before any court, administrative board or other tribunal.

(b) Submit to arbitration or mediation or settle any claim in favor of or against me or any litigation to which I am a party, pay any judgment or settlement and receive any money or other things of value paid in settlement.

(10) Personal and family maintenance

Do all acts necessary to maintain my customary standard of living, and that of my spouse and children and other persons customarily supported by or legally entitled to be supported by me. My attorney-in-fact's powers include but are not limited to the power to:

(a) Pay for medical, dental and surgical care, living quarters, usual vacations and travel expenses, shelter, clothing, food, appropriate education and other living costs.

(b) Continue arrangements with respect to automobiles or other means of transportation, charge accounts, discharge of any services or duties assumed by me to any parent, relative or friend, contributions or payments incidental to membership or affiliation in any church, club, society or other organization.

(11) Government benefits

Act for me in all matters that affect my right to government benefits, including Social Security, Medicare, Medicaid, or other governmental programs, or civil or military service. My attorney-in-fact's powers include but are not limited to the power to:

(a) Prepare, execute, file, prosecute, defend, submit to arbitration or settle a claim on my behalf to benefits or assistance, financial or otherwise.

(b) Receive the proceeds of such a claim and conserve, invest, disburse or use them on my behalf.

(12) Retirement plan transactions

Act for me in all matters that affect my retirement plans. My attorney-in-fact's powers include but are not limited to the power to select payment options under any retirement plan in which I participate, make contributions to those plans, exercise investment options, receive payment from a plan, roll over plan benefits into other retirement plans, designate beneficiaries under those plans and change existing beneficiary designations.

(13) Tax matters

Act for me in all matters that affect my local, state and federal taxes. My attorney-in-fact's powers include but are not limited to the power to:

(a) Prepare, sign and file federal, state, local and foreign income, gift, payroll, Federal Insurance Contributions Act returns and other tax returns, claims for refunds, requests for extension of time, petitions, any power of attorney required by the Internal Revenue Service or other taxing authority, and other documents.

(b) Pay taxes due, collect refunds, post bonds, receive confidential information, exercise any election available to me and contest deficiencies determined by a taxing authority.

I understand the importance of the powers I delegate to my attorney-in-fact in this document. I recognize that the document gives my attorney-in-fact broad powers over my assets.

Signed this _____ day of _____, _____,

at _____
                                                        Address

_____   _____
Signature   Social Security Number

WITNESSES

On the date written above, the principal declared to me that this instrument is his or her financial power of attorney, and that he or she willingly executed it as a free and voluntary act. The principal signed this instrument in my presence.

_____   _____
Name   Name

_____   _____
Address   Address

_____   _____

_____   _____
County   County

CERTIFICATE OF ACKNOWLEDGMENT OF NOTARY PUBLIC

District of Columbia: ss

Subscribed and Sworn to before me this _____ day _____ of _____.

_____
Notary Public, D.C.

[NOTARIAL SEAL]   My commission expires: _____

Financial Power of Attorney: NEW MEXICO

> ## WARNING TO PERSON EXECUTING THIS DOCUMENT
>
> THIS IS AN IMPORTANT LEGAL DOCUMENT. IT CREATES A POWER OF ATTORNEY FOR FINANCES. BEFORE EXECUTING THIS DOCUMENT, YOU SHOULD KNOW THESE IMPORTANT FACTS:
>
> THIS DOCUMENT MAY PROVIDE THE PERSON YOU DESIGNATE AS YOUR ATTORNEY-IN-FACT WITH BROAD LEGAL POWERS, INCLUDING THE POWERS TO MANAGE, DISPOSE, SELL AND CONVEY YOUR REAL AND PERSONAL PROPERTY AND TO BORROW MONEY USING YOUR PROPERTY AS SECURITY FOR THE LOAN.
>
> THESE POWERS WILL EXIST UNTIL YOU REVOKE OR TERMINATE THIS POWER OF ATTORNEY. IF YOU SO STATE, THESE POWERS WILL CONTINUE TO EXIST EVEN IF YOU BECOME DISABLED OR INCAPACITATED. YOU HAVE THE RIGHT TO REVOKE OR TERMINATE THIS POWER OF ATTORNEY AT ANY TIME.
>
> THIS DOCUMENT DOES NOT AUTHORIZE ANYONE TO MAKE MEDICAL OR OTHER HEALTHCARE DECISIONS FOR YOU.
>
> IF THERE IS ANYTHING ABOUT THIS FORM THAT YOU DO NOT UNDERSTAND, YOU SHOULD ASK A LAWYER TO EXPLAIN IT TO YOU.

1. Principal and Attorney-in-Fact

I, _____,

of _____,

appoint _____

_____

_____

as my attorney-in-fact to act for me in any lawful way with respect to the powers delegated in Part 6 below. If that person (or all of those persons, if I name more than one) is unable or unwilling to serve as attorney-in-fact, I appoint the following alternates, to serve alone in the order named:

First Alternate

_____
Name

_____
Address

Second Alternate

_____
Name

_____
Address

2. Authorization of Attorneys-in-Fact

If I have named more than one attorney-in-fact, they are authorized to act:

☐ jointly.

☐ independently.

3. Delegation of Authority

☐ My attorney-in-fact may delegate, in writing, any authority granted under this power of attorney to a person he or she selects. Any such delegation shall state the period during which it is valid and specify the extent of the delegation.

☐ My attorney-in-fact may not delegate any authority granted under this power of attorney.

4. Effective Date and Durability

☐ This power of attorney is not durable. It is effective immediately, and shall terminate on

_____.

☐ This power of attorney is durable. It is effective immediately, and shall continue in effect if I become incapacitated or disabled.

☐ This power of attorney is durable. It shall take effect only if I become incapacitated or disabled and unable to manage my financial affairs.

5. Determination of Incapacity

If I am creating a springing durable power of attorney under Part 4 of this document, my incapacity or disability shall be determined by written declaration of two licensed healthcare professionals, one of whom is a physician. Each declaration shall be made under penalty of perjury and shall state that in the healthcare professional's opinion I am substantially unable to manage my financial affairs. If possible, the declarations shall be made by _____

_____

_____.

No licensed physician shall be liable to me for any actions taken under this part which are done in good faith.

6. Powers of the Attorney-in-Fact

I grant my attorney-in-fact power to act on my behalf in the following matters, as indicated by my initials next to each granted power or on line (14), granting all the listed powers. Powers that are struck through are not granted.

_____ (1) Real estate transactions.

_____ (2) Tangible personal property transactions.

_____ (3) Stock and bond, commodity and option transactions.

_____ (4) Banking and other financial institution transactions.

_____ (5) Business operating transactions.

_____ (6) Insurance and annuity transactions.

_____ (7) Estate, trust, and other beneficiary transactions.

_____ (8) Living trust transactions.

_____ (9) Legal actions.

_____ (10) Personal and family care.

_____ (11) Government benefits.

_____ (12) Retirement plan transactions.

_____ (13) Tax matters.

_____ (14) ALL POWERS (1 THROUGH 13) LISTED ABOVE.

These powers are defined in Part 14, below.

7. Special Instructions to the Attorney-in-Fact

_____

_____

_____

_____

_____

_____

_____

_____

_____

_____

_____

_____

_____

_____

_____

_____

8. Compensation and Reimbursement of the Attorney-in-Fact

☐ My attorney-in-fact shall not be compensated for services, but shall be entitled to reimbursement, from my assets, for reasonable expenses. Reasonable expenses include but are not limited to reasonable fees for information or advice from accountants, lawyers or investment experts relating to my attorney-in-fact's responsibilities under this power of attorney.

☐ My attorney-in-fact shall be entitled to reimbursement for reasonable expenses and reasonable compensation for services. What constitutes reasonable compensation shall be determined exclusively by my attorney-in-fact. If more than one attorney-in-fact is named in this document, each shall have the exclusive right to determine what constitutes reasonable compensation for his or her own duties.

☐ My attorney-in-fact shall be entitled to reimbursement for reasonable expenses and compensation for services in the amount of $_____.
If more than one attorney-in-fact is named in this document, each shall be entitled to receive this amount.

9. Personal Benefit to the Attorney-in-Fact

☐ My attorney-in-fact may buy any assets of mine or engage in any transaction he or she deems in good faith to be in my interest, no matter what the interest or benefit to my attorney-in-fact.

☐ My attorney-in-fact may not benefit personally from any transaction engaged in on my behalf.

☐ Although my attorney-in-fact may receive gifts of my property as described in Part 7 of this document, my attorney-in-fact may not benefit personally from any other transaction he or she engages in on my behalf.

10. Commingling by the Attorney-in-Fact

☐ My attorney-in-fact may commingle any of my funds with any funds of his or hers.

☐ My attorney-in-fact may not commingle any of my funds with any funds of his or hers.

11. Liability of the Attorney-in-Fact

My attorney-in-fact shall not incur any liability to me, my estate, my heirs, successors or assigns for acting or refraining from acting under this document, except for willful misconduct or gross negligence. My attorney-in-fact is not required to make my assets produce income, increase the value of my estate, diversify my investments or enter into transactions authorized by this document, as long as my attorney-in-fact believes his or her actions are in my best interests or in the interests of my estate and of those interested in my estate. A successor attorney-in-fact shall not be liable for acts of a prior attorney-in-fact.

12. Reliance on This Power of Attorney

Any third party who receives a copy of this document may rely on and act under it. Revocation of the power of attorney is not effective as to a third party until the third party has actual knowledge of the revocation. I agree to indemnify the third party for any claims that arise against the third party because of reliance on this power of attorney.

13. Severability

If any provision of this document is ruled unenforceable, the remaining provisions shall stay in effect.

14. Definition of Powers Granted to the Attorney-in-Fact

The powers granted in Part 6 of this document authorize my attorney-in-fact to do the following.

(1) Real estate transactions

Act for me in any manner to deal with all or any part of any interest in real property that I own at the time of execution of this document or later acquire, under such terms, conditions and covenants as my attorney-in-fact deems proper. My attorney-in-fact's powers include but are not limited to the power to:

(a) Accept as a gift, or as security for a loan, reject, demand, buy, lease, receive or otherwise acquire ownership of possession of any estate or interest in real property.

(b) Sell, exchange, convey with or without covenants, quitclaim, release, surrender, mortgage, encumber, partition or consent to the partitioning of, grant options concerning, lease, sublet or otherwise dispose of any interest in real property.

(c) Maintain, repair, improve, insure, rent, lease, and pay or contest taxes or assessments on any estate or interest in real property I own or claim to own.

(d) Prosecute, defend, intervene in, submit to arbitration, settle and propose or accept a compromise with respect to any claim in favor of or against me based on or involving any real estate transaction.

(2) Tangible personal property transactions

Act for me in any manner to deal with all or any part of any interest in personal property that I own at the time of execution of this document or later acquire, under such terms as my attorney-in-fact deems proper. My attorney-in-fact's powers include but are not limited to the power to lease, buy, exchange, accept as a gift or as security for a loan, acquire, possess, maintain, repair, improve, insure, rent, convey, mortgage, pledge, and pay or contest taxes and assessments on any tangible personal property.

(3) Stock and bond, commodity, option and other securities transactions

Do any act which I can do through an agent, with respect to any interest in a bond, share, other instrument of similar character or commodity. My attorney-in-fact's powers include but are not limited to the power to:

(a) Accept as a gift or as security for a loan, reject, demand, buy, receive or otherwise acquire ownership or possession of any bond, share, instrument of similar character, commodity interest or any investment with respect thereto, together with the interest, dividends, proceeds or other distributions connected with it.

(b) Sell (including short sales), exchange, transfer, release, surrender, pledge, trade in or otherwise dispose of any bond, share, instrument of similar character or commodity interest.

(c) Demand, receive and obtain any money or other thing of value to which I am or may become or may claim to be entitled as the proceeds of any interest in a bond, share, other instrument of similar character or commodity interest.

(d) Agree and contract, in any manner, and with any broker or other person and on any terms, for the accomplishment of any purpose listed in this section.

(e) Execute, acknowledge, seal and deliver any instrument my attorney-in-fact thinks useful to accomplish a purpose listed in this section, or any report or certificate required by law or regulation.

(4) Banking and other financial institution transactions

Do any act that I can do through an agent in connection with any banking transaction that might affect my financial or other interests. My attorney-in-fact's powers include but are not limited to the power to:

(a) Continue, modify and terminate any deposit account or other banking arrangement, or open either in the name of the agent alone or my name alone or in both our names jointly, a deposit account of any type in any financial institution, rent a safe deposit box or vault space, have access to a safe deposit box or vault to which I would have access, and make other contracts with the institution.

(b) Make, sign and deliver checks or drafts, and withdraw my funds or property from any financial institution by check, order or otherwise.

(c) Prepare financial statements concerning my assets and liabilities or income and expenses and deliver them to any financial institution, and receive statements, notices or other documents from any financial institution.

(d) Borrow money from a financial institution on terms my attorney-in-fact deems acceptable, give security out of my assets, and pay, renew or extend the time of payment of any note given by or on my behalf.

(5) Business operating transactions

Do any act that I can do through an agent in connection with any business operated by me that my attorney-in-fact deems desirable. My attorney-in-fact's powers include but are not limited to the power to:

(a) Perform any duty and exercise any right, privilege or option which I have or claim to have under any contract of partnership, enforce the terms of any partnership agreement, and defend, submit to arbitration or settle any legal proceeding to which I am a party because of membership in a partnership.

(b) Exercise in person or by proxy and enforce any right, privilege or option which I have as the holder of any bond, share or instrument of similar character and defend, submit to arbitration or settle a legal proceeding to which I am a party because of any such bond, share or instrument of similar character.

(c) With respect to a business owned solely by me, continue, modify, extend or terminate any contract on my behalf, demand and receive all money that is due or claimed by me and use such funds in the operation of the business, engage in banking transactions my attorney-in-fact deems desirable, determine the location of the operation, the nature of the business it undertakes, its name, methods of manufacturing, selling, marketing, financing, accounting, form of organization and insurance, and hiring and paying employees and independent contractors.

(d) Execute, acknowledge, seal and deliver any instrument of any kind that my attorney-in-fact thinks useful to accomplish any purpose listed in this section.

(e) Pay, compromise or contest business taxes or assessments.

(f) Demand and receive money or other things of value to which I am or claim to be entitled as the proceeds of any business operation, and conserve, invest, disburse or use anything so received for purposes listed in this section.

(6) Insurance and annuity transactions

Do any act that I can do through an agent, in connection with any insurance or annuity policy, that my attorney-in-fact deems desirable. My attorney-in-fact's powers include but are not limited to the power to:

(a) Continue, pay the premium on, modify, rescind or terminate any annuity or policy of life, accident, health, disability or liability insurance procured by me or on my behalf before the execution of this power of attorney. My attorney-in-fact cannot name himself or herself as beneficiary of a renewal, extension or substitute for such a policy unless he or she was already the beneficiary before I signed the power of attorney.

(b) Procure new, different or additional contracts of health, disability, accident or liability insurance on my life, modify, rescind or terminate any such contract and designate the beneficiary of any such contract.

(c) Sell, assign, borrow on, pledge, or surrender and receive the cash surrender value of any policy.

(7) Estate, trust and other beneficiary transactions

Act for me in all matters that affect a trust, probate estate, guardianship, conservatorship, escrow, custodianship or other fund from which I am, may become or claim to be entitled, as a beneficiary, to a share or payment. My attorney-in-fact's authority includes the power to disclaim any assets which I am, may become or claim to be entitled, as a beneficiary, to a share or payment.

(8) Living trust transactions

Transfer any of my interests in real property, stocks, bonds, accounts with financial institutions, insurance or other property to the trustee of a revocable trust I have created as settlor.

(9) Legal actions

Act for me in all matters that affect claims in favor of or against me and proceedings in any court or administrative body. My attorney-in-fact's powers include but are not limited to the power to:

(a) Hire an attorney to assert any claim or defense before any court, administrative board or other tribunal.

(b) Submit to arbitration or mediation or settle any claim in favor of or against me or any litigation to which I am a party, pay any judgment or settlement and receive any money or other things of value paid in settlement.

(10) Personal and family maintenance

Do all acts necessary to maintain my customary standard of living, and that of my spouse and children and other persons customarily supported by or legally entitled to be supported by me. My attorney-in-fact's powers include but are not limited to the power to:

(a) Pay for medical, dental and surgical care, living quarters, usual vacations and travel expenses, shelter, clothing, food, appropriate education and other living costs.

(b) Continue arrangements with respect to automobiles or other means of transportation, charge accounts, discharge of any services or duties assumed by me to any parent, relative or friend, contributions or payments incidental to membership or affiliation in any church, club, society or other organization.

(11) Government benefits

Act for me in all matters that affect my right to government benefits, including Social Security, Medicare, Medicaid, or other governmental programs, or civil or military service. My attorney-in-fact's powers include but are not limited to the power to:

(a) Prepare, execute, file, prosecute, defend, submit to arbitration or settle a claim on my behalf to benefits or assistance, financial or otherwise.

(b) Receive the proceeds of such a claim and conserve, invest, disburse or use them on my behalf.

(12) Retirement plan transactions

Act for me in all matters that affect my retirement plans. My attorney-in-fact's powers include but are not limited to the power to select payment options under any retirement plan in which I participate, make contributions to those plans, exercise investment options, receive payment from a plan, roll over plan benefits into other retirement plans, designate beneficiaries under those plans and change existing beneficiary designations.

(13) Tax matters

Act for me in all matters that affect my local, state and federal taxes. My attorney-in-fact's powers include but are not limited to the power to:

(a) Prepare, sign and file federal, state, local and foreign income, gift, payroll, Federal Insurance Contributions Act returns and other tax returns, claims for refunds, requests for extension of time, petitions, any power of attorney required by the Internal Revenue Service or other taxing authority, and other documents.

(b) Pay taxes due, collect refunds, post bonds, receive confidential information, exercise any election available to me and contest deficiencies determined by a taxing authority.

I understand the importance of the powers I delegate to my attorney-in-fact in this document. I recognize that the document gives my attorney-in-fact broad powers over my assets.

Signed this _____ day of _____, _____.

State of New Mexico, County of _____.

_____   _____
Signature   Social Security Number

CERTIFICATE OF ACKNOWLEDGMENT OF NOTARY PUBLIC

State of New Mexico

County of _____ } ss

The foregoing instrument was acknowledged before me this _____ day of

_____, _____, by _____

_____.

_____
Notary Public

[NOTARIAL SEAL]   My commission expires: _____

Financial Power of Attorney: NORTH CAROLINA

WARNING TO PERSON EXECUTING THIS DOCUMENT

THIS IS AN IMPORTANT LEGAL DOCUMENT. IT CREATES A POWER OF ATTORNEY FOR FINANCES. BEFORE EXECUTING THIS DOCUMENT, YOU SHOULD KNOW THESE IMPORTANT FACTS:

THIS DOCUMENT MAY PROVIDE THE PERSON YOU DESIGNATE AS YOUR ATTORNEY-IN-FACT WITH BROAD LEGAL POWERS, INCLUDING THE POWERS TO MANAGE, DISPOSE, SELL AND CONVEY YOUR REAL AND PERSONAL PROPERTY AND TO BORROW MONEY USING YOUR PROPERTY AS SECURITY FOR THE LOAN.

THESE POWERS WILL EXIST UNTIL YOU REVOKE OR TERMINATE THIS POWER OF ATTORNEY. IF YOU SO STATE, THESE POWERS WILL CONTINUE TO EXIST EVEN IF YOU BECOME DISABLED OR INCAPACITATED. YOU HAVE THE RIGHT TO REVOKE OR TERMINATE THIS POWER OF ATTORNEY AT ANY TIME.

THIS DOCUMENT DOES NOT AUTHORIZE ANYONE TO MAKE MEDICAL OR OTHER HEALTHCARE DECISIONS FOR YOU.

IF THERE IS ANYTHING ABOUT THIS FORM THAT YOU DO NOT UNDERSTAND, YOU SHOULD ASK A LAWYER TO EXPLAIN IT TO YOU.

1. Principal and Attorney-in-Fact

I, _____,

of _____,

appoint _____

_____

_____

as my attorney-in-fact to act for me in any lawful way with respect to the powers delegated in Part 6 below. If that person (or all of those persons, if I name more than one) is unable or unwilling to serve as attorney-in-fact, I appoint the following alternates, to serve alone in the order named:

First Alternate

_____
Name

_____
Address

Second Alternate

_____
Name

_____
Address

2. Authorization of Attorneys-in-Fact

If I have named more than one attorney-in-fact, they are authorized to act:

☐ jointly.

☐ independently.

3. Delegation of Authority

☐ My attorney-in-fact may delegate, in writing, any authority granted under this power of attorney to a person he or she selects. Any such delegation shall state the period during which it is valid and specify the extent of the delegation.

☐ My attorney-in-fact may not delegate any authority granted under this power of attorney.

4. Effective Date and Durability

☐ This power of attorney is not durable. It is effective immediately, and shall terminate on

_____.

☐ This power of attorney is durable. It is effective immediately, and shall continue in effect if I become incapacitated or disabled.

☐ This power of attorney is durable. It shall take effect only if I become incapacitated or disabled and unable to manage my financial affairs.

5. Determination of Incapacity

If I am creating a springing durable power of attorney under Part 4 of this document, my incapacity or disability shall be determined by written declaration of ☐ one ☐ two licensed physician(s). Each declaration shall be made under penalty of perjury and shall state that in the physician's opinion I am substantially unable to manage my financial affairs. If possible, the declaration(s) shall be made by _____

_____

_____.

No licensed physician shall be liable to me for any actions taken under this part which are done in good faith.

6. Powers of the Attorney-in-Fact

I grant my attorney-in-fact power to act on my behalf in the following matters, as indicated by my initials next to each granted power or on line (14), granting all the listed powers. Powers that are struck through are not granted.

INITIALS

_____ (1) Real estate transactions.

_____ (2) Tangible personal property transactions.

_____ (3) Stock and bond, commodity and option transactions.

_____ (4) Banking and other financial institution transactions.

_____ (5) Business operating transactions.

_____ (6) Insurance and annuity transactions.

_____ (7) Estate, trust, and other beneficiary transactions.

_____ (8) Living trust transactions.

_____ (9) Legal actions.

_____ (10) Personal and family care.

_____ (11) Government benefits.

_____ (12) Retirement plan transactions.

_____ (13) Tax matters.

_____ (14) ALL POWERS (1 THROUGH 13) LISTED ABOVE.

These powers are defined in Part 15, below.

7. Special Instructions to the Attorney-in-Fact

_____

_____

_____

_____

_____

_____

_____

_____

_____

_____

_____

_____

_____

_____

_____

_____

8. Waiver of Attorney-in-Fact's Duty to File and Render Accounts

I waive the requirement, set out in North Carolina Gen. Stat. § 32A-11, that my attorney-in-fact file this power of attorney with the clerk of the superior court and render inventories and accounts, after my incapacity or mental incompetence, to the clerk of the superior court.

9. Compensation and Reimbursement of the Attorney-in-Fact

☐ My attorney-in-fact shall not be compensated for services, but shall be entitled to reimbursement, from my assets, for reasonable expenses. Reasonable expenses include but are not limited to reasonable fees for information or advice from accountants, lawyers or investment experts relating to my attorney-in-fact's responsibilities under this power of attorney.

☐ My attorney-in-fact shall be entitled to reimbursement for reasonable expenses and reasonable compensation for services. What constitutes reasonable compensation shall be determined exclusively by my attorney-in-fact. If more than one attorney-in-fact is named in this document, each shall have the exclusive right to determine what constitutes reasonable compensation for his or her own duties.

☐ My attorney-in-fact shall be entitled to reimbursement for reasonable expenses and compensation for services in the amount of $_____.
If more than one attorney-in-fact is named in this document, each shall be entitled to receive this amount.

10. Personal Benefit to the Attorney-in-Fact

☐ My attorney-in-fact may buy any assets of mine or engage in any transaction he or she deems in good faith to be in my interest, no matter what the interest or benefit to my attorney-in-fact.

☐ My attorney-in-fact may not benefit personally from any transaction engaged in on my behalf.

☐ Although my attorney-in-fact may receive gifts of my property as described in Part 7 of this document, my attorney-in-fact may not benefit personally from any other transaction he or she engages in on my behalf.

11. Commingling by the Attorney-in-Fact

☐ My attorney-in-fact may commingle any of my funds with any funds of his or hers.

☐ My attorney-in-fact may not commingle any of my funds with any funds of his or hers.

12. Liability of the Attorney-in-Fact

My attorney-in-fact shall not incur any liability to me, my estate, my heirs, successors or assigns for acting or refraining from acting under this document, except for willful misconduct or gross negligence. My attorney-in-fact is not required to make my assets produce income, increase the value of my estate, diversify my investments or enter into transactions authorized by this document, as long as my attorney-in-fact believes his or her actions are in my best interests or in the interests of my estate and of those interested in my estate. A successor attorney-in-fact shall not be liable for acts of a prior attorney-in-fact.

13. Reliance on This Power of Attorney

Any third party who receives a copy of this document may rely on and act under it. Revocation of the power of attorney is not effective as to a third party until the third party has actual knowledge of the revocation. I agree to indemnify the third party for any claims that arise against the third party because of reliance on this power of attorney.

14. Severability

If any provision of this document is ruled unenforceable, the remaining provisions shall stay in effect.

15. Definition of Powers Granted to the Attorney-in-Fact

The powers granted in Part 6 of this document authorize my attorney-in-fact to do the following.

(1) Real estate transactions

Act for me in any manner to deal with all or any part of any interest in real property that I own at the time of execution of this document or later acquire, under such terms, conditions and covenants as my attorney-in-fact deems proper. My attorney-in-fact's powers include but are not limited to the power to:

(a) Accept as a gift, or as security for a loan, reject, demand, buy, lease, receive or otherwise acquire ownership of possession of any estate or interest in real property.

(b) Sell, exchange, convey with or without covenants, quitclaim, release, surrender, mortgage, encumber, partition or consent to the partitioning of, grant options concerning, lease, sublet or otherwise dispose of any interest in real property.

(c) Maintain, repair, improve, insure, rent, lease, and pay or contest taxes or assessments on any estate or interest in real property I own or claim to own.

(d) Prosecute, defend, intervene in, submit to arbitration, settle and propose or accept a compromise with respect to any claim in favor of or against me based on or involving any real estate transaction.

(2) Tangible personal property transactions

Act for me in any manner to deal with all or any part of any interest in personal property that I own at the time of execution of this document or later acquire, under such terms as my attorney-in-fact deems proper. My attorney-in-fact's powers include but are not limited to the power to lease, buy, exchange, accept as a gift or as security for a loan, acquire, possess, maintain, repair, improve, insure, rent, convey, mortgage, pledge, and pay or contest taxes and assessments on any tangible personal property.

(3) Stock and bond, commodity, option and other securities transactions

Do any act which I can do through an agent, with respect to any interest in a bond, share, other instrument of similar character or commodity. My attorney-in-fact's powers include but are not limited to the power to:

(a) Accept as a gift or as security for a loan, reject, demand, buy, receive or otherwise acquire ownership or possession of any bond, share, instrument of similar character, commodity interest or any investment with respect thereto, together with the interest, dividends, proceeds or other distributions connected with it.

(b) Sell (including short sales), exchange, transfer, release, surrender, pledge, trade in or otherwise dispose of any bond, share, instrument of similar character or commodity interest.

(c) Demand, receive and obtain any money or other thing of value to which I am or may become or may claim to be entitled as the proceeds of any interest in a bond, share, other instrument of similar character or commodity interest.

(d) Agree and contract, in any manner, and with any broker or other person and on any terms, for the accomplishment of any purpose listed in this section.

(e) Execute, acknowledge, seal and deliver any instrument my attorney-in-fact thinks useful to accomplish a purpose listed in this section, or any report or certificate required by law or regulation.

(4) Banking and other financial institution transactions

Do any act that I can do through an agent in connection with any banking transaction that might affect my financial or other interests. My attorney-in-fact's powers include but are not limited to the power to:

(a) Continue, modify and terminate any deposit account or other banking arrangement, or open either in the name of the agent alone or my name alone or in both our names jointly, a deposit account of any type in any financial institution, rent a safe deposit box or vault space, have access to a safe deposit box or vault to which I would have access, and make other contracts with the institution.

(b) Make, sign and deliver checks or drafts, and withdraw my funds or property from any financial institution by check, order or otherwise.

(c) Prepare financial statements concerning my assets and liabilities or income and expenses and deliver them to any financial institution, and receive statements, notices or other documents from any financial institution.

(d) Borrow money from a financial institution on terms my attorney-in-fact deems acceptable, give security out of my assets, and pay, renew or extend the time of payment of any note given by or on my behalf.

(5) Business operating transactions

Do any act that I can do through an agent in connection with any business operated by me that my attorney-in-fact deems desirable. My attorney-in-fact's powers include but are not limited to the power to:

(a) Perform any duty and exercise any right, privilege or option which I have or claim to have under any contract of partnership, enforce the terms of any partnership agreement, and defend, submit to arbitration or settle any legal proceeding to which I am a party because of membership in a partnership.

(b) Exercise in person or by proxy and enforce any right, privilege or option which I have as the holder of any bond, share or instrument of similar character and defend, submit to arbitration or settle a legal proceeding to which I am a party because of any such bond, share or instrument of similar character.

(c) With respect to a business owned solely by me, continue, modify, extend or terminate any contract on my behalf, demand and receive all money that is due or claimed by me and use such funds in the operation of the business, engage in banking transactions my attorney-in-fact deems desirable, determine the location of the operation, the nature of the business it undertakes, its name, methods of manufacturing, selling, marketing, financing, accounting, form of organization and insurance, and hiring and paying employees and independent contractors.

(d) Execute, acknowledge, seal and deliver any instrument of any kind that my attorney-in-fact thinks useful to accomplish any purpose listed in this section.

(e) Pay, compromise or contest business taxes or assessments.

(f) Demand and receive money or other things of value to which I am or claim to be entitled as the proceeds of any business operation, and conserve, invest, disburse or use anything so received for purposes listed in this section.

(6) Insurance and annuity transactions

Do any act that I can do through an agent, in connection with any insurance or annuity policy, that my attorney-in-fact deems desirable. My attorney-in-fact's powers include but are not limited to the power to:

(a) Continue, pay the premium on, modify, rescind or terminate any annuity or policy of life, accident, health, disability or liability insurance procured by me or on my behalf before the execution of this power of attorney. My attorney-in-fact cannot name himself or herself as beneficiary of a renewal, extension or substitute for such a policy unless he or she was already the beneficiary before I signed the power of attorney.

(b) Procure new, different or additional contracts of health, disability, accident or liability insurance on my life, modify, rescind or terminate any such contract and designate the beneficiary of any such contract.

(c) Sell, assign, borrow on, pledge, or surrender and receive the cash surrender value of any policy.

(7) Estate, trust and other beneficiary transactions

Act for me in all matters that affect a trust, probate estate, guardianship, conservatorship, escrow, custodianship or other fund from which I am, may become or claim to be entitled, as a beneficiary, to a share or payment. My attorney-in-fact's authority includes the power to disclaim any assets which I am, may become or claim to be entitled, as a beneficiary, to a share or payment.

(8) Living trust transactions

Transfer any of my interests in real property, stocks, bonds, accounts with financial institutions, insurance or other property to the trustee of a revocable trust I have created as settlor.

(9) Legal actions

Act for me in all matters that affect claims in favor of or against me and proceedings in any court or administrative body. My attorney-in-fact's powers include but are not limited to the power to:

(a) Hire an attorney to assert any claim or defense before any court, administrative board or other tribunal.

(b) Submit to arbitration or mediation or settle any claim in favor of or against me or any litigation to which I am a party, pay any judgment or settlement and receive any money or other things of value paid in settlement.

(10) Personal and family maintenance

Do all acts necessary to maintain my customary standard of living, and that of my spouse and children and other persons customarily supported by or legally entitled to be supported by me. My attorney-in-fact's powers include but are not limited to the power to:

(a) Pay for medical, dental and surgical care, living quarters, usual vacations and travel expenses, shelter, clothing, food, appropriate education and other living costs.

(b) Continue arrangements with respect to automobiles or other means of transportation, charge accounts, discharge of any services or duties assumed by me to any parent, relative or friend, contributions or payments incidental to membership or affiliation in any church, club, society or other organization.

(11) Government benefits

Act for me in all matters that affect my right to government benefits, including Social Security, Medicare, Medicaid, or other governmental programs, or civil or military service. My attorney-in-fact's powers include but are not limited to the power to:

(a) Prepare, execute, file, prosecute, defend, submit to arbitration or settle a claim on my behalf to benefits or assistance, financial or otherwise.

(b) Receive the proceeds of such a claim and conserve, invest, disburse or use them on my behalf.

(12) Retirement plan transactions

Act for me in all matters that affect my retirement plans. My attorney-in-fact's powers include but are not limited to the power to select payment options under any retirement plan in which I participate, make contributions to those plans, exercise investment options, receive payment from a plan, roll over plan benefits into other retirement plans, designate beneficiaries under those plans and change existing beneficiary designations.

(13) Tax matters

Act for me in all matters that affect my local, state and federal taxes. My attorney-in-fact's powers include but are not limited to the power to:

(a) Prepare, sign and file federal, state, local and foreign income, gift, payroll, Federal Insurance Contributions Act returns and other tax returns, claims for refunds, requests for extension of time, petitions, any power of attorney required by the Internal Revenue Service or other taxing authority, and other documents.

(b) Pay taxes due, collect refunds, post bonds, receive confidential information, exercise any election available to me and contest deficiencies determined by a taxing authority.

I understand the importance of the powers I delegate to my attorney-in-fact in this document. I recognize that the document gives my attorney-in-fact broad powers over my assets.

Signed this _____ day of _____, _____.

State of North Carolina, County of _____.

_____   _____
Signature   Social Security Number

CERTIFICATE OF ACKNOWLEDGMENT OF NOTARY PUBLIC

On this _____ day _____, _____, personally appeared

before me, the said named _____

to me known and known to be the person described in and who executed the foregoing instrument and he or she acknowledged that he or she executed the same and being duly sworn by me, made oath that the statements in the foregoing instrument are true.

My commission expires: _____

_____
Signature of Notary Public

Notary Public [Official Seal]

Financial Power of Attorney: OKLAHOMA

1. Principal and Attorney-in-Fact

I, _____,

of _____,

appoint _____

_____

_____

as my attorney-in-fact to act for me in any lawful way with respect to the powers delegated in Part 6 below. If that person (or all of those persons, if I name more than one) is unable or unwilling to serve as attorney-in-fact, I appoint the following alternates, to serve alone in the order named:

First Alternate

_____
Name

_____
Address

Second Alternate

_____
Name

_____
Address

2. **Authorization of Attorneys-in-Fact**

   If I have named more than one attorney-in-fact, they are authorized to act:

   ☐ jointly.

   ☐ independently.

3. **Delegation of Authority**

   ☐ My attorney-in-fact may delegate, in writing, any authority granted under this power of attorney to a person he or she selects. Any such delegation shall state the period during which it is valid and specify the extent of the delegation.

   ☐ My attorney-in-fact may not delegate any authority granted under this power of attorney.

4. **Effective Date and Durability**

   ☐ This power of attorney is not durable. It is effective immediately, and shall terminate on

   _____.

   ☐ This power of attorney is durable. It is effective immediately, and shall continue in effect if I become incapacitated or disabled.

   ☐ This power of attorney is durable. It shall take effect only if I become incapacitated or disabled and unable to manage my financial affairs.

5. **Determination of Incapacity**

   If I am creating a springing durable power of attorney under Part 4 of this document, my incapacity or disability shall be determined by written declaration of ☐ one ☐ two licensed physician(s). Each declaration shall be made under penalty of perjury and shall state that in the physician's opinion I am substantially unable to manage my financial affairs. If possible, the declaration(s) shall be made by _____

   _____

   _____.

   No licensed physician shall be liable to me for any actions taken under this part which are done in good faith.

6. **Powers of the Attorney-in-Fact**

   I grant my attorney-in-fact power to act on my behalf in the following matters, as indicated by my initials next to each granted power or on line (14), granting all the listed powers. Powers that are struck through are not granted.

   INITIALS

   _____ (1) Real estate transactions.

   _____ (2) Tangible personal property transactions.

_____ (3) Stock and bond, commodity and option transactions.

_____ (4) Banking and other financial institution transactions.

_____ (5) Business operating transactions.

_____ (6) Insurance and annuity transactions.

_____ (7) Estate, trust, and other beneficiary transactions.

_____ (8) Living trust transactions.

_____ (9) Legal actions.

_____ (10) Personal and family care.

_____ (11) Government benefits.

_____ (12) Retirement plan transactions.

_____ (13) Tax matters.

_____ (14) ALL POWERS (1 THROUGH 13) LISTED ABOVE.

These powers are defined in Part 14, below.

7. **Special Instructions to the Attorney-in-Fact**

_____

_____

_____

_____

_____

_____

_____

_____

_____

_____

_____

_____

_____

_____

8. **Compensation and Reimbursement of the Attorney-in-Fact**

☐ My attorney-in-fact shall not be compensated for services, but shall be entitled to reimbursement, from my assets, for reasonable expenses. Reasonable expenses include but are not limited to reasonable fees for information or advice from accountants, lawyers or investment experts relating to my attorney-in-fact's responsibilities under this power of attorney.

☐ My attorney-in-fact shall be entitled to reimbursement for reasonable expenses and reasonable compensation for services. What constitutes reasonable compensation shall be determined exclusively by my attorney-in-fact. If more than one attorney-in-fact is named in this document, each shall have the exclusive right to determine what constitutes reasonable compensation for his or her own duties.

☐ My attorney-in-fact shall be entitled to reimbursement for reasonable expenses and compensation for services in the amount of $_____. If more than one attorney-in-fact is named in this document, each shall be entitled to receive this amount.

9. Personal Benefit to the Attorney-in-Fact

☐ My attorney-in-fact may buy any assets of mine or engage in any transaction he or she deems in good faith to be in my interest, no matter what the interest or benefit to my attorney-in-fact.

☐ My attorney-in-fact may not benefit personally from any transaction engaged in on my behalf.

☐ Although my attorney-in-fact may receive gifts of my property as described in Part 7 of this document, my attorney-in-fact may not benefit personally from any other transaction he or she engages in on my behalf.

10. Commingling by the Attorney-in-Fact

☐ My attorney-in-fact may commingle any of my funds with any funds of his or hers.

☐ My attorney-in-fact may not commingle any of my funds with any funds of his or hers.

11. Liability of the Attorney-in-Fact

My attorney-in-fact shall not incur any liability to me, my estate, my heirs, successors or assigns for acting or refraining from acting under this document, except for willful misconduct or gross negligence. My attorney-in-fact is not required to make my assets produce income, increase the value of my estate, diversify my investments or enter into transactions authorized by this document, as long as my attorney-in-fact believes his or her actions are in my best interests or in the interests of my estate and of those interested in my estate. A successor attorney-in-fact shall not be liable for acts of a prior attorney-in-fact.

12. Reliance on This Power of Attorney

Any third party who receives a copy of this document may rely on and act under it. Revocation of the power of attorney is not effective as to a third party until the third party has actual knowledge of the revocation. I agree to indemnify the third party for any claims that arise against the third party because of reliance on this power of attorney.

13. Severability

If any provision of this document is ruled unenforceable, the remaining provisions shall stay in effect.

14. Definition of Powers Granted to the Attorney-in-Fact

The powers granted in Part 6 of this document authorize my attorney-in-fact to do the following.

(1) Real estate transactions

Act for me in any manner to deal with all or any part of any interest in real property that I own at the time of execution of this document or later acquire, under such terms, conditions and covenants as my attorney-in-fact deems proper. My attorney-in-fact's powers include but are not limited to the power to:

(a) Accept as a gift, or as security for a loan, reject, demand, buy, lease, receive or otherwise acquire ownership of possession of any estate or interest in real property.

(b) Sell, exchange, convey with or without covenants, quitclaim, release, surrender, mortgage, encumber, partition or consent to the partitioning of, grant options concerning, lease, sublet or otherwise dispose of any interest in real property.

(c) Maintain, repair, improve, insure, rent, lease, and pay or contest taxes or assessments on any estate or interest in real property I own or claim to own.

(d) Prosecute, defend, intervene in, submit to arbitration, settle and propose or accept a compromise with respect to any claim in favor of or against me based on or involving any real estate transaction.

(2) Tangible personal property transactions

Act for me in any manner to deal with all or any part of any interest in personal property that I own at the time of execution of this document or later acquire, under such terms as my attorney-in-fact deems proper. My attorney-in-fact's powers include but are not limited to the power to lease, buy, exchange, accept as a gift or as security for a loan, acquire, possess, maintain, repair, improve, insure, rent, convey, mortgage, pledge, and pay or contest taxes and assessments on any tangible personal property.

(3) Stock and bond, commodity, option and other securities transactions

Do any act which I can do through an agent, with respect to any interest in a bond, share, other instrument of similar character or commodity. My attorney-in-fact's powers include but are not limited to the power to:

(a) Accept as a gift or as security for a loan, reject, demand, buy, receive or otherwise acquire ownership or possession of any bond, share, instrument of similar character, commodity interest or any investment with respect thereto, together with the interest, dividends, proceeds or other distributions connected with it.

(b) Sell (including short sales), exchange, transfer, release, surrender, pledge, trade in or otherwise dispose of any bond, share, instrument of similar character or commodity interest.

(c) Demand, receive and obtain any money or other thing of value to which I am or may become or may claim to be entitled as the proceeds of any interest in a bond, share, other instrument of similar character or commodity interest.

(d) Agree and contract, in any manner, and with any broker or other person and on any terms, for the accomplishment of any purpose listed in this section.

(e) Execute, acknowledge, seal and deliver any instrument my attorney-in-fact thinks useful to accomplish a purpose listed in this section, or any report or certificate required by law or regulation.

(4) Banking and other financial institution transactions

Do any act that I can do through an agent in connection with any banking transaction that might affect my financial or other interests. My attorney-in-fact's powers include but are not limited to the power to:

(a) Continue, modify and terminate any deposit account or other banking arrangement, or open either in the name of the agent alone or my name alone or in both our names jointly, a deposit account of any type in any financial institution, rent a safe deposit box or vault space, have access to a safe deposit box or vault to which I would have access, and make other contracts with the institution.

(b) Make, sign and deliver checks or drafts, and withdraw my funds or property from any financial institution by check, order or otherwise.

(c) Prepare financial statements concerning my assets and liabilities or income and expenses and deliver them to any financial institution, and receive statements, notices or other documents from any financial institution.

(d) Borrow money from a financial institution on terms my attorney-in-fact deems acceptable, give security out of my assets, and pay, renew or extend the time of payment of any note given by or on my behalf.

(5) Business operating transactions

Do any act that I can do through an agent in connection with any business operated by me that my attorney-in-fact deems desirable. My attorney-in-fact's powers include but are not limited to the power to:

(a) Perform any duty and exercise any right, privilege or option which I have or claim to have under any contract of partnership, enforce the terms of any partnership agreement, and defend, submit to arbitration or settle any legal proceeding to which I am a party because of membership in a partnership.

(b) Exercise in person or by proxy and enforce any right, privilege or option which I have as the holder of any bond, share or instrument of similar character and defend, submit to arbitration or settle a legal proceeding to which I am a party because of any such bond, share or instrument of similar character.

(c) With respect to a business owned solely by me, continue, modify, extend or terminate any contract on my behalf, demand and receive all money that is due or claimed by me and use such funds in the operation of the business, engage in banking transactions my attorney-in-fact deems desirable, determine the location of the operation, the nature of the business it undertakes, its name, methods of manufacturing, selling, marketing, financing, accounting, form of organization and insurance, and hiring and paying employees and independent contractors.

(d) Execute, acknowledge, seal and deliver any instrument of any kind that my attorney-in-fact thinks useful to accomplish any purpose listed in this section.

(e) Pay, compromise or contest business taxes or assessments.

(f) Demand and receive money or other things of value to which I am or claim to be entitled as the proceeds of any business operation, and conserve, invest, disburse or use anything so received for purposes listed in this section.

(6) Insurance and annuity transactions

Do any act that I can do through an agent, in connection with any insurance or annuity policy, that my attorney-in-fact deems desirable. My attorney-in-fact's powers include but are not limited to the power to:

(a) Continue, pay the premium on, modify, rescind or terminate any annuity or policy of life, accident, health, disability or liability insurance procured by me or on my behalf before the execution of this power of attorney. My attorney-in-fact cannot name himself or herself as beneficiary of a renewal, extension or substitute for such a policy unless he or she was already the beneficiary before I signed the power of attorney.

(b) Procure new, different or additional contracts of health, disability, accident or liability insurance on my life, modify, rescind or terminate any such contract and designate the beneficiary of any such contract.

(c) Sell, assign, borrow on, pledge, or surrender and receive the cash surrender value of any policy.

(7) Estate, trust and other beneficiary transactions

Act for me in all matters that affect a trust, probate estate, guardianship, conservatorship, escrow, custodianship or other fund from which I am, may become or claim to be entitled, as a beneficiary, to a share or payment. My attorney-in-fact's authority includes the power to disclaim any assets which I am, may become or claim to be entitled, as a beneficiary, to a share or payment.

(8) Living trust transactions

Transfer any of my interests in real property, stocks, bonds, accounts with financial institutions, insurance or other property to the trustee of a revocable trust I have created as settlor.

(9) Legal actions

Act for me in all matters that affect claims in favor of or against me and proceedings in any court or administrative body. My attorney-in-fact's powers include but are not limited to the power to:

(a) Hire an attorney to assert any claim or defense before any court, administrative board or other tribunal.

(b) Submit to arbitration or mediation or settle any claim in favor of or against me or any litigation to which I am a party, pay any judgment or settlement and receive any money or other things of value paid in settlement.

(10) Personal and family maintenance

Do all acts necessary to maintain my customary standard of living, and that of my spouse and children and other persons customarily supported by or legally entitled to be supported by me. My attorney-in-fact's powers include but are not limited to the power to:

(a) Pay for medical, dental and surgical care, living quarters, usual vacations and travel expenses, shelter, clothing, food, appropriate education and other living costs.

(b) Continue arrangements with respect to automobiles or other means of transportation, charge accounts, discharge of any services or duties assumed by me to any parent, relative or friend, contributions or payments incidental to membership or affiliation in any church, club, society or other organization.

(11) Government benefits

Act for me in all matters that affect my right to government benefits, including Social Security, Medicare, Medicaid, or other governmental programs, or civil or military service. My attorney-in-fact's powers include but are not limited to the power to:

(a) Prepare, execute, file, prosecute, defend, submit to arbitration or settle a claim on my behalf to benefits or assistance, financial or otherwise.

(b) Receive the proceeds of such a claim and conserve, invest, disburse or use them on my behalf.

(12) Retirement plan transactions

Act for me in all matters that affect my retirement plans. My attorney-in-fact's powers include but are not limited to the power to select payment options under any retirement plan in which I participate, make contributions to those plans, exercise investment options, receive payment from a plan, roll over plan benefits into other retirement plans, designate beneficiaries under those plans and change existing beneficiary designations.

(13) Tax matters

Act for me in all matters that affect my local, state and federal taxes. My attorney-in-fact's powers include but are not limited to the power to:

(a) Prepare, sign and file federal, state, local and foreign income, gift, payroll, Federal Insurance Contributions Act returns and other tax returns, claims for refunds, requests for extension of time, petitions, any power of attorney required by the Internal Revenue Service or other taxing authority, and other documents.

(b) Pay taxes due, collect refunds, post bonds, receive confidential information, exercise any election available to me and contest deficiencies determined by a taxing authority.

I understand the importance of the powers I delegate to my attorney-in-fact in this document. I recognize that the document gives my attorney-in-fact broad powers over my assets.

Signed this _____ day of _____, _____.

State of Oklahoma, County of _____.

_____   _____
Signature   Social Security Number

WITNESSES

The principal is personally known to me and I believe the principal to be of sound mind. I am eighteen (18) years of age or older. I am not related to the principal by blood or marriage, or related to the attorney-in-fact by blood or marriage. The principal has declared to me that this instrument is his power of attorney granting to the named attorney-in-fact the power and authority specified herein, and that he or she has willingly made and executed it as his or her free and voluntary act for the purposes herein expressed.

_____   _____
Name   Name

_____   _____
Address   Address

_____   _____

_____   _____
County   County

CERTIFICATE OF ACKNOWLEDGMENT OF NOTARY PUBLIC

State of Oklahoma

County of _____ } ss

Before me, the undersigned authority, on this _____ day of _____,

personally appeared _____ (principal),

_____ (witness), and

_____ (witness),

whose names are subscribed to the foregoing instrument in their respective capacities, and all of said persons being by me duly sworn, the principal declared to me and to the said witnesses in my presence that the instrument is his or her power of attorney, and that the principal has willingly and voluntarily made and executed it as the free act and deed of the principal for the purposes therein expressed, and the witnesses declared to me that they were each eighteen (18) years of age or over, and that neither of them is related to the principal by blood or marriage, or related to the attorney-in-fact by blood or marriage.

_____
Notary Public

[NOTARIAL SEAL]   My commission expires: _____

PREPARATION STATEMENT

This document was prepared by:

_____
Name

_____
Address

_____

_____

_____

Power of Attorney

I, _____,
name of principal

of _____, _____,
city   county

_____, appoint _____
state   name of attorney-in-fact

_____, of _____,
city

_____, _____,
county   state

as my attorney-in-fact to act in my place for the purposes of:

_____

_____

_____

_____

_____

_____

_____

_____

_____

_____

_____

_____

_____

This power of attorney takes effect on _____, and shall continue

until terminated in writing, or until _____,whichever comes first.

I grant my attorney-in-fact full authority to act in any manner both proper and necessary to the exercise of the foregoing powers, and I ratify every act that my attorney-in-fact may lawfully perform in exercising those powers.

[continued on next page]

I agree that any third party who receives a copy of this document may act under it. Revocation of the power of attorney is not effective as to a third party until the third party has actual knowledge of the revocation. I agree to indemnify the third party for any claims that arise against the third party because of reliance on this power of attorney.

Signed this _____ day of _____, _____.

State of _____, County of _____.

_____   _____
Signature   Social Security Number

CERTIFICATE OF ACKNOWLEDGMENT OF NOTARY PUBLIC

State of _____ ⎫
                                                               ⎬ ss
County of _____ ⎭

On _____, _____, before me, _____

_____, a notary public in and for said state, personally appeared

_____, personally

known to me (or proved on the basis of satisfactory evidence) to be the person whose name is subscribed to the within instrument, and acknowledged to me that he or she executed the same in his or her authorized capacity and that by his or her signature on the instrument the person, or the entity upon behalf of which the person acted, executed the instrument.

WITNESS my hand and official seal.

_____

Notary Public for the State of _____

[NOTARIAL SEAL]   My commission expires: _____

PREPARATION STATEMENT

This document was prepared by:

_____
Name

_____
Address

I agree that any third party who receives a copy of this document may act under it. Revocation of the power of attorney is not effective as to a third party until the third party has actual knowledge of the revocation. I agree to indemnify the third party for any claims that arise against the third party because of reliance on this power of attorney.

Signed this _____ day of _____, _____.

State of _____, County of _____.

_____   _____
Signature   Social Security Number

WITNESSES

On the date written above, the principal declared to me that this instrument is his or her financial power of attorney, and that he or she willingly executed it as a free and voluntary act. The principal signed this instrument in my presence.

_____
Name

_____
Address

_____
County

CERTIFICATE OF ACKNOWLEDGMENT OF NOTARY PUBLIC

State of _____ ⎫
                                                          ⎬ ss
County of _____ ⎭

On _____, _____, before me, _____

_____, a notary public in and for said state, personally appeared

_____, personally

known to me (or proved on the basis of satisfactory evidence) to be the person whose name is subscribed to the within instrument, and acknowledged to me that he or she executed the same in his or her authorized capacity and that by his or her signature on the instrument the person, or the entity upon behalf of which the person acted, executed the instrument.

WITNESS my hand and official seal.

_____

Notary Public for the State of _____

[NOTARIAL SEAL]   My commission expires: _____

PREPARATION STATEMENT

This document was prepared by:

_____
Name

_____
Address

_____

I agree that any third party who receives a copy of this document may act under it. Revocation of the power of attorney is not effective as to a third party until the third party has actual knowledge of the revocation. I agree to indemnify the third party for any claims that arise against the third party because of reliance on this power of attorney.

Signed this _____ day of _____, _____.

State of _____, County of _____.

_____   _____
Signature   Social Security Number

WITNESSES

On the date written above, the principal declared to me that this instrument is his or her financial power of attorney, and that he or she willingly executed it as a free and voluntary act. The principal signed this instrument in my presence.

_____   _____
Name   Name

_____   _____
Address   Address

_____   _____
County   County

CERTIFICATE OF ACKNOWLEDGMENT OF NOTARY PUBLIC

State of _____ ⎫
                                                             ⎬ ss
County of _____ ⎭

On _____, _____, before me, _____

_____, a notary public in and for said state, personally appeared

_____, personally

known to me (or proved on the basis of satisfactory evidence) to be the person whose name is subscribed to the within instrument, and acknowledged to me that he or she executed the same in his or her authorized capacity and that by his or her signature on the instrument the person, or the entity upon behalf of which the person acted, executed the instrument.

WITNESS my hand and official seal.

_____

Notary Public for the State of _____

[NOTARIAL SEAL]   My commission expires: _____

PREPARATION STATEMENT

This document was prepared by:

_____
Name

_____
Address

Power of Attorney for Real Estate

I, _____,
name of principal

of _____, _____,
city   county

_____, appoint _____
state   name of attorney-in-fact

_____, of _____,
city

_____, _____,
county   state

to act in my place with respect to the real property described as follows:

_____

_____

_____

_____

_____

_____

_____

_____

_____

_____

_____

_____

_____

_____

_____

_____

_____

_____

_____

_____

_____

My attorney-in-fact may act for me in any manner to deal with all or any part of any interest in the real property described in this document, under such terms, conditions and covenants as my attorney-in-fact deems proper. My attorney-in-fact's powers include but are not limited to the power to:

1. Accept as a gift, or as security for a loan, reject, demand, buy, lease, receive or otherwise acquire ownership of possession of any estate or interest in real property.

2. Sell, exchange, convey with or without covenants, quitclaim, release, surrender, mortgage, encumber, partition or consent to the partitioning of, grant options concerning, lease, sublet or otherwise dispose of any interest in the real property described in this document.

3. Maintain, repair, improve, insure, rent, lease, and pay or contest taxes or assessments on any estate or interest in the real property described in this document.

4. Prosecute, defend, intervene in, submit to arbitration, settle and propose or accept a compromise with respect to any claim in favor of or against me based on or involving the real property described in this document.

However, my attorney in fact shall not have the power to:

_____

_____

_____

_____

_____

_____

_____

_____

_____

_____

_____

_____

_____

_____

I further grant to my attorney-in-fact full authority to act in any manner both proper and necessary to the exercise of the foregoing powers, including _____

_____

_____

and I ratify every act that my attorney-in-fact may lawfully perform in exercising those powers.

This power of attorney takes effect on _____, and shall continue until terminated in writing, or until _____, whichever comes first.

I agree that any third party who receives a copy of this document may act under it. Revocation of the power of attorney is not effective as to a third party until the third party has actual knowledge of the revocation. I agree to indemnify the third party for any claims that arise against the third party because of reliance on this power of attorney.

Signed this _____ day of _____, _____.

State of _____, County of _____.

_____   _____
Signature   Social Security Number

CERTIFICATE OF ACKNOWLEDGMENT OF NOTARY PUBLIC

State of _____
County of _____ } ss

On _____, _____, before me, _____
_____, a notary public in and for said state, personally appeared
_____, personally known to me (or proved on the basis of satisfactory evidence) to be the person whose name is subscribed to the within instrument, and acknowledged to me that he or she executed the same in his or her authorized capacity and that by his or her signature on the instrument the person, or the entity upon behalf of which the person acted, executed the instrument.

WITNESS my hand and official seal.

_____

Notary Public for the State of _____

[NOTARIAL SEAL]   My commission expires: _____

PREPARATION STATEMENT

This document was prepared by:

_____
Name

_____
Address

_____

This power of attorney is effective immediately, and shall continue until terminated in writing, or until _____, whichever comes first.

Signed this _____ day of _____, _____.

State of _____, County of _____.

_____   _____
Signature   Social Security Number

WITNESSES

On the date written above, the principal declared to me that this instrument is his or her power of attorney, and that he or she willingly executed it as a free and voluntary act. The principal signed this instrument in my presence.

_____
Name

_____
Address

_____
County

CERTIFICATE OF ACKNOWLEDGMENT OF NOTARY PUBLIC

State of _____ ⎫
                                            ⎬ ss
County of _____ ⎭

On _____, _____, before me, _____

_____, a notary public in and for said state, personally appeared

_____, personally known to me (or proved on the basis of satisfactory evidence) to be the person whose name is subscribed to the within instrument, and acknowledged to me that he or she executed the same in his or her authorized capacity and that by his or her signature on the instrument the person, or the entity upon behalf of which the person acted, executed the instrument.

WITNESS my hand and official seal.

_____

Notary Public for the State of _____

[NOTARIAL SEAL]   My commission expires: _____

PREPARATION STATEMENT

This document was prepared by:

_____
Name

_____
Address

This power of attorney is effective immediately, and shall continue until terminated in writing, or until _____ whichever comes first.

Signed this _____ day of _____, _____.

State of _____, County of _____.

_____ _____
Signature   Social Security Number

WITNESSES

On the date written above, the principal declared to me that this instrument is his or her financial power of attorney, and that he or she willingly executed it as a free and voluntary act. The principal signed this instrument in my presence.

_____ _____
Name   Name

_____ _____
Address   Address

_____ _____
County   County

CERTIFICATE OF ACKNOWLEDGMENT OF NOTARY PUBLIC

State of _____ ⎫
                                                                 ⎬ ss
County of _____ ⎭

On _____, _____, before me, _____

_____, a notary public in and for said state, personally appeared

_____, personally known to me (or proved on the basis of satisfactory evidence) to be the person whose name is subscribed to the within instrument, and acknowledged to me that he or she executed the same in his or her authorized capacity and that by his or her signature on the instrument the person, or the entity upon behalf of which the person acted, executed the instrument.

WITNESS my hand and official seal.

_____

Notary Public for the State of _____

[NOTARIAL SEAL]   My commission expires: _____

PREPARATION STATEMENT

This document was prepared by:

_____
Name

_____
Address

_____

Power of Attorney for Child Care

I, _____ ,

name of principal

of _____ , _____ ,

city   county

_____ , am the parent of and have legal custody of

state

_____ .

name of child

I appoint _____ ,

name of attorney-in-fact

of _____ , _____ ,

city   county

_____ , as my attorney-in-fact to take any of the actions

state

with respect to the care of my child. My attorney-in-fact's powers include, but are not limited to, the following:

1. Enroll or withdraw my child from school or any similar institution.
2. Hire, retain or fire a third person to care for, counsel, treat or otherwise assist my child.
3. Consent to any necessary medical treatment, surgery, medication, therapy, hospitalization or similar care for my child.
4. Exercise the same parental rights I may exercise with respect to the care, custody and control of my child.

I further grant my attorney-in-fact full authority to act in any manner both proper and necessary to the exercise of the foregoing powers, including _____

_____

_____

_____

and I ratify every act that my attorney-in-fact may lawfully perform in exercising those powers.

This power of attorney takes effect on _____ , and shall continue until terminated in writing, or until _____ , whichever comes first.

I agree that any third party who receives a copy of this document may act under it. Revocation of the power of attorney is not effective as to a third party until the third party has actual knowledge of the revocation. I agree to indemnify the third party for any claims that arise against the third party because of reliance on this power of attorney.

Signed this _____ day of _____, _____.

State of _____, County of _____.

_____   _____
Signature   Social Security Number

CERTIFICATE OF ACKNOWLEDGMENT OF NOTARY PUBLIC

State of _____ ⎫

County of _____ ⎬ ss

On _____, _____, before me, _____

_____, a notary public in and for said state, personally appeared

_____, personally

known to me (or proved on the basis of satisfactory evidence) to be the person whose name is
subscribed to the within instrument, and acknowledged to me that he or she executed the same in
his or her authorized capacity and that by his or her signature on the instrument the person, or the
entity upon behalf of which the person acted, executed the instrument.

WITNESS my hand and official seal.

_____

Notary Public for the State of _____

[NOTARIAL SEAL]   My commission expires: _____

Power of Attorney for Child Care

We, _____
name of principal

and _____,
name of principal

of _____, _____,
city   county

_____, are the parents of and have legal custody of
state

_____.
name of child

We appoint _____,
name of attorney-in-fact

of _____, _____,
city   county

_____, as our attorney-in-fact to take any of the actions
state

with respect to the care of our child. Our attorney-in-fact's powers include, but are not limited to, the following:

1. Enroll or withdraw our child from school or any similar institution.

2. Hire, retain or fire a third person to care for, counsel, treat or otherwise assist our child.

3. Consent to any necessary medical treatment, surgery, medication, therapy, hospitalization or similar care for our child.

4. Exercise the same parental rights we may exercise with respect to the care, custody and control of our child.

We further grant our attorney-in-fact full authority to act in any manner both proper and necessary to the exercise of the foregoing powers, including _____

_____

_____

_____

_____

and we ratify every act that our attorney-in-fact may lawfully perform in exercising those powers.

This power of attorney takes effect on _____, and shall continue until terminated in writing, or until _____, whichever comes first.

We agree that any third party who receives a copy of this document may act under it. Revocation of the power of attorney is not effective as to a third party until the third party has actual knowledge of the revocation. We agree to indemnify the third party for any claims that arise against the third party because of reliance on this power of attorney.

Signed this _____ day of _____, _____.

State of _____, County of _____.

_____
Signature

Social Security Number _____

_____
Signature

Social Security Number _____

CERTIFICATE OF ACKNOWLEDGMENT OF NOTARY PUBLIC

State of _____

County of _____ } ss

On _____, _____, before me, _____

_____, a notary public in and for said state, personally appeared

_____ and

_____, personally

known to me (or proved on the basis of satisfactory evidence) to be the persons whose names are subscribed to the within instrument, and acknowledged to me that he or she executed the same in their authorized capacities and that by their signatures on the instrument the persons, or the entity upon behalf of which the persons acted, executed the instrument.

WITNESS my hand and official seal.

_____

Notary Public for the State of _____

[NOTARIAL SEAL]   My commission expires: _____

Information for an Attorney-in-Fact

An attorney-in-fact is someone who agrees to manage financial matters for someone else. Some attorneys-in-fact assist a relative or friend who just wants some help with paying bills or managing investments. Others take over complete control of the financial matters of someone who can no longer handle them. It all depends on the circumstances and on the document, called a "power of attorney for finances," which sets out your duties.

Serving as an attorney-in-fact is a serious responsibility, but in most situations, it involves little legal risk. In most cases, you don't need special financial or legal knowledge. Common sense, dependability and complete honesty are more important.

Your Duties as an Attorney-in-Fact

The power of attorney document is prepared and signed by the person who is granting you authority over his or her finances. (This person is called the principal.) It spells out exactly what authority has been granted. Read the document carefully. If there is anything you don't understand, talk to the principal or ask a lawyer to explain it to you.

Depending on the circumstances, your duties may include, among others:

- Handling banking transactions for the principal—writing checks, paying bills, depositing checks.
- Claiming Social Security and other benefits for the principal.
- Managing the principal's investments.
- Paying everyday expenses of the principal and his or her family.
- Managing real estate.
- Preparing and filing tax returns for the principal.
- Running the principal's small business.

Keep in mind that you can hire experts, if necessary, to help you with any of these tasks. Their fees are paid out of the principal's assets.

Your Legal Responsibilities

An attorney-in-fact holds a position of great trust. As you perform your duties, the law requires you to be scrupulously honest and act only in the best interests of the principal. Specifically, you must:

- Manage the principal's assets prudently, steering well clear of risky investments. You don't, however, need to worry about getting sued for honest mistakes you make while handling someone else's money. Under the Nolo Press power of attorney form, you will be liable for losses only if you are extremely careless or intentionally do wrong.
- Avoid conflicts of interest. If you benefit personally from an action taken on the principal's behalf, the transaction is presumed to be fraudulent—no matter how pure your motives. You must avoid all such transactions unless the durable power of attorney document specifically allows them.
- Keep your property and the principal's separate, unless the power of attorney document expressly allows you to mix them.
- Keep in contact with the principal, to the extent possible. If you are acting on behalf of a principal who is incapacitated, and he or she gives you instructions that you believe are not in his or her best interest, you should seek court approval before you disobey his or her wishes.
- Keep good records. You must keep accurate and separate records of all transactions made on the principal's behalf. This shouldn't be an onerous requirement. In most situations, it's enough to have a balanced checkbook and receipts for bills paid and claims made. You may, however, be required to furnish periodic reports of income and expenses to persons the principal named in the durable power of attorney.

Should You Take the Job?

You do not have to accept the responsibility of serving as an attorney-in-fact. Before you decide, discuss these issues with the principal:

- How the principal wants you to make financial decisions.
- The potential for conflicts and tension if others close to the principal disapprove of your actions.
- If you would become attorney-in-fact only if the principal becomes incapacitated, how the determination of incapacity will be made, and by whom.
- What expertise you need to manage the principal's property and keep necessary records.
- How much time your duties will require. If you are to be paid for your time, the power of attorney document should spell out the terms of the agreement.

Resigning

You can resign at any time. If you do, the alternate (successor) named in the power of attorney document will take over. If no alternate is named or none is available, you can, if the power of attorney allows it, delegate the job to a person you choose. Otherwise, the principal or a court (if the principal is incapacitated) will have to turn the job over to someone else.

If you need to step down temporarily, the power of attorney document may allow you to delegate your duties to someone else for a certain period of time. If the document doesn't permit this, you will have to resign and the principal or a court (if the principal is incapacitated) will assign the job to another person.

—From *The Financial Power of Attorney Workbook*, by Shae Irving (Nolo Press)

Physician's Determination of Incapacity

I, _____,

of the City of _____, County of _____,

State of _____, declare under penalty of perjury that:

    1. I am a physician licensed to practice in the state of _____.

    2. I examined _____

       on _____, _____. It is my professional opinion that

       _____

is currently incapacitated and unable to mange his/her finances and property.

Dated: _____

_____
(Signature of Physician)

_____, Physician

CERTIFICATE OF ACKNOWLEDGMENT OF NOTARY PUBLIC

State of _____

County of _____ } ss

On _____, _____, before me, _____

_____, a notary public in and for said state, personally appeared

_____, personally
known to me (or proved on the basis of satisfactory evidence) to be the person whose name is
subscribed to the within instrument, and acknowledged to me that he or she executed the same in
his or her authorized capacity and that by his or her signature on the instrument the person, or the
entity upon behalf of which the person acted, executed the instrument.

                WITNESS my hand and official seal.

                _____

                Notary Public for the State of _____

[NOTARIAL SEAL]   My commission expires: _____

Healthcare Professional's Determination of Incapacity

I, _____,

of the City of _____, County of _____,

State of New Mexico, declare under penalty of perjury that:

1. I am a healthcare professional licensed to practice in the state of New Mexico.

2. I examined _____

    on _____, _____. It is my professional opinion that

    _____

    is currently incapacitated and unable to manage his/her finances and property.

Dated: _____

_____
Signature of Healthcare Professional

_____, Healthcare Professional

CERTIFICATE OF ACKNOWLEDGMENT OF NOTARY PUBLIC

State of New Mexico

County of _____ } ss

The foregoing instrument was acknowledged before me this _____

day of _____, _____, by _____

_____.

_____
Notary Public

[NOTARIAL SEAL]   My commission expires: _____

Delegation of Authority

I, _____,

of the City of _____, County of _____,

State of _____, am currently serving as attorney-in-fact for

_____

under the Financial Power of Attorney dated _____.

Under the power granted to me in that document, I delegate the following authority to

_____

for the period beginning _____ and ending

_____:

_____

_____

_____

_____

_____

_____

_____

_____

_____

_____

_____

_____

_____

_____

Dated: _____

_____
Signature of Attorney-in-Fact

_____, Attorney-in-Fact

Resignation of Attorney-in-Fact

I, _____,

of the City of _____, County of _____,

State of _____, resign as attorney-in-fact under the

Financial Power of Attorney created by _____

_____

and dated _____. My resignation is effective _____

_____.

Dated: _____

_____
Signature of Attorney-in-Fact

_____, Attorney-in-Fact

CERTIFICATE OF ACKNOWLEDGMENT OF NOTARY PUBLIC

State of _____ }

County of _____ } ss

On _____, _____, before me, _____

_____, a notary public in and for said state, personally appeared

_____, personally

known to me (or proved on the basis of satisfactory evidence) to be the person whose name is

subscribed to the within instrument, and acknowledged to me that he or she executed the same in

his or her authorized capacity and that by his or her signature on the instrument the person, or the

entity upon behalf of which the person acted, executed the instrument.

WITNESS my hand and official seal.

_____

Notary Public for the State of _____

[NOTARIAL SEAL]   My commission expires: _____

Notice of Revocation of Durable Power of Attorney

I, _____,

of the City of _____, County of _____,

State of _____, revoke the power of attorney dated

_____, empowering _____

_____

to act as my attorney-in-fact. I revoke and withdraw all power and authority granted under that

power of attorney.Power of Attorney for Child Care

Dated: _____

_____
Signature of Principal

_____, Principal

CERTIFICATE OF ACKNOWLEDGMENT OF NOTARY PUBLIC

State of _____ } ss

County of _____

On _____, _____, before me, _____

_____, a notary public in and for said state, personally appeared

_____, personally

known to me (or proved on the basis of satisfactory evidence) to be the person whose name is

subscribed to the within instrument, and acknowledged to me that he or she executed the same in

his or her authorized capacity and that by his or her signature on the instrument the person, or the

entity upon behalf of which the person acted, executed the instrument.

WITNESS my hand and official seal.

_____

Notary Public for the State of _____

[NOTARIAL SEAL]   My commission expires: _____

Notice of Revocation of Durable Power of Attorney

I, _____,

of the City of _____, County of _____,

State of _____, revoke the power of attorney dated

_____, empowering _____

_____

to act as my attorney-in-fact. I revoke and withdraw all power and authority granted under that

power of attorney.

    That power of attorney was recorded on _____, _____, in Book

_____, at Page _____ of the Official Records, County of _____,

State of _____.

Dated: _____

_____

Signature of Principal

_____, Principal

CERTIFICATE OF ACKNOWLEDGMENT OF NOTARY PUBLIC

State of _____ }

County of _____ } ss

On _____, _____, before me, _____

_____, a notary public in and for said state, personally appeared

_____, personally

known to me (or proved on the basis of satisfactory evidence) to be the person whose name is

subscribed to the within instrument, and acknowledged to me that he or she executed the same in

his or her authorized capacity and that by his or her signature on the instrument the person, or the

entity upon behalf of which the person acted, executed the instrument.

             WITNESS my hand and official seal.

_____

Notary Public for the State of _____

[NOTARIAL SEAL]   My commission expires: _____

Index

A

Accountants' fee, 3/3, 8/4
Address on forms, 6/4, 8/8, 9/6, 10/6
Adoption, and attorney-in-fact, 3/4
Advance Directives (Directives to Physician), 2/5, 2/6
Agent. *See* Attorney-in-fact
Alabama, 11/4
    power of attorney statutes, 12/6
Alaska, 3/7, 6/2, 6/6, 8/6, 11/4, 11/5
    power of attorney statutes, 12/6
    special state form, Appendix B
Alternate attorney-in-fact, 3/11, 4/5-6, 6/4, 8/5, 8/10
    defined, 1/3
    duties and responsibilities, 4/10
American Association of Retired Persons (AARP)
  Legal Plan, 12/3
Annuity transactions, 5/4-5
Arizona, 6/2, 7/3, 8/6, 8/22, 9/12, 11/4
    power of attorney statutes, 12/6
    special state form, Appendix B
Arkansas, 7/3, 8/22, 9/12, 11/4
    power of attorney statutes, 12/6
Assets, protecting, 2/7
Attorney-in-fact, 4/2-12
    alternate, 1/3, 3/11, 4/5-6, 4/10, 6/4, 8/5, 8/10
    authority, delegation of, 5/12-14, 6/4, 7/6, 8/10
    choosing, 4/2-6, 8/5, 9/4
    compensation/reimbursement, 3/3, 4/10, 4/12,
      6/8, 8/3-4, 8/14, 9/3
    defined, 1/2, 1/3
    duties and responsibilities, 4/6-10, 4/11, 8/6
    instructions, special, 5/7-12, 6/8, 8/12
    liability, 4/10, 6/10, 8/14
    more than one, 4/4-5, 4/6, 4/12, 5/13, 6/4, 7/5,
      8/23-24
    powers, 3/3-4, 5/2-14, 6/6, 8/6-7, 8/10, 8/12,
      8/18, 9/5, 9/8
    reports by, 5/11-12
    resignation, 4/8-10, 4/12, 7/6
    supervision, 4/8
    when takes over, 3/5-8
Attorneys. *See* Lawyers

B

Banks
    as attorney-in-fact, 4/5
    power of attorney forms, 1/4, 5/4, 6/2, 8/7
    transactions, 5/3
Beneficiaries, to insurance/annuity policies, 5/5
Beneficiary transactions, 5/5
Bond transactions, 5/3
Borrowing money, 5/3
Business operating transactions, 5/4, 5/11

C

California, 4/3, 4/8, 8/5, 9/4, 11/4, 11/5
    power of attorney statutes, 12/6
Certificate of Acknowledgment of Notary Public
    form, blank, 3/9, 4/9
    form, filled-in sample, 6/12, 8/16, 8/21, 11/6,
      11/7
Challenges to power of attorney, 3/2
Child(ren)
    custody, 10/3
    guardian, 10/2, 10/4, 10/5
    power of attorney for child care, 1/5, 8/3, 8/7,
      10/2-10
    travel across border, 10/3
Claims and litigation, 5/5-6, 6/6
Closely held corporations, 5/4
Co-agents. *See* Attorney-in-fact, more than one
Colorado, 11/4
    power of attorney statutes, 12/6
Commingling of funds, 4/7, 6/10, 8/14

Commodity transactions, 5/3

Compensation/reimbursement, of attorney-in-fact, 3/3, 4/10, 4/12. *See also specific power of attorney type*

Conflicts of interest, 4/7

Connecticut, 7/3, 8/22, 9/12, 11/4
    power of attorney statutes, 12/6

Conservators/conservatorship proceedings, 2/2, 2/5, 3/11, 4/8, 4/10, 5/12
    and revocation of power of attorney, 11/3, 11/4

Conventional power of attorney. *See* Conventional power of attorney for finances; Limited power of attorney; Power of attorney for child care; Power of attorney for real estate

Conventional power of attorney for finances, 1/4, 8/2-24
    and attorney-in-fact, 4/2-12
    cost, 8/3-4
    defined, 1/3, 8/2
    effective date, 8/4, 8/10
    form, blank, Appendix B
    form, filled-in sample, 8/9, 8/11, 8/13, 8/15-16
    form, instructions, 8/2-8, 8/10, 8/12, 8/14, 8/17
    legal steps, final, 8/20-24
    notarization, 8/20-22
    recording, 8/23
    revocation, 8/5, 8/17, 8/24
    storage, 8/23-24
    termination, 8/4-5
    validity and acceptance, 8/2, 8/4, 8/17
    witnesses, 8/7, 8/22

Copies of power of attorney form, 7/5, 8/24, 9/13, 10/10

Cost. *See specific power of attorney type*

Courts
    invalidation of durable power of attorney, 3/11
    supervision of attorney-in-fact, 4/8

Custody of child, 10/3

D

Date power of attorney ends. *See specific power of attorney form*

Death
    of attorney-in-fact, 4/6, 9/4, 10/4
    of principal, 2/7, 3/11, 8/5, 9/4, 10/4

Delaware, 11/4
    power of attorney statutes, 12/6

Delegation of authority, by attorney-in-fact, 5/12-14, 6/4, 7/6, 8/10
    form, blank, 5/14, Appendix B

Directives to Physician, 2/5, 2/6

"Disabled." *See* Incapacity

Disclaiming property, 5/5

District of Columbia, 6/2, 7/3, 8/6, 8/22, 9/12, 11/4
    power of attorney statutes, 12/6
    special state form, Appendix B

Divorce, 3/11, 4/3, 8/5, 8/24, 9/4, 11/5

Doctors. *See* Physicians

Durable power of attorney
    defined, 1/3
    revocation, 11/2-3
    See also Durable power of attorney for finances

Durable power of attorney for finances, 1/3-4, 3/2-11, 6/2-12, 8/3
    and attorney-in-fact, 3/3-8, 4/2-12
    challenges to, 3/2
    clauses, sample, 5/9-10, 5/11, 5/12
    cost, 3/3
    effective date, 3/6, 6/4, 6/6
    expiration, 7/5
    form, blank, Appendix B
    form, filled-in sample, 6/5, 6/7, 6/9, 6/11-2
    form, instructions, 6/2-4, 6/6, 6/8, 6/10
    legal steps, final, 7/2-5
    need for, 2/2-7
    notarization, 7/2
    recording, 7/4-5
    revocation, 3/10-11, 6/10, 7/5, 11/2-3
    storage, 7/5
    termination, 3/10-11
    validity and acceptance, 3/8, 3/10, 6/10, 7/5
    witnesses, 6/2-3, 7/2-4
    See also Springing durable power of attorney

Durable power of attorney for healthcare, 1/3, 1/4, 2/6

E

Erasures on forms, 6/3, 8/8, 9/6, 10/6

Estate planning, 2/5-7
    and gifts, 5/7-8

Estate transactions, 5/5

F

Families
  conflicts, and challenges to power of attorney,
    2/5, 4/3, 4/8
  emergencies, 5/8
  maintenance, 5/6
Fiduciary, defined, 4/6
Filing fees, 3/3, 8/3
Financial advisers' fee, 3/3, 8/4, 9/3
Financial institutions' power of attorney forms, 1/4,
  5/4, 6/2, 8/7
Financial power of attorney. *See* Conventional
  power of attorney for finances; Durable power of
  attorney for finances
Financial powers, of attorney-in-fact, 5/2-14
Financial transactions, 5/3
Florida, 7/3, 8/22, 9/12, 11/4
  power of attorney statutes, 12/6
Forgery, 2/3

G

Gay couples, 1/3
General power of attorney. *See* Durable power of
  attorney
Georgia, 7/3, 8/22, 9/12, 11/4
  power of attorney statutes, 12/6
Gifts, 2/7, 5/7-10
  to attorney-in-fact, 5/8-9
  taxes, 5/8
Government benefits, 5/6
Guardian, 11/3, 11/4
  of child, 10/2, 10/4, 10/5
  of the person, 11/3

H

Handwritten forms, 6/3, 8/8, 9/6, 10/6
Hawaii, 11/4
  power of attorney statutes, 12/6
Healthcare decisions, 2/5-6, 3/4
Healthcare directives, 2/5-6
Healthcare forms, obtaining, 2/6
Healthcare power of attorney, 1/3, 1/4, 2/6

Healthcare Professional's Determination of
  Incapacity form (New Mexico), Appendix B
Home sale, 5/10-11

I

Icons used in book, 1/5
Idaho, 11/4
  power of attorney statutes, 12/6
Illinois, 4/3, 8/5, 9/4, 11/4, 11/5
  power of attorney statutes, 12/6
Incapacity, 3/5-8
  and conventional power of attorney, 8/5
  defined, 1/3, 3/5-6
  determination of, 6/6
"Incompetent." *See* Incapacity
Indiana, 4/3, 8/5, 9/4, 11/4, 11/5
  power of attorney statutes, 12/6
Information sheet for attorney-in-fact, 4/10, 4/11-12,
  7/6, Appendix B
Institutions, as attorney-in-fact, 4/5
Insurance transactions, 5/4-5
Internet, 12/7-8
Iowa, 11/4
  power of attorney statutes, 12/6
IRS power of attorney form, 5/7

J

Joint custody of child, and power of attorney, 10/3
Joint tenancy property, 2/4-5

K

Kansas, 11/4
  power of attorney statutes, 12/6
Kentucky, 11/4
  power of attorney statutes, 12/6

L

Law libraries, 12/5, 12/7
Lawyers, 3/3, 12/2-5
  and challenges to power of attorney, 3/2
  fees, 12/4-5
  need for, 1/5
Legal description of property, 9/6, 9/8
Legal research, 12/5-8
Legal typing services, 12/2

Liability of attorney-in-fact, 4/10, 6/10, 8/14

Libraries, legal, 12/5, 12/7

Limited liability companies, 5/4

Limited power of attorney, 8/6-7

    form, blank, Appendix B

    form, filled-in sample, 8/19

    form, instructions, 8/17-18, 8/20

    termination date, 8/18, 8/20

    See also Financial institutions' power of attorney
        forms; Power of attorney for child care; Power
        of attorney for real estate

Litigation and claims, 5/5-6, 6/6

Living trusts, 2/3-4, 3/4, 4/3-4, 5/5

Living wills (Directives to Physician), 1/4, 2/5, 2/6

Loans, 5/3

Louisiana, 11/4

    power of attorney statutes, 12/6

M

Maine, 11/4

    power of attorney statutes, 12/6

Married couples, 2/3, 4/3, 11/5

    and attorney-in-fact, 3/4

    and insurance, 5/5

Maryland, 11/4

    power of attorney statutes, 12/6

Massachusetts, 11/4

    power of attorney statutes, 12/6

Medicaid, 5/6

Medical decisions. *See* Healthcare decisions

Medical power of attorney. *See* Durable power of
    attorney for healthcare

Medicare, 5/6

Mental competency ("sound mind") requirement,
    3/2, 8/3, 9/3, 10/3

Michigan, 7/3, 8/22, 9/12, 11/4

    power of attorney statutes, 12/6

Minnesota, 11/4

    power of attorney statutes, 12/6

Mississippi, 11/4

    power of attorney statutes, 12/6

Missouri, 4/3, 8/5, 9/4, 11/4, 11/5

    power of attorney statutes, 12/6

Montana, 11/4

    power of attorney statutes, 12/6

Moving to another state, and revocation of power of
    attorney, 3/10, 8/24, 11/3

N

Name

    changing, 6/4, 8/8, 8/18, 9/6

    on forms, 6/3-4, 8/8, 8/17-18, 9/6, 10/6

Nebraska, 11/4

    power of attorney statutes, 12/6

Nevada, 11/4

    power of attorney statutes, 12/6

New Hampshire, 11/4

    power of attorney statutes, 12/6

New Jersey, 11/4

    power of attorney statutes, 12/6

New Mexico, 6/2, 6/6, 8/6, 11/4

    healthcare form, 3/7, Appendix B

    power of attorney statutes, 12/6

    special state form, Appendix B

New York, 11/4

    power of attorney statutes, 12/6

North Carolina, 6/2, 7/4, 8/6, 11/4

    power of attorney statutes, 12/6

    proof of service, 11/8

    special state form, Appendix B

North Dakota, 11/4

    power of attorney statutes, 12/6

Notarization of forms. *See specific power of attorney
    type*

Notice of Revocation, 11/5-8

    Recorded Power of Attorney form, 7/6, 11/7,
        Appendix B

    Unrecorded Power of Attorney form, 7/6, 11/6,
        Appendix B

O

Ohio, 7/3, 8/22, 9/12, 11/4

    power of attorney statutes, 12/6

Oklahoma, 6/2, 7/3, 8/6, 8/22, 9/12, 11/4

    power of attorney statutes, 12/6

    special state form, Appendix B

Online legal research, 12/7-8

Option transactions, 5/3

Oregon, 11/4

    power of attorney statutes, 12/6

P

Partnerships, business, 5/4

Patient advocate, named in living will, 2/6

Pennsylvania, 7/3, 8/22, 9/12, 11/4
power of attorney statutes, 12/6

Personal benefit, by attorney in fact, 4/6, 6/8, 8/14

Personal guardian, of child, 10/5

Personal maintenance, 5/6

Personal property transactions, 5/3

Physicians
and determining incapacity, 3/8, 6/6
statement, and challenges to power of attorney, 3/2

Physician's Determination of Incapacity form, 3/7-8, 7/6
form, blank, 3/9, Appendix B

Power of attorney
defined, 1/2
forms from financial institution, 1/4, 5/4, 6/3, 8/7
statutes, state by state, 12/6
See also specific power of attorney type

Power of attorney for child care, 1/5, 8/3, 8/7, 10/2-10
clauses, sample, 10/6,10/8
cost, 10/3-4
effective date, 10/4
form, blank, Appendix B
form, filled-in sample, 10/7, 10/9
form, instructions, 10/6, 10/8
legal steps, final, 10/8
notarization, 10/8
revocation, 10/4, 10/10
for single parents, 10/5, Appendix B
termination, 10/4, 10/8
for two parents, 10/5, 10/7, 10/9, Appendix B
validity and acceptance, 10/4

Power of attorney for finances, conventional. *See* Conventional power of attorney for finances

Power of attorney for real estate, 1/4-5, 8/3, 8/7, 9/2-13
clauses, sample, 9/5
cost, 9/3
effective date, 9/4
form, blank, Appendix B
form, filled-in sample, 9/7, 9/9, 9/11
form, instructions, 9/6, 9/8, 9/10

legal steps, final, 9/109/12-13
notarization, 9/10
recording, 9/12, 9/13
revocation, 9/4, 9/13
storage, 9/13
termination, 9/4, 9/8
validity and acceptance, 9/3-4
witnesses, 9/5-6, 9/10, 9/12

Preparation statement, 7/4, 8/23, 9/12-13

Principal, defined, 1/2

Probate, avoiding, 2/7

Proof of service (North Carolina), 11/8

Proxy, named in living will, 2/6

"Prudent person" concept, 4/6

R

Real estate transactions, 1/4-5, 5/2, 7/4, 7/5, 8/23, 9/2-13

Real property, legal description, 9/6, 9/8

Recording of form. *See specific power of attorney type*

Recordkeeping, 4/7-8

Reimbursement. *See* Compensation/reimbursement

Reports, periodic, by attorney-in-fact, 5/11-12

Representative payee, and Social Security checks, 5/6

Resignation of attorney-in-fact, 4/8-10, 4/12, 7/6
form, blank, 4/9, Appendix B

Retirement plan transactions, 5/6

Revocable living trusts, 2/3-3, 3/4, 4/3-4, 5/5

Revocation of power of attorney, 3/10-11, 11/2-9
forms, 3/11, Appendix B
process, 11/5-8
reasons for, 11/3-5
See also specific power of attorney form

Rhode Island, 11/4
power of attorney statutes, 12/6

S

Safe deposit boxes, 5/3, 7/5

Sale of home, 5/10-11

Search engines on Internet, 12/7-8

Self-dealing activities, 4/7

Severability clause, 6/10, 8/17

Signatures
of attorney-in-fact, 6/22, 7/3, 9/12

forging, 2/3

and Notice of Revocation, 11/8

of principal, 7/2-3, 8/20, 8/22, 9/10, 10/8

Small business operating transactions, 5/4, 5/11

Social Security Administration, telephone, 5/6

Social Security checks, 5/6

Sole proprietorships, 5/4

"Sound mind" requirement. *See* Mental competency ("sound mind") requirement

South Carolina, 7/3, 7/4, 8/22, 9/12, 11/4

power of attorney statutes, 12/6

South Dakota, 11/4

power of attorney statutes, 12/6

Springing durable power of attorney for finances, 1/3, 3/5, 3/6-8

revocation, 11/2-3

storage, 7/5

Stock transactions, 5/3

Storage of power of attorney form. *See specific power of attorney type*

Successor attorney-in-fact. *See* Alternate attorney-in-fact

Successor trustees, 2/3-4

T

Tangible personal property transactions, 5/3

Taxes, 5/7, 5/8

Tennessee, 4/8, 11/4

power of attorney statutes, 12/6

Termination of power of attorney. *See specific power of attorney type*

Texas, 11/4

power of attorney statutes, 12/6

Trust fund transactions, 5/5

Trusts, 2/3-4, 3/4, 4/3-4, 5/5

U

Unmarried couples, 1/3

Utah, 11/4

power of attorney statutes, 12/6

V

Vermont, 7/3, 8/22, 9/12, 11/4

power of attorney statutes, 12/6

Videotapes, and challenges to power of attorney, 3/2

Virginia, 11/4

power of attorney statutes, 12/6

Voting, and attorney-in-fact, 3/4

W

Washington, 11/4

power of attorney statutes, 12/6

West Virginia, 11/4

power of attorney statutes, 12/6

WillMaker software program, 2/6

Wills, and attorney-in-fact, 3/4

Wisconsin, 11/4

power of attorney statutes, 12/6

Witnesses

and challenges to power of attorney, , 3/2

and revocation of power of attorney, 11/8

statement form, blank, 11/8

See also specific power of attorney type

World Wide Web, 12/7-8

Wyoming, 11/4

power of attorney statutes, 12/6

CATALOG

...more from Nolo Press

	EDITION	PRICE	CODE

BUSINESS

	EDITION	PRICE	CODE
The California Nonprofit Corporation Handbook	7th	$29.95	NON
The California Professional Corporation Handbook	5th	$34.95	PROF
The Employer's Legal Handbook	2nd	$29.95	EMPL
Form Your Own Limited Liability Company	1st	$24.95	LIAB
▣ Hiring Independent Contractors: The Employer's Legal Guide, (Book w/Disk—PC)	2nd	$29.95	HICI
▣ How to Form a CA Nonprofit Corp.—w/Corp. Records Binder & PC Disk	1st	$49.95	CNP
▣ How to Form a Nonprofit Corp., Book w/Disk (PC)—National Edition	3rd	$39.95	NNP
▣ How to Form Your Own Calif. Corp.—w/Corp. Records Binder & Disk—PC	1st	$39.95	CACI
How to Form Your Own California Corporation	8th	$29.95	CCOR
▣ How to Form Your Own Florida Corporation, (Book w/Disk—PC)	3rd	$39.95	FLCO
▣ How to Form Your Own New York Corporation, (Book w/Disk—PC)	3rd	$39.95	NYCO
▣ How to Form Your Own Texas Corporation, (Book w/Disk—PC)	4th	$39.95	TCOR
How to Handle Your Workers' Compensation Claim (California Edition)	1st	$29.95	WORK
How to Market a Product for Under $500	1st	$29.95	UN500
How to Mediate Your Dispute	1st	$18.95	MEDI

▣ Book with disk
⦿ Book with CD-ROM

	EDITION	PRICE	CODE
How to Write a Business Plan	4th	$21.95	SBS
The Independent Paralegal's Handbook	4th	$29.95	PARA
Legal Guide for Starting & Running a Small Business, Vol. 1	3rd	$24.95	RUNS
Marketing Without Advertising	2nd	$19.00	MWAD
⊟ The Partnership Book: How to Write a Partnership Agreement, (Book w/Disk—PC)	5th	$34.95	PART
Sexual Harassment on the Job	2nd	$18.95	HARS
Starting and Running a Successful Newsletter or Magazine	1st	$24.95	MAG
⊟ Taking Care of Your Corporation, Vol. 1, (Book w/Disk—PC)	1st	$29.95	CORK
⊟ Taking Care of Your Corporation, Vol. 2, (Book w/Disk—PC)	1st	$39.95	CORK2
Tax Savvy for Small Business	2nd	$26.95	SAVVY
Trademark: How to Name Your Business & Product	2nd	$29.95	TRD
Your Rights in the Workplace	3rd	$19.95	YRW

CONSUMER

	EDITION	PRICE	CODE
Fed Up With the Legal System: What's Wrong & How to Fix It	2nd	$9.95	LEG
How to Win Your Personal Injury Claim	2nd	$24.95	PICL
Nolo's Everyday Law Book	1st	$21.95	EVL
Nolo's Pocket Guide to California Law	5th	$11.95	CLAW
Trouble-Free Travel...And What to Do When Things Go Wrong	1st	$14.95	TRAV

ESTATE PLANNING & PROBATE

	EDITION	PRICE	CODE
8 Ways to Avoid Probate (Quick & Legal Series)	1st	$15.95	PRO8
How to Probate an Estate (California Edition)	9th	$34.95	PAE
Make Your Own Living Trust	2nd	$21.95	LITR
⊟ Nolo's Will Book, (Book w/Disk—PC)	3rd	$29.95	SWIL
Plan Your Estate	3rd	$24.95	NEST
The Quick and Legal Will Book	1st	$15.95	QUIC
Nolo's Law Form Kit: Wills	1st	$14.95	KWL

⊟ Book with disk
● Book with CD-ROM

	EDITION	PRICE	CODE

FAMILY MATTERS

	EDITION	PRICE	CODE
A Legal Guide for Lesbian and Gay Couples	9th	$24.95	LG
California Marriage Law	12th	$19.95	MARR
Child Custody: Building Parenting Agreements that Work	2nd	$24.95	CUST
Divorce & Money: How to Make the Best Financial Decisions During Divorce	3rd	$26.95	DIMO
Get A Life: You Don't Need a Million to Retire Well	1st	$18.95	LIFE
The Guardianship Book (California Edition)	2nd	$24.95	GB
How to Adopt Your Stepchild in California	4th	$22.95	ADOP
How to Do Your Own Divorce in California	21st	$24.95	CDIV
How to Do Your Own Divorce in Texas	6th	$19.95	TDIV
How to Raise or Lower Child Support in California	3rd	$18.95	CHLD
The Living Together Kit	8th	$24.95	LTK
Nolo's Law Form Kit: Hiring Childcare & Household Help	1st	$14.95	KCHLO
Nolo's Pocket Guide to Family Law	4th	$14.95	FLD
Practical Divorce Solutions	1st	$14.95	PDS
Smart Ways to Save Money During and After Divorce	1st	$14.95	SAVMO

GOING TO COURT

	EDITION	PRICE	CODE
Collect Your Court Judgment (California Edition)	3rd	$24.95	JUDG
How to Seal Your Juvenile & Criminal Records (California Edition)	6th	$24.95	CRIM
How to Sue For Up to 25,000...and Win!	2nd	$29.95	MUNI
Everybody's Guide to Small Claims Court in California	12th	$18.95	CSCC
Everybody's Guide to Small Claims Court (National Edition)	6th	$18.95	NSCC
Fight Your Ticket ... and Win! (California Edition)	6th	$19.95	FYT
How to Change Your Name (California Edition)	6th	$24.95	NAME
Mad at Your Lawyer	1st	$21.95	MAD
Represent Yourself in Court: How to Prepare & Try a Winning Case	1st	$29.95	RYC

⬛ Book with disk
⬤ Book with CD-ROM

CALL 800-992-6656 OR USE THE ORDER FORM IN THE BACK OF THE BOOK

EDITION PRICE CODE

HOMEOWNERS, LANDLORDS & TENANTS

The Deeds Book (California Edition) .... 4th $16.95 DEED

Dog Law .... 3rd $14.95 DOG

▣ Every Landlord's Legal Guide (National Edition) .... 1st $34.95 ELLI

For Sale by Owner (California Edition) .... 2nd $24.95 FSBO

Homestead Your House (California Edition) .... 8th $9.95 HOME

How to Buy a House in California .... 4th $24.95 BHCA

The Landlord's Law Book, Vol. 1: Rights & Responsibilities (California Edition) .... 5th $34.95 LBRT

The Landlord's Law Book, Vol. 2: Evictions (California Edition) .... 6th $34.95 LBEV

Leases & Rental Agreements (Quick & Legal Series) .... 1st $18.95 LEAR

Neighbor Law: Fences, Trees, Boundaries & Noise .... 2nd $16.95 NEI

Safe Homes, Safe Neighborhoods: Stopping Crime Where You Live .... 1st $14.95 SAFE

Tenants' Rights (California Edition) .... 13th $19.95 CTEN

HUMOR

29 Reasons Not to Go to Law School 4th $9.95 29R

Poetic Justice .... 1st $9.95 PJ

IMMIGRATION

How to Become a United States Citizen .... 5th $14.95 CIT

How to Get a Green Card: Legal Ways to Stay in the U.S.A. .... 2nd $24.95 GRN

U.S. Immigration Made Easy .... 5th $39.95 IMEZ

MONEY MATTERS

Chapter 13 Bankruptcy: Repay Your Debts 2nd $29.95 CH13

Credit Repair (Quick & Legal Series) .... 1st $15.95 CREP

How to File for Bankruptcy .... 6th $26.95 HFB

Money Troubles: Legal Strategies to Cope With Your Debts .... 4th $19.95 MT

Nolo's Law Form Kit: Personal Bankruptcy .... 1st $14.95 KBNK

Simple Contracts for Personal Use .... 2nd $16.95 CONT

Stand Up to the IRS .... 3rd $24.95 SIRS

▣ Book with disk

◉ Book with CD-ROM

| | EDITION | PRICE | CODE |

PATENTS AND COPYRIGHTS

The Copyright Handbook: How to Protect and Use Written Works .... 4th $29.95 COHA

Copyright Your Software .... 1st $39.95 CYS

The Patent Drawing Book .... 1st $29.95 DRAW

Patent, Copyright & Trademark: A Desk Reference to Intellectual Property Law .... 1st $24.95 PCTM

Patent It Yourself .... 6th $44.95 PAT

⊡ Software Development: A Legal Guide (Book with disk—PC) .... 1st $44.95 SFT

The Inventor's Notebook .... 2nd $19.95 INOT

RESEARCH & REFERENCE

● Law on the Net, (Book w/CD-ROM—Windows/Macintosh) .... 2nd $39.95 LAWN

Legal Research: How to Find & Understand the Law .... 4th $19.95 LRES

Legal Research Made Easy (Video) .... 1st $89.95 LRME

SENIORS

Beat the Nursing Home Trap .... 2nd $18.95 ELD

Social Security, Medicare & Pensions .... 6th $19.95 SOA

The Conservatorship Book (California Edition) .... 2nd $29.95 CNSV

SOFTWARE

Call for special direct discounts on Software

California Incorporator 2.0—DOS .... 2.0 $79.95 INCI

Living Trust Maker 2.0—Macintosh 2.0 $79.95 LTM2

Living Trust Maker 2.0—Windows 2.0 $79.95 LTWI2

Small Business Legal Pro Deluxe CD—Windows/Macintosh CD-ROM .... 2.0 $79.95 SBCD

Nolo's Partnership Maker 1.0—DOS 1.0 $79.95 PAGI1

Personal RecordKeeper 4.0—Macintosh 4.0 $49.95 RKM4

Personal RecordKeeper 4.0—Windows 4.0 $49.95 RKP4

Patent It Yourself 1.0—Windows 1.0 $229.95 PYP12

WillMaker 6.0—Macintosh 6.0 $49.95 WM6B

WillMaker 6.0—Windows 6.0 $49.95 WIW6B

⊡ Book with disk
● Book with CD-ROM

CALL 800-992-6656 OR USE THE ORDER FORM IN THE BACK OF THE BOOK